The Dessert Lover's Cookbook

By the same author

Cookery for Entertaining

Marlene Sorosky's
Year-Round Holiday Cookbook

Marlene Sorosky

Photographs by Robert Stein

The Dessert Lover's Cookbook

HARPER & ROW, PUBLISHERS, New York
Cambridge, Philadelphia, San Francisco, London
Mexico City, São Paulo, Singapore, Sydney

1817

FIRST EDITION

Designed by Kao & Kao Associates

Food stylist: Marlene Sorosky

Library of Congress Cataloging in Publication Data

Sorosky, Marlene.
  The dessert lover's cookbook.

  Includes index.
  1. Desserts. I. Title.
TX773.S675 1985   641.8'6   84-43119
ISBN 0-06-181781-3

85 86 87 88 89 SCP 10 9 8 7 6 5 4 3 2 1

The Dessert Lover's Cookbook
is dedicated to dessert lovers everywhere.

Definition of a dessert lover:

One who plans an entire meal around dessert.

One who knows what he/she will order for dessert even before being seated in a restaurant.

One whose motto is, "It's better to fast tomorrow than pass up dessert today."

Contents

ACKNOWLEDGMENTS	xi
INTRODUCTION	xiii
ABOUT BAKING	1
EQUIPMENT AND INGREDIENTS	6
CAKES AND TORTES	11

Layer Cakes — 12

Coffee Macadamia Torte · Absolutely Divine Devil's Food Cake · Orange Sponge Cake · Fresh Banana Cake with Banana Frosting · Chocolate Kahlúa Cream Torte · White Chocolate Cake

Flourless Cakes — 23

Bittersweet Fudge Torte · Chocolate Nut Torte · Mocha Fudge Torte

Cake Rolls — 27

Lemon Meringue Spiral · Strawberry Shortcake Roll · Sherbet Alaska Roll · Espresso Chocolate Soufflé Roll

Cakes with Fruit — 35

Hot Apple Cake · Apricot Upside-Down Ginger Cake · Strawberry Cream Sponge Tart · Glazed Almond Date Cake

Bundt Cakes — 39

Bourbon Street Fudge Cake · Persimmon Spice Cake · Holiday Egg Nog Cake · Orange-Apricot Bundt Cake · Grand Marnier Nut Cake

CHEESECAKES — 45

White Chocolate Cheesecake · Triple Cheese Flan · Classic New York Cheesecake · Oreo Cheesecake · Chocolate Truffle Cheesecake · Lemonade Chiffon Cheesecake · Miniature Fruit-Glazed Cheesecakes · Piña Colada Cheesecake · Peanut Butter Chocolate Chip Cheesecake · Banana Fudge Cheesecake · My Favorite Cheesecake · Hazelnut Praline Cheesecake · Apricot Cheesecake

PUDDINGS AND OLD-FASHIONED FRUIT DESSERTS   63

Puddings   65

Light and Dark Steamed Pudding · Steamed Blueberry Pudding · Steamed Chocolate Pudding · Orange Sponge Pudding · Caramel Pumpkin Pudding · Christmas Cranberry Pudding

Bread Puddings   71

Cinnamon Apple Bread Pudding · Olde English Bread Pudding · Mexican Bread and Cheese Pudding

Old-Fashioned Fruit Desserts   75

Mixed Fruit Cobbler · Fresh Peach Cobbler · Fresh Blackberry Cobbler · Rhubarb-Peach Cobbler with Lattice Biscuit · Warm Blueberry Puff · Blueberry Fritters · Chocolate Strawberry Shortcake

PIES, TARTS AND TARTLETS   83

Pastry Crusts   85

Rich All-Purpose Pastry · Shortening Pastry · Cookie Pastry · Chocolate Pastry · Cream Cheese Pastry for Tartlets

Fruit Pies and Tarts   91

Apple Lemon Tart · Double-Crust Apple Pie with Custard · Apple Streusel Tart · Pineapple Banana Pie · Berries and Cream Tart · Purple Plum Tart · Brandy and Ginger Peach Tart · Cherry Quiche · Cranberry Pear Pie · Pear and Cheddar Tart

Cream and Chiffon Pies   103

Pumpkin Praline Chiffon Pie · White Chocolate Mousse Pie · Caramel Custard Fruit Tart · Zesty Lemon Custard Pie

Nut Tarts   109

Lemon Almond Tart · Regal Pecan Tart

Ice Cream Pies   113

Praline Ice Cream Pie · Peanut Butter Ice Cream Pie with Hot Fudge Sauce · Coffee Fudge Ice Cream Torte · Ice Cream Cone Pie

Tartlets   116

Sour Cream Lime Tartlets · Amaretti Fruit Tartlets · Chocolate Truffle Tartlets · Honey Walnut Tartlets · Toasted Coconut Cream Tartlets

PRESENTATIONS IN PASTRY 121

Easy Puff Pastry · Open-Face Apple Tart · Fresh Blueberry Turnovers · Apricot Strudel · Almond Paste Chocolate Chip Strudel · Viennese Apple Strudel · Cherry Goat Cheese Strudel · Pineapple Cheese Baklava · Strawberry Phyllo Napoleon · Black Forest Soufflé in Phyllo · Gorgonzola Pear Dumplings · Chocolate Cream Puffs with Chocolate Mocha Mousse · Almond Cream Puff Ring with Strawberries · Lacy Almond Cookie Cups and Saucers

MOUSSES, CUSTARDS AND ICE CREAMS 141

Mousses 143

Citrus Mousse · Kiwi Mousse with Kiwi Sauce · Lemon Mousse with Crème Fraîche Sauce · Irish Cream Mousse · Chocolate Mocha Mousse · Southern Praline Maple Mousse · Chocolate Raspberry Dessert · Chocolate Velvet Crown · Frozen Crunchy Strawberry Cloud · Chocolate Shells · Chocolate Cups · Chocolate Peppermint Angel Dessert

Creams and Custards 155

Warm Champagne Zabaglione · Chilled Raspberry-Rimmed Zabaglione · Duke of Nottingham's Fruit Trifle · Flaming Caramel Flan · Classic Caramel Custard · Crème Brûlée · Vanilla Pots de Crème · Coffee Pots de Crème · Chocolate Pots de Crème

Ice Creams 164

Irish Whiskey Ice Cream · Oreo Espresso Ice Cream · Marvelous Mango Ice Cream · Fresh Peach Ice Cream · Incredible White Coffee Ice Cream · White Chocolate Ice Cream

SOUFFLÉS AND MERINGUES 169

Soufflés 171

Iced Lemon Soufflé · Chilled Mandarin Orange Soufflé · Frosty Daiquiri Soufflé · Fudgy Brownie Soufflé · Amaretto Soufflé · Hot Raspberry Soufflé · Candlelight Chocolate Soufflés for Two

Meringues 178

Heavenly Fruit-Filled Meringue · Toffee-Crunch Meringue Torte · Raspberry Floating Islands · Crunchy Meringue Ice Cream Sandwich · Chocolate Meringue Butterflies · Hazelnut Meringue Torte · Coffee Meringues · Chocolate Meringue Shells · Meringue Swans

FRUITS   191

Fresh from the Orchard   192

Tropical Fruit in Pineapple Rickshaw · Cantaloupe Alaska · Minted-Melon Mélange · Macaroon-Filled Apricots · Hawaiian Fruit in Honey-Nut Yogurt · Strawberries in Crème de Grand Marnier · Chocolate-Nougat Fondue with Fresh Fruit · Fresh Fruit Medley · Fluffy Orange Dip · Fresh Raspberry Alaska · Orange-Glazed Oranges · Baby Papaya Birds · Cinnamon-Scented Winter Fruit · Fresh Figs in Vanilla-Lemon Syrup

Cooked Fruit   202

Pears in Praline Cream · Prunes in Port · Lemon-Cream Peaches with Blueberry Sauce · Peach Melba · Pineapple and Bananas Flambé · Baked Grapefruit Streusel · Spiced Fruit Compote · Truffle-Filled Chocolate-Glazed Pears · Sugar-and-Spice Baked Apples

Frozen Fruit   210

Tangerine Slush · Papaya-Yogurt Freeze · Lemon Chardonnay Snow · Piña Colada Sherbet · Fresh Strawberry Ice · Honeydew Melon Sherbet

SAUCES AND TOPPINGS   215

Vanilla Custard Sauce · Creamy Vanilla Sauce · Hard Sauce · Ruby-Red Raspberry Sauce · Satin Strawberry Sauce · Blueberry Sauce · Berries and Cherries Jubilee · Crème Fraîche Sauce · Lemon Sauce · Hot Chocolate Fudge Sauce · Hot Bittersweet Fudge Sauce · Sabayon Sauce · Rum Sauce · Brandy Cream Sauce · Crème de Grand Marnier · Irish Cream Liqueur

GARNISHES AND FLOURISHES   225

Chocolate Dough · Chocolate Shavings · Chocolate Leaves · Notched Lemon or Orange Slices · Candied Citrus Peel

INDEX   231

Acknowledgments

I wish to express my gratitude to several very special people who generously gave their time, energy and talents to help enhance my book:

Edon Kreitler, a skilled cook and gifted artist, whose warmth, enthusiasm and devotion helped make this book a joy to write. Her superb taste, talent and creativity were a continual source of inspiration and I thank her for so openheartedly sharing them with me. Through our laughter, tears, trials and tribulations, I have found a very dear and cherished friend. A big thank you also to Brad and Jennifer, who spent many late nights and lonely weekends patiently waiting for their mom to come home.

Jimmy Dodge, the talented pastry chef at Fournous' Ovens, the prestigious restaurant in the Stanford Court Hotel in San Francisco, for being such a wonderful friend and spending two hectic weeks in Los Angeles helping me prepare and style food for photography.

Dierdra Bugli, a noted food stylist, who devotedly assisted me whenever and wherever she was needed.

Lane Crowther, whose special flair with food greatly enhanced the photographs.

Bob Stein, my photographer, for his deep commitment to excellence. His caring, humor and patience provided us all with an enjoyable and congenial environment through many long and difficult hours.

Charles Pollack, owner of "Charles Pollack's Antiques" in Los Angeles, for lending us many of his wonderful antiques and accessories for photography.

Lee Gelfond, owner of "Chocolate" in Los Angeles, for sharing her expertise and ingredients so generously.

Janice Wald Henderson, who cheerfully and unhesitatingly found time, day or night, to help me structure a sentence, edit a thought or compile an idea.

And last, but not least, my loyal and hard-working testers, who never flinched when asked to retest "just one more time"—Michele Davidson, Gloria Mitchell, Laurel Lyle, Carol Magness, Mitzi Costin, Shirley Wilcox and Mary Waycott.

(*) This symbol is used throughout
to indicate the point to which a recipe
may be prepared in advance.

Introduction

This book is written from the heart, for I have been obsessed by a wondrous love affair with desserts ever since I can remember. I continuously crave, certainly savor and definitely devour them. There's no doubt about it; I simply can not—and will not—resist them.

The more time and energy I poured into creating this cookbook, the more I realized that desserts play such a vital role as one of life's greatest pleasures. Indeed, they are one of the precious few pleasures that you can bestow upon yourself as well as loved ones. What a serendipitous discovery!

Although you must follow instructions for the actual preparation of these sweet finales, your imagination is given free rein to soar when you are decorating them. In this respect, desserts can be touted as the most artistic type of cooking—the ultimate culinary art form.

The Dessert Lover's Cookbook is filled with the consummate results of my countless hours of experimentation. Many of these recipes were tested as many as thirty times. My first goal was to ensure their superlative taste. When I was more than pleased, I then tested for technique. Was I employing the simplest means for obtaining the desired result? Was the texture ideal, the appearance outstanding? How far in advance could it be prepared, refrigerated and/or frozen before serving?

And these explorations were only the beginning. Several testers—amateur cooks who had never seen these recipes—then prepared the desserts and answered a two-page questionnaire about them. Did they find the recipes easy to make? Did they discover any difficulties with the instructions or techniques? Would they want to prepare them again? These questions are only a sampling of the many that had to be answered satisfactorily. Only when a recipe received unanimously positive response did it qualify for inclusion in this book.

You will discover upon reviewing *The Dessert Lover's Cookbook* that the recipes don't stop once the desserts are removed from the oven. I take each one an important step further—up to the moment it's served. Is a white chocolate cheesecake tastier when presented chilled or at room temperature? Should you spoon or slice a molded kiwi mousse? I may have tested a recipe many additional times to discover the answers to such questions, but it was worth the work knowing that you will be able to present the desserts confidently and proudly.

This book is meant for you. As every recipe is designed for the home cook, all ingredients are readily obtainable from most supermarkets. Even the necessary baking utensils are stocked at any well-equipped cookware shop or department store. And as an extra advantage, there's no need to own every pan that exists; I deliberately use the same sizes in recipes throughout the book.

I do not assume that you already know how to make a flaky pie crust or a delicately textured sponge cake roll, or any other of the baking basics. Thus, detailed explanations of important culinary techniques are given as well as easy-to-understand visual demonstrations through step-by-step color photographs.

Accomplished bakers, however, are promised a wealth of creative desserts with which to experiment, from cream puffs flavored with chocolate, pastry enriched with zippy Gorgonzola cheese, to a doubly moist and undeniably rich chocolate cake enlivened with the unusual addition of beets. They will discover this book to be a bountiful blend of my favorite renditions of superb classics and exciting, contemporary twists on traditional themes.

There is only one shortcut that I did not take when writing this book: ingredients. I could create new techniques and recipes that simplified baking, but I could not compromise when it came to great taste. I insist upon using only the purest, freshest ingredients so that these desserts sparkle with intense, simple, yet sublime flavors.

My responsibility is to give everyone who buys this book the very best. I believe that once you try just one recipe, you'll discover that you can't wait to make them all. As for me, every time I sample these desserts, I can't help but fall in love with them over and over again.

With *The Dessert Lover's Cookbook,* I can now turn my labors of love over to you. As extensions of your own love of delectable desserts, I hope that these recipes will bring much happiness into your lives and the lives of those you love.

Marlene Sorosky

The Dessert Lover's Cookbook

About Baking

Throughout the fifteen years that I have been a culinary instructor, I have continually encountered the same questions about baking and dessert-making over and over again. There are tricky spots which seem to be universal. I have compiled a list of those questions most frequently asked and my answers to them. I hope that the following information will assist you in becoming a more knowledgeable and confident dessert-maker and ensure your success when making my recipes.

1 *What is the easiest method of separating egg whites from yolks?*

Eggs are simpler to separate when they are cold. Separation can be accomplished in a variety of ways; but the easiest method is really up to you. Here are three of the most common ways: (1) Cup the fingers of one hand together and curl them over your palm. Crack the egg into this hand. Open your fingers slightly and shake your hand over a bowl, letting the white drop through your fingers. Place the yolk in a separate bowl. (2) Crack all the eggs necessary for the recipe into a bowl. Using your hand as a scoop, remove the yolks to a separate bowl. (3) Crack the shell on the side of a bowl. Break the shell in half, and using each half as a holder, tip the yolk back and forth carefully, letting the white fall into a nearby bowl. Probably the safest method is to separate eggs one at a time, placing each in individual custard cups and then transferring the whites to a bowl. That way, if any of the yolk should spill into the white, you only lose one egg. If a small amount of egg yolk falls into the white, use the jagged edge of a shell or a small piece of paper towel to remove it.

2 *When whipping egg whites, how can you ensure that they will become light, fluffy and billowy?*

If egg whites come in contact with fat, oil or grease, they simply will not whip. It is, therefore, very important that the bowl and beater be absolutely clean and that there is not even one drop of yolk in the whites.

3 *Is it necessary for egg whites to be at room temperature before beating them?*

If egg whites are cold, it will take them longer to reach their fullest volume. For best results, separate eggs while they're cold and cover the whites and yolks tightly with plastic wrap. Let stand until they reach room temperature. If you are in a hurry, place the bowl with the cold whites into a bowl of tepid water, swirling the bowl occasionally until the whites reach room temperature. Be careful that the water is not too hot, or it will cook the eggs.

4 *Why are egg whites sometimes difficult to fold into a mixture? Why do they clump?*

This problem is a trouble spot for so many of my students. Whites clump because they are overbeaten. The solution is a simple one. Beat them only until rounded, very soft peaks form when the beater is lifted from the whites. Do not beat them stiff unless sugar is added, and then beat them until the whites form firm, shiny, but still moist peaks. If the mixture to which the whites are being added is very stiff, it is helpful to stir in a small portion of whites to lighten the mixture before folding in all the whites.

5 *Can leftover egg whites and yolks be frozen? How can they be used?*

Yes, both whites and yolks can be frozen. Egg whites should be frozen in a labeled, airtight container. Or, place individual egg whites in ice cube trays. Freeze them into solid cubes, and then run them under hot water to release. Place them in a plastic bag tied tightly and return to the freezer. Defrost as needed in a bowl covered with plastic wrap until they reach room temperature. Defrosted egg whites can be used in any recipe. Many baking authorities believe they actually whip up to a greater volume. Yolks may be frozen in a container topped with a thin film of oil and a tight-fitting lid. When defrosted, they can be used successfully in sauces like hollandaise or mayonnaise.

6 *How can you ensure that whipping cream will always whip?*

In order to whip cream, it must be cold. Many pastry chefs recommend refrigerating the bowl and beaters along with the cream to ensure that the cream will whip. If the cream takes a while to thicken, don't worry. Most supermarket cream is now ultra-pasteurized, which gives it a much longer shelf life. Although ultra-pasteurized cream seems to whip more consistently, it does take more time to thicken.

7 *Why aren't all mousses and chiffon pies light?*

Because too many home cooks beat whipping cream and egg whites much too stiff. In these recipes especially, egg whites should be whipped only until soft, rounded peaks form when the beater is lifted, not until stiff peaks form. And they should be folded in as soon as they are beaten or they will deflate. Whipping cream should be beaten only until it thickens enough to hold a very soft peak. Since most mousses and chiffon pies contain unflavored gelatin to give them substance, the main function of egg whites and cream is to contribute a soft, creamy texture.

8 *Why does unflavored gelatin sometimes not gel?*

> In order for unflavored gelatin to work, it must first be softened in liquid for about five minutes. Then it must be dissolved by heat, either by being stirred into a hot mixture, or by being brought to a simmer with the liquid in which it was softened.

9 *When using unflavored gelatin to make a mousse, cold soufflé or chiffon pie, why does a layer of gelatin sometimes form on the bottom of the mold or pie?*

> The custard or cream base containing the dissolved gelatin mixture must be thickened before egg whites or whipped cream are folded in. If the gelatin mixture is too thin, it will sink to the bottom of the dessert. The fastest way to thicken a custard-gelatin mixture is to place the bowl in a larger bowl of ice water, and to stir occasionally until it begins to set and thicken.

10 *Why do recipes call for unsalted butter when salt is listed as one of the ingredients?*

> Unsalted butter is usually fresher than lightly salted or salted butter. Salt, which acts as a preservative, gives butter a longer shelf life, thereby reducing its quality. If you wish to substitute salted butter for unsalted, omit the salt called for in the recipe. One stick (¼ pound) of salted butter contains approximately ½ teaspoon salt.

11 *Can salt be omitted from dessert recipes?*

> Generally speaking, yes. Other than in recipes using yeast, salt is not added for chemical or scientific reasons, but primarily for taste. It is believed that it enhances the sweetness of sugar and the flavor of chocolate. If you are watching your sodium intake, you can omit salt from all my recipes.

12 *What is the difference between cake, pastry, bread and all-purpose flours?*

> All flour is comprised of several different components, one of which is called gluten or protein. Cake flour, made from soft wheat, is very fine and soft and possesses the lowest amount of gluten. This flour contains just enough protein for a cake to hold its shape while baking. The result is an extremely light, tender cake. Pastry flour has a slightly higher amount of gluten and is ideal for pie and tart crusts. When fat is worked into it, the pastry will not become tough. Bread flour is made from hard wheat and contains the greatest amount of gluten. When combined with yeast in a dough, it contains the necessary strength to allow bread to rise and stay risen. Somewhere in between lies the versatile all-purpose flour. It is a blend of hard and soft wheat and is exactly what its name states—it's good for every

purpose. To make things easy, I use all-purpose flour and obtain excellent results in all my recipes. The only exception is Easy Puff Pastry (see page 122), which is softened with some cake flour. If a recipe calls for cake flour, you can substitute all-purpose. One cup all-purpose flour equals 1 cup less 2 tablespoons cake flour.

13 *Does flour need to be sifted?*

Since all-purpose flour is pre-sifted it is not necessary to sift it for most baking purposes, unless it is lumpy. (A humid climate sometimes causes flour to become lumpy.) In my cake recipes, I combine the flour with the other dry ingredients before adding it to the batter to ensure that the baking powder and soda are well distributed. To accurately measure flour, scoop the specified size measuring cup into the flour. Lift the cup out and without pushing down on the flour, level off the top with a knife.

14 *What is the difference between flour, cornstarch and arrowroot?*

When thickening dessert sauces or making glazes, cornstarch or arrowroot are the preferred choices. Flour is a more durable thickener and is used for dishes that require a long cooking time or for thick heavy gravies. Arrowroot is the most fragile of the three. Although it makes a shinier and more translucent sauce, it should only be used in recipes which cook quickly, since it loses its thickening power if boiled for any length of time. Arrowroot and cornstarch are more powerful thickeners than flour. As a general rule, use half as much of either of these as flour.

15 *Why does cornstarch sometimes lump in a sauce?*

Cornstarch should be dissolved in a cold or room temperature liquid before it's added to a sauce. And the sauce should not be boiling when it's added since the bubbling can cause the cornstarch to lump. It's best to remove the pan containing the sauce from the heat and whisk in the dissolved cornstarch until smooth. Then return the sauce to the heat and whisk constantly until it boils and thickens.

16 *Can margarine be successfully substituted for butter?*

Although butter possesses more flavor, it is more expensive and is also higher in saturated fats. On the other hand, margarine contains additives, perservatives and flavor enhancers. Many people choose to use margarine for dietary reasons. For that purpose, margarine is certainly an acceptable substitute. I think, however, that whenever possible, substituting margarine for half of the butter required in a recipe is a better, tastier solution.

17 *Why does chocolate sometimes become granular or solidify when melted?*

Chocolate can become stiff if even a drop of steam falls into it when it is melting. Also, if too small an amount of liquid has been added to the melting chocolate the chocolate will stiffen. It is safe to add 1 tablespoon or more of liquid per ounce, or square, of chocolate, but not less. To smooth out lumpy chocolate, stir in 1 teaspoon of solid vegetable shortening for each ounce of chocolate. Do not try using butter since it contains water.

18 *What is the safest way to melt chocolate?*

To ensure that chocolate does not scorch or turn gray, melt the chocolate using as little heat as possible. First, chop the chocolate into small pieces with a knife or, for large amounts, use a food processor fitted with a metal blade, using on-and-off pulses. Place the chocolate in the top of a double boiler off the heat. Fill the bottom with an inch or two of water. Bring to a boil, then remove it from the heat. Place the top of the double boiler with the chocolate over the water and cover with a lid. Let stand off the heat until the chocolate is melted. Stir until smooth.

19 *Why is pastry so difficult to roll?*

There can be a number of reasons, but the one I have observed most frequently is that the pastry is too warm. Pastry is much easier to roll when it is cold—even if it takes more muscle. Don't be afraid to pound on it with your rolling pin to make it more pliable. If you still have trouble, try rolling it between 2 sheets of lightly floured waxed paper.

20 *Can bottled lemon juice be substituted for fresh?*

Yes, if you don't mind sacrificing some flavor. There are two brands of bottled lemon juice currently on the market. One is sold on the supermarket shelf and contains preservatives. It does not possess a fresh lemon taste. The other is a frozen product and must be defrosted before using. I find the latter variety an acceptable substitute, although it occasionally has become rancid in less than one month after being defrosted and stored in the refrigerator. Therefore, I prefer squeezing my own lemon juice and getting the freshest flavor possible.

21 *How do you prevent cheesecakes from cracking?*

I discovered the answer to this question after experimenting with countless cheesecakes. If you begin by baking the cake at very high heat, 400° to 425°, for 10 to 15 minutes, and then reducing the temperature to low, 225° to 250°, for the duration of the cooking time, your cake will not form large cracks. It is also important to slowly cool the cake in the oven with the heat turned off and the oven door closed for at least one hour before removing it. Then let it cool completely in a draft-free place before refrigerating it.

Equipment and Ingredients

The quality of home cookware and baking equipment has improved markedly in recent years along with the increasing awareness of good food. The importance of high quality equipment cannot be over emphasized, especially for baking. A pastry cannot brown evenly on a baking sheet that tilts and bends in the oven. Cakes cannot rise properly in a flimsy pan that burns the batter before it bakes it. I recommend purchasing, whenever possible, commercial or professional bakeware. It is heavier, conducts the heat better and is available in various shapes and sizes made expressly for home use.

Equipment

BAKING SHEETS

The heavier the baking sheet, the more evenly it will bake. Heavy gauge aluminum is a better conductor than stainless steel. Teflon-coated baking sheets are fine when you need a non-stick pan, but they are usually not very heavy. Air-cushioned baking sheets are excellent for cookies and pastries. Rimmed baking sheets (15½ x 10½ x 1 inch) are used for making jelly rolls or baking desserts, such as strudels, which might spill over into the oven.

BUNDT PANS

There are two types of bundt pans on the market. One is lightweight aluminum, usually weighing under 1 pound. The heavier variety, usually enamel-coated aluminum, weighs about 2 pounds. Because the heavy weight pan retains the heat, it is important to decrease the baking temperature by 25°. The baking time remains the same.

CAKE PANS

I use two standard-size round layer-cake pans. They may be either 8 inches or 9 inches in diameter, and either 1½ inches or 2 inches deep.

GRATERS AND ZESTERS

The easiest way to grate the peel or zest from lemons and oranges is with a standard metal grater. Hold the grater and the fruit over a sheet of wax paper. Rub the peel against the small round holes in the grater until the outer peel is removed. (Do not rub the inner white part or your grated peel will have a bitter taste.) Another tool which works well for small amounts of grated peel is a zester (see picture in Garnishes, page 229). Hold the zester in one hand and the fruit in the other over a sheet of wax paper. Scrape the zester along the peel of the fruit, making the strokes as long or short as desired.

SPRINGFORM PANS

Pans with a removable bottom and sides that spring loose are called springforms (see picture on page 51). Before serving a dessert made in a springform, remove the sides of the pan, but leave the dessert on the bottom of the pan. If you freeze a dessert in a springform, you may be able to remove the bottom of the pan once the dessert is frozen. Gently try prying the dessert loose with the tip of a sharp knife. If you are successful, the dessert can be wrapped in foil and the springform will be free for other uses.

The different sizes of springform pans available on the market are confusing. They measure either 8 x 3, 9 x 3 or 10 x 3 inches; or, they come in half sizes, 8½ x 2, 9½ x 2 or 10½ x 2. A number of my cheesecakes, specifically the Classic New York, Oreo, Banana Fudge, and My Favorite, are made in large pans. If you use a smaller pan than specified, you will have some batter left over. If using smaller pans, decrease the baking time by 10 to 15 minutes.

TART PANS

Although my tart recipes specify tart pans with removable bottoms, loose flan rings, rectangles or flower shapes without bottoms may be substituted. Place the flan sides on a baking sheet and line with pastry as directed in the recipe.

THERMOMETERS

Correct oven temperature is essential for good baking. Don't trust your luck—test the temperature of your oven often with an oven thermometer, preferably a mercury one.

WHISKS

Two types of whisks are helpful when making desserts. One with a balloon bottom is good for whipping air into egg whites and whipping cream. Even if you beat whites and cream in a machine, it is helpful to finish whipping them by hand for added control. The other type of whisk with a narrow, more pointed bottom is designed to get into the corners of a saucepan when whisking sauces and custards.

Ingredients

APPLES

In my apple pies and tarts, I specify using either Golden Delicious apples or tart green ones such as Granny Smith, Greening or Pippin. Golden Delicious are a softer variety suited for recipes in which the apples do not bake for a long time, such as my Open-Face Apple Tart and Double-Crust Apple Pie with Custard (see pages 124 and 92). If you were to use tart green apples in those recipes, the pastry would be golden, but the apples would be crunchily undercooked. In recipes calling for whole baked apples, you may use either Rome Beauty, Jonathan or Cortland. Three medium-size apples equal approximately 1 pound and yield about 2¾ cups sliced apples.

BUTTER

Unsalted butter, also called sweet butter, is the best choice for baking since it is generally fresher and contains less water than salted butter. I tested all my recipes with Land O'Lakes unsalted butter. I recommend this particular brand because of its superior quality. Fortunately, it's now on the market in most parts of the country. Unsalted butter may be refrigerated for several days, but should be frozen for longer storage. For more information on salted and unsalted butter, see baking question 10, page 3.

CHOCOLATE

There are four categories of chocolate used in baking: unsweetened, semi- or bittersweet, unsweetened cocoa powder, and white chocolate. Unsweetened, or bitter chocolate as it is also called, is widely available from either Baker's or Hersheys. Either brand can be used in those recipes specifying unsweetened chocolate.

The terms semisweet and bittersweet chocolate are interchangeable. That does not mean, however, that all semisweet or bittersweet chocolate tastes the same. Every manufacturer has its own recipe for making these chocolates, and the amounts of pure chocolate, cocoa butter, sugar, flavorings and other ingredients will vary. All my recipes were tested with Baker's semisweet chocolate, because it is readily available nationwide. You may, of course, substitute your favorite brand—the richer the chocolate, the higher the percentage of cocoa butter, and the richer and denser the dessert. Semisweet chocolate chips may be substituted for semisweet chocolate squares, if desired. Unsweetened cocoa powder is pulverized unsweetened chocolate. I use either Hershey's or Droste, a Dutch brand.

White chocolate is not technically considered chocolate since it contains no brown chocolate liquor, the liquid extracted from the cocoa bean. White chocolate consists of cocoa butter, milk, sugar and flavorings. Not all white chocolate melts smoothly. I recommend either Tobler Narcisse, Toblerone Blanc or Lindt Blancor.

For information on melting chocolate, see baking questions 17 and 18, pages 4–5.

CREAM OF TARTAR

If you do not whip your egg whites in a copper bowl, you may wish to add ¼ teaspoon cream of tartar to every 4 whites to provide extra stability. Beat in the cream of tartar when the whites reach the foamy stage. Although the addition of cream of tartar is not mandatory, it is a good security measure, especially when making meringue.

EGGS

I use only U.S. Graded Large size eggs for baking. According to the U.S. Standard Weights and Measures, a large egg weighs 2 ounces and approximately 7 large eggs will fill a 1 cup measure. For information on how to separate, freeze and whip eggs, see baking questions 1–5, pages 1–2.

FLOUR

I use all-purpose, pre-sifted, unbleached flour in all my desserts unless a recipe specifies otherwise. Flour should be stored in an airtight container. It can also be frozen and used in pastries directly from the freezer. For definitions of different types of flour, see baking question 12, page 3. For information on sifting flour, see baking question 13, page 4.

NUTS

As a general rule, nuts in recipes can be interchanged as desired. To grind nuts in the food processor, take 2 tablespoons of flour or sugar from the recipe and add it to the nuts in the processor bowl. Process with the metal blade using on and off pulses to achieve the desired consistency. The sugar or flour will coat the nuts and keep them from becoming oily. If not stored in vacuum sealed bags, shelled nuts should be kept in the freezer since they become rancid very rapidly. One pound of nuts in the shell provides approximately ½ pound of nut meats.

PEARS

The most popular pears for slicing, baking and poaching are Anjou, Comice and Bartlett. Anjou and Comice are available in late fall and winter; Bartlett, from mid summer through winter. The slender brown-skinned Bosc pear, with its tapered neck and long stem, is especially attractive for poaching.

SUGAR

Although granulated sugar is the most common sweetener, other sugars play an important role in dessert making.

Powdered sugar, 10X sugar, or confectioners' sugar as it is also called, is very finely ground granulated sugar with a small amount of cornstarch added to keep it smooth and powdery. It is mainly used in frostings, as a glaze or sprinkled on desserts as a garnish. To sift powdered sugar, place it in a fine strainer over a bowl and push it through the strainer using the back of a spoon. To dust a cake or pastry with powdered sugar, place the sugar in a strainer held over the dessert and tap the side of the strainer lightly while shaking it gently.

Light and dark brown sugar can be used interchangeably in recipes, although dark brown sugar possesses more flavor and adds a deeper color. Brown sugar is always measured firmly packed, unless a recipe states otherwise. Store brown sugar in an airtight container with a slice of apple in it. Although the apple slice will shrivel and look unattractive, the sugar will never get hard and lumpy. If brown sugar has become hard, it may be softened in a microwave oven on low power.

Superfine sugar is finely ground granulated sugar. I use it when making hard meringue shells since it dissolves more rapidly in egg whites and helps assure a dry, crisp meringue.

WHIPPING CREAM

Most of the cream for whipping available in our supermarkets is ultra-pasteurized, which gives it a 6 to 8 week refrigerator shelf life. (See baking question 6, page 2.) To successfully whip cream, place the cold cream in a large bowl, preferably metal so it remains cold. Begin beating at low speed until the cream thickens slightly. Then gradually increase the mixer speed to medium or high until the desired consistency is obtained. To frost and decorate cakes with whipped cream, add 2 tablespoons powdered sugar for each cup of cream to give it greater stability. If cream is overwhipped slightly, fold in some additional unwhipped cream to help smooth it out. If whipping cream reaches the expiration date and you have not yet used it, it may be frozen. When defrosted, it may be successfully whipped, but do not try to use it in sauces or custards.

Cakes and Tortes

Cakes can be grandiose or simple, and everything in between. This chapter includes a sampling, from a sophisticated four-layer Chocolate Kahlúa Cream Torte for elegant dinner parties to a homey Apricot Upside-Down Ginger Cake for backyard barbeques.

TIPS

- All ingredients must be at room temperature.
- KNOW YOUR OVEN—every one bakes differently. If you're baking more than one layer at a time, be sure to stagger the placement of the pans so that the heat will circulate evenly.
- Always bake cakes in the center of the oven, unless a recipe specifies otherwise.
- Use the baking pan the recipe recommends. If you choose another size, the cake or torte may underbake or overbake, or it may not even rise.
- I seldom sift flour. But I do mix it with other dry ingredients—like baking powder or soda—to make sure they're evenly incorporated. Then I add it to the liquid.
- Do not overbeat cake batter when adding dry ingredients. Mix only until the dry ingredients are incorporated.
- It is important to beat eggs until they're very thick and creamy, to ensure a light-textured cake.
- When beating together butter and sugar, ensure that the butter is at room temperature. Otherwise, the mixture will not become light and fluffy.
- To test if a cake is done, a cake tester or a wooden toothpick inserted halfway into the cake should come out free without any batter or crumbs adhering to it. Also, the cake edges should pull away slightly from the sides of the pan and the top of the cake should spring back when pressed lightly with your fingertips.
- Pans may be greased with butter, shortening or margarine. Butter may add a bit of flavor. Shortening is less expensive.
- To flour pans, sprinkle some flour in the pans, shake to evenly coat, then rap the pan on the corner of the sink and knock out the excess.
- If paper is called for in a recipe to line pans, I prefer to use parchment paper rather than wax paper or aluminum foil. It works especially well when you're making a rolled cake like a jelly roll: Leave a 2-inch overlap on the narrow ends (photo page 30). Parchment is truly non-stick paper.
- If you're having problems setting the second layer evenly over the first when frosting layer cakes, flip the bottom layer over so that its flat surface meets the flat surface of the second layer. This will avoid the cake slipping and appearing crooked.

CLOCKWISE FROM TOP: *Orange-Apricot Bundt Cake, page 42; Fresh Banana Cake with Banana Frosting, page 18; Chocolate Kahlúa Cream Torte, page 20.*

Coffee Macadamia Torte

Substitute ground nuts for flour and presto! you create a light-textured, amazingly moist, very European-style torte. An unbeatable complement to the macadamia flavor is the coffee both in the cake layers and the ultra-buttery butter cream. Although this torte is made with macadamias and pecans, 2 cups of any type of ground nuts may be used.

CAKE

1¼ cups salted or unsalted
   macadamia nuts (about 5 ounces)
¾ cup shelled pecans (about 3
   ounces)
2 tablespoons plus ¾ cup plus
   ¼ cup sugar
4 large eggs, separated and at room
   temperature
2 tablespoons all-purpose flour
½ teaspoon baking powder
¼ teaspoon salt
1½ tablespoons instant coffee,
   powder or crystals, dissolved in
   2 teaspoons boiling water
Dash of cream of tartar

COFFEE BUTTER CREAM

4 large egg yolks, at room
   temperature
¼ cup light corn syrup
⅓ cup sugar
½ pound (2 sticks) unsalted
   butter, at room temperature
2 tablespoons instant coffee
   dissolved in 2 teaspoons boiling
   water
2 tablespoons Kahlúa, or to taste

BAKING PANS

Two 9 x 1½-inch or 9 x 2-inch
   round layer-cake pans

Grease bottom and sides of cake pans. Cut a circle of wax paper or parchment to fit in bottom of each pan. Grease paper.

Preheat oven to 350°. If using salted macadamia nuts, place them in a tea towel and rub together to remove as much salt as possible. Place macadamia nuts, pecans and 2 tablespoons sugar in a food processor fitted with a metal blade. Pulse on and off until finely ground. You should have about 2 cups ground nuts. Spread evenly on baking sheet and bake in the 350° oven until lightly browned, stirring occasionally, about 10 to 12 minutes. Cool to room temperature. Leave oven at 350°.

CAKE

Beat egg yolks in a small mixing bowl with an electric mixer on high speed until thickened, about 3 minutes. Gradually beat in ¾ cup sugar. Continue beating until mixture is pale yellow and very thick, about 5 minutes. Beat in flour, baking powder, salt and coffee on low speed just until incorporated. The mixture will be very stiff.

In a separate medium-size mixing bowl, beat egg whites with electric mixer on low speed until frothy. Add the dash of cream of tartar and beat on high speed until soft peaks form. Gradually add ¼ cup sugar, a tablespoon at a time, beating until the mixture forms stiff but moist peaks. Spoon a third of the yolk mixture and a third of the nuts over top of whites. Fold together until partially blended. Repeat with second third of yolk mixture and nuts, folding only until partially blended. Repeat with remaining third, folding just until incorporated. Do not overmix.

Divide mixture equally between the 2 prepared pans, spreading the

tops evenly with a spatula. Bake in the 350° oven for 18 to 20 minutes or until cakes pull away slightly from sides of pans and tops are lightly browned. Remove from oven and immediately invert cakes onto wire racks. Remove pans and cool cakes completely.
(*) If desired, cakes may be frozen, wrapped tightly in foil. Defrost wrapped cakes at room temperature.

COFFEE BUTTER CREAM

Beat the egg yolks in a medium-size mixing bowl with an electric mixer on high speed until very thick, about 5 minutes. Meanwhile, combine corn syrup and ⅓ cup sugar in a small, heavy saucepan. Bring to a full boil, stirring constantly. Transfer to a heatproof glass measuring cup. Reduce mixer speed to medium and slowly pour hot syrup into yolks in a thin, steady stream. Continue beating until mixture feels cool to the touch, about 5 minutes. Gradually beat in softened butter, a few tablespoons at a time, mixing until incorporated. Mix in coffee and Kahlúa.

To assemble torte, line a cake plate with four strips of wax paper placed at right angles to each other and overlapping. Place one cake layer top-side down on plate. Spread with approximately a third of the Coffee Butter Cream. Top with second cake layer bottom-side down. Frost top and sides with remaining Coffee Butter Cream, swirling with a spatula. Refrigerate for several hours or until well chilled.

(*) If desired, the torte may be refrigerated overnight or frozen. Freeze uncovered until solid, then wrap in plastic wrap and foil. Defrost wrapped cake overnight in refrigerator.

Remove from refrigerator 30 minutes before serving. Remove wax paper strips.

Serves 10 to 12.

Absolutely Divine Devil's Food Cake

One Easter, I brought this cake to Julia Child's for lunch. Neither she nor our dear friend and excellent cook, Rosemary Manell, could guess the mystery ingredient—beets. They turn the cake a beautiful deep dark—almost black—color and add a moistness and depth of flavor. When you think of beet sugar and the use of beet coloring in dyes, this uncommon ingredient seems less unusual. The frosting is pure fudge. The cake is truly out of this world.

CAKE

3 squares (3 ounces) unsweetened chocolate, chopped
1 can (8¼ ounces) julienne beets
¼ pound (1 stick) unsalted butter, at room temperature
2½ cups firmly packed golden brown sugar
3 large eggs, at room temperature
2 teaspoons vanilla
2 cups all-purpose flour
2 teaspoons baking soda
½ teaspoon salt
½ cup buttermilk

FUDGE FROSTING

2 cups whipping cream
1 pound semisweet chocolate, chopped
2 teaspoons vanilla

BAKING PAN

Two 9 x 1½-inch or 9 x 2-inch round layer-cake pans

CAKE

Preheat oven to 350°. Grease bottom and sides of pans. Dust with flour and shake out excess. Melt chocolate in double boiler over hot water. Set aside to cool slightly. Drain beet juice into small bowl. Place beets on cutting board and chop into very small pieces. Add to beet juice and set aside.

Beat butter, sugar, eggs and vanilla in a large bowl with an electric mixer on high speed until very fluffy, about 5 minutes, scraping sides occasionally. Reduce speed to low and beat in melted chocolate.

Stir together flour, baking soda and salt in a medium-size bowl. With mixer on low speed, alternately beat flour in fourths and buttermilk in thirds into chocolate mixture, beginning and ending with flour. Mix until incorporated, about 1 minute. Add beets and juice and mix on medium speed until blended, about 1 minute. The batter will be thin and you will see pieces of beets.

Divide the batter equally between the 2 prepared pans. Bake in the 350° oven for 30 to 35 minutes or until cake tester inserted in center comes out clean and top of cake springs back when lightly pressed with fingertips. Do not overbake or cake will be dry. Cool cakes in pans on wire racks for 10 minutes and then invert onto racks. (*) If desired, cake layers may be wrapped in foil and kept at room temperature overnight, or they may be frozen. Defrost wrapped cake at room temperature before frosting.

FROSTING

Heat cream in a medium-size saucepan just until it comes to a boil. Remove from heat and add chocolate and vanilla, stirring until mixture is smooth and chocolate is melted. Transfer mixture to a plastic or glass bowl (metal causes the sides to get too cold and set up too quickly.) Refrigerate, stirring every 10 minutes until mixture is as thick as pudding, about 50 to 60 minutes. At this point the

Absolutely Divine Devil's Food Cake

frosting will begin to set up very quickly. Leave in refrigerator and stir every 5 minutes until frosting is as thick as fudge, about 15 more minutes. Alternatively, the frosting may be placed over ice water and stirred constantly until spreading consistency. If it begins to get too thick, immediately remove it from the water.

To assemble the cake, place one cake layer top-side down on serving platter. Spread with a third of the frosting and top with second layer, bottom-side up. Spread remaining frosting over top and sides. Let stand at room temperature for frosting to set. (*) The frosted cake may be held at room temperature, uncovered, overnight or refrigerated up to 2 days. Bring to room temperature before serving.

Serves 10 to 12.

Orange Sponge Cake

This tall, feathery light sponge cake has a delicate hint of fresh orange flavor. Cut into three layers, it's filled either with Orange Custard Filling and topped with Coconut Marshmallow Frosting, or with Strawberry Cream Filling covered with Whipped Cream Frosting. Either choice will give you a delightful dessert to serve to a crowd for any occasion.

6 large eggs, separated and at room temperature
2 tablespoons finely grated orange peel
½ cup fresh orange juice
1 cup plus ½ cup sugar
1¼ cups all-purpose flour
¼ teaspoon salt
½ teaspoon cream of tartar
1 recipe Orange Custard Filling and Coconut Marshmallow Frosting (see page 17) OR
1 recipe Strawberry Filling and Whipped Cream Frosting (see page 18)

BAKING PAN
10 x 4-inch angel-food cake pan with removable center

Preheat oven to 325°. Beat egg yolks in a medium-size bowl with an electric mixer on high speed until very thick, about 5 minutes. Beating continuously, gradually add grated orange peel, orange juice and 1 cup of the sugar, beating about 5 more minutes until the mixture is very pale, thick and creamy. Sift flour and salt over top of batter and gently fold in. Beat egg whites in another mixing bowl with an electric mixer on low speed until foamy. Add cream of tartar and continue beating at high speed until soft peaks form. Add remaining ½ cup sugar, 2 tablespoons at a time, until whites form stiff but moist peaks. Gently fold whites into yolks, being careful not to overmix and deflate the whites.

Turn batter into ungreased angel-food cake pan. Bake cake in the 325° oven for 50 to 60 minutes or until top of cake springs back when lightly pressed with fingertips. Remove cake from oven and immediately turn pan upside down over neck of a narrow bottle or onto the pan's feet. It is important that the cake cool at least 1 inch from the counter. Let cake cool completely in this position.

To remove cake from pan, run a sharp knife around edge of cake and around tube. Remove sides of pan and invert cake onto plate. Remove center of pan and leave cake upside down. (*) If desired, the cake may be frozen, wrapped tightly in foil. Defrost wrapped cake at room temperature.

Make Orange Custard Filling and Coconut Marshmallow Frosting or Strawberry Filling and Whipped Cream Frosting as directed.

To cut cake horizontally into 3 equal layers, measure cake from top to bottom; it will be very close to 3 inches high. Measure 1 inch down from top and mark with a toothpick. Continue marking by placing toothpicks at 2 inch intervals around cake. Measure 2 inches down from top of cake and place toothpicks around second layer in same manner. Using a long, serrated bread knife, cut layers, using toothpicks as guides.

Place one cake layer cut-side up on serving platter. Divide filling in half and spread cake with half the filling. Top with second cake layer cut-side down. Spread with remaining filling. Top with third layer, cut-side down. Frost top and sides as directed in recipe.

Serves 12.

ORANGE CUSTARD FILLING AND COCONUT MARSHMALLOW FROSTING

EQUIPMENT
Candy Thermometer

ORANGE CUSTARD FILLING

1 cup sugar
3 tablespoons cornstarch
¼ teaspoon salt
¾ cup fresh orange juice with pulp
¼ cup fresh lemon juice
½ cup water
3 large egg yolks
1 tablespoon grated orange peel

COCONUT MARSHMALLOW FROSTING

4 large egg whites, at room temperature
1 cup sugar
½ teaspoon cream of tartar
½ cup water
1 teaspoon vanilla
¾ cup shredded coconut

CUSTARD FILLING

Combine sugar, cornstarch and salt in a medium-size heavy saucepan. Gradually stir in orange juice, lemon juice and water. Bring to a boil over moderate heat, stirring constantly. Remove from heat and whisk in egg yolks, one at a time, mixing well after each. Return to moderately low heat, bring to a boil and boil for 1 minute, stirring constantly. Remove from heat and stir in orange peel. Cool to room temperature before using.

FROSTING

Beat egg whites in a medium-size bowl with electric mixer on medium speed until soft peaks form. Meanwhile, combine sugar, cream of tartar and water in a medium-size saucepan. Bring to a simmer over moderate heat, stirring until sugar is dissolved and syrup is clear. Insert candy thermometer. Increase heat to moderately high and cook, without stirring, until sugar reaches the soft ball stage, 236° to 238°. Immediately remove from heat. With mixer on medium speed, slowly pour the syrup in a thin, steady stream over the egg whites. Do not be concerned with syrup that splatters onto sides of bowl. Add vanilla and continue beating until frosting forms stiff peaks and maintains a good spreading consistency, about 5 minutes. Spread over top and sides of filled cake and sprinkle with shredded coconut. (*) The filled and frosted cake may be refrigerated up to 8 hours, if desired.

**STRAWBERRY FILLING AND
WHIPPED CREAM FROSTING**

*2 cups fresh strawberries (about
    1½ pint boxes)*
*1½ cups plus 1½ cups whipping
    cream (1½ pints)*
2 tablespoons Grand Marnier
*3 tablespoons plus 3 tablespoons
    powdered sugar*
Mint leaves for garnish (optional)

Set 8 to 12 perfect strawberries aside for garnish. Remove stems and slice remaining berries into a bowl. Whip 1½ cups cream in large bowl with electric mixer until soft peaks form. Add Grand Marnier and 3 tablespoons powdered sugar. Beat on high speed until stiff enough to spread. Fold in sliced strawberries. Use to fill Orange Sponge Cake as directed.

To make frosting, whip the remaining 1½ cups cream in large bowl with electric mixer on low speed until soft peaks form. Add 3 tablespoons powdered sugar and beat on high speed until firm peaks form. Spread over top and sides of cake. (*) The filled and frosted cake may be refrigerated up to 8 hours, if desired.

Before serving, garnish the top with reserved strawberries and mint leaves.

Fresh Banana Cake with Banana Frosting

To make this super-moist, fresh banana cake you will need 3 very ripe bananas for the cake and frosting and 1 or 2 firm bananas for slicing and decorating. This cake is pictured on page 10.

CAKE

*½ pound (2 sticks) unsalted butter,
    at room temperature*
1 cup sugar
2 large eggs, at room temperature
*1 cup mashed ripe banana (2 very
    ripe medium-size bananas)*
1¾ cups all-purpose flour
¼ teaspoon salt
1 teaspoon baking soda
⅓ cup buttermilk
1 teaspoon vanilla

BANANA FROSTING

*12 ounces cream cheese, at room
    temperature about 30 minutes*
*⅓ cup mashed ripe banana (about
    ½ a ripe banana)*
1 cup powdered sugar
*1 to 2 firm-ripe bananas for
    layering and garnishining*
*½ cup coarsely chopped pecans or
    walnuts, for garnishing*
*Powdered sugar for sprinkling
    on top*

BAKING PANS

*Two 8 x 1½-inch or 8 x 2-inch
    round layer-cake pans*

Preheat oven to 350°. Grease bottom and sides of cake pans. Dust with flour and shake out excess. Set aside.

CAKE

Beat together butter and sugar in a large mixing bowl with electric mixer on medium speed until light and fluffy. Add eggs one at a time, beating well after each addition. Add 1 cup mashed banana to batter, mixing until incorporated.

Stir together the flour, salt and baking soda in a small bowl. With mixer on low speed, alternately mix flour in fourths and buttermilk in thirds into batter, beginning and ending with flour. Add vanilla and beat 1 minute on medium speed.

Divide batter equally between prepared pans. Place the pans in the center of the 350° oven for 30 to 35 minutes or until the tops are golden and spring back when lightly pressed with fingertips. Remove to wire racks and cool in pans 10 minutes. Invert cakes onto racks and cool completely. (*) If desired, cakes may be wrapped in foil and kept at room temperature overnight, or frozen. Defrost wrapped cakes at room temperature.

FROSTING

Beat cream cheese in small bowl with electric mixer on medium speed until smooth. Mix in mashed banana. Scrape sides of bowl and slowly beat in sugar until mixture is light and creamy, about 1 minute.

To assemble cake, line a serving platter with 4 strips of wax paper placed at right angles to each other and overlapping. Place one cake layer flat-side up on platter. Spread with a quarter of the frosting. Thinly slice 1 firm-ripe banana and arrange a layer of slices over frosting. Top with second cake layer, flat-side down. Frost top and sides. Garnish with a 1-inch border of nuts around top of cake. Sift powdered sugar over top of cake to cover it lightly. Refrigerate until serving time. (*) The filled and frosted cake may be refrigerated uncovered overnight, if desired.

Before serving, remove strips of wax paper. Slice remaining firm-ripe banana and arrange in overlapping circles in center of cake.

Serves 8 to 10.

Chocolate Kahlúa Cream Torte

Four luscious layers of chocolate cake are filled with a mocha cream and glazed with rich, dark chocolate. Although it looks and tastes as if you spent hours in the kitchen, it's actually simple to prepare. The trick is to bake the cake in a jelly-roll pan, then cut it into equal layers. This cake is pictured on page 10.

CAKE

6 large eggs, separated and at
 room temperature
½ cup plus ½ cup powdered sugar
3 tablespoons unsweetened cocoa
 powder
Dash of cream of tartar

FILLING

1½ cups whipping cream
¼ cup unsweetened cocoa powder
½ cup powdered sugar
2 tablespoons Kahlúa

FROSTING

6 ounces chocolate chips
2 tablespoons unsalted butter
2 tablespoons light corn syrup
3 tablespoons milk
Chocolate Curls for garnish
 (optional) (see page 227)
Powdered sugar for garnish
 (optional)

BAKING PAN

15½ x 10½ x 1-inch jelly-roll
 pan.

Preheat oven to 400°. Grease jelly-roll pan. Line with parchment or wax paper, leaving a 2-inch overlap on each end. Grease paper.

CAKE

Beat egg yolks in large bowl with an electric mixer on high speed until thick and creamy, about 3 minutes. Reduce speed to low and gradually beat in ½ cup powdered sugar and the cocoa, mixing until incorporated. Beat egg whites in another mixing bowl with an electric mixer on low speed, until foamy. Add cream of tartar, increase speed to high and beat until soft peaks form. Add remaining ½ cup sugar, a tablespoon at at time, beating continuously until mixture forms stiff but not dry peaks. Gently fold whites into yolks until incorporated.

Turn batter into prepared pan and spread top evenly with a spatula. Bake in the 400° oven for 12 to 15 minutes or until top springs back when lightly pressed with fingertips and cake shrinks slightly from side of pan. While cake bakes, place a clean dish towel on counter. Sift some extra cocoa over the towel. Carefully invert cake onto towel. Remove pan and then gently pull off paper. Cool thoroughly.

FILLING

Beat cream in a large bowl with electric mixer on low speed until soft peaks form. Add cocoa, powdered sugar and Kahlúa. Beat on medium speed until spreading consistency.

Line the edges of a long, narrow platter with 4 strips of wax paper. Using a long serrated knife, cut cake crosswise into 4 slices, each about 3½ inches wide. Place one cake layer on platter. Spread with a third of the filling. Top with second layer and a third of the filling. Repeat with third layer and filling. Place final cake layer on top. Trim edges even, if necessary. (*) If desired, the filled torte may be refrigerated, covered with foil, overnight, or frozen wrapped in foil. Defrost wrapped cake in refrigerator overnight.

FROSTING

Several hours before serving, melt chocolate chips and butter in the top of a double boiler over hot water. Remove from heat and add corn syrup and milk, whisking until smooth. If frosting is too thin to spread, refrigerate, stirring occasionally, until slightly thickened. Spread frosting over top and sides of torte, covering it completely. Garnish the top with Chocolate Curls. To duplicate the effect shown on page 10, place a strip of wax paper down the center of the curls. Sift powdered sugar over the tips of the curls and carefully lift off the wax paper. Remove strips of wax paper from platter. Refrigerate torte until frosting is set or up to 8 hours. It is easiest to cut this creamy-textured torte with a serrated knife.

Serves 8.

White Chocolate Cake

This magnificent recipe, adapted from food stylist Lane Crowther, is the ultimate celebration cake—perfect for weddings, anniversaries and birthdays. Four luscious layers of white chocolate cake are moistened with crème de cacao syrup and layered with ultra-creamy white chocolate butter cream. The cake is frosted with more butter cream and then, if desired, majestically wrapped in a dark chocolate band and topped with layers of dark chocolate leaves. See cover photo or page 224.

CAKE

4 ounces white chocolate (see page 7), chopped
½ cup whipping cream
¼ pound (1 stick) unsalted butter, at room temperature
1 cup sugar
1 teaspoon vanilla
3 large eggs, at room temperature
2 cups all-purpose flour
1 teaspoon baking soda
¼ teaspoon salt
⅔ cup buttermilk

SYRUP

⅓ cup sugar
⅓ cup water
4 tablespoons crème de cacao

WHITE CHOCOLATE BUTTER CREAM

14 ounces white chocolate, chopped
½ cup whipping cream
½ pound (2 sticks) unsalted butter, at room temperature
5 large egg yolks
3 tablespoons crème de cacao

GARNISH (optional)
Chocolate Band (page 227)
Chocolate Leaves (page 228)

BAKING PANS
Two 9 x 1½-inch or 9 x 2-inch round layer-cake pans

Preheat oven to 350°. Grease and flour pans, shaking out excess flour.

CAKE

Melt chocolate with cream in top of double boiler over simmering water, whisking until smooth. Set aside to cool. Beat butter and sugar in medium-size bowl with electric mixer on medium speed until light and fluffy, about 3 minutes. Add vanilla and eggs one at a time, beating well after each addition. Mix in melted chocolate on low speed. Stir together flour, baking soda and salt in medium-size bowl. Alternately add flour in fourths and buttermilk in thirds on low speed, beginning and ending with flour, mixing until batter is smooth. Divide batter between pans and spread with a spatula.

continued

Bake in the 350° oven for 25 to 30 minutes or until cake tester comes out clean and top springs back when lightly pressed with fingertips. The sides will begin to turn golden, but the top will remain white.

Remove cakes from oven and cool in pans 10 minutes. Invert onto cooling racks and cool completely. (*) Cakes may be wrapped and held at room temperature overnight, or they may be frozen, if desired. Defrost wrapped cakes at room temperature.

SYRUP

Combine sugar and water in a heavy small saucepan. Bring to a boil over moderate heat, stirring until sugar is dissolved. Remove from the heat and cool to room temperature. Stir in crème de cacao. (*) Syrup may be made ahead and refrigerated, covered, indefinitely.

BUTTER CREAM

Melt chocolate with cream in top of double boiler over simmering water, stirring until smooth. Set aside until cool.

Beat butter in medium-size bowl with electric mixer on high speed until light and fluffy, about 2 minutes. Beat in egg yolks, one at a time, mixing until well blended. Mix in cooled chocolate and crème de cacao on low speed. Refrigerate butter cream for 20 to 30 minutes or until firm enough to frost and pipe.

To assemble cake, cut each cake in half horizontally, making 4 layers. Line cake plate with four strips of wax paper placed at right angles to each other and overlapping. Place 1 cake layer top-side down on serving platter. Brush top generously with the syrup and spread with ⅓ cup butter cream. Top with second cake layer cut-side down. Brush with syrup and spread with ⅓ cup butter cream. Place third layer top-side down and brush with syrup (you will not use it all) and spread with ⅓ cup butter cream. Top with last layer cut-side down. Frost top and sides with half the remaining butter cream. Place remaining butter cream in pastry bag fitted with ¾-inch rosette or star tip and pipe a border of rosettes around top of cake. Refrigerate for at least 30 minutes for frosting to set. (*) Frosted cake may be covered with plastic wrap and refrigerated up to 2 days.

If decorating with dark chocolate band, as pictured on page 224, remove cake from refrigerator and leave at room temperature, uncovered, for 30 minutes for butter cream to soften. Gently place chocolate band around sides of cake. Decorate top with overlapping rows of chocolate leaves, beginning on the outside border and working towards the center. The cake may be refrigerated up to 8 hours. Before serving, remove wax paper strips and allow cake to stand at room temperature for 30 minutes.

Serves 10 to 12.

Bittersweet Fudge Torte

It's not really a cake or a torte—it tastes more like a fallen soufflé. This flourless, black-as-midnight, chocolate treat is super-moist, slightly dense and sensationally fudgy. Served topped with a dollop of Creamy Vanilla Sauce or sweetened whipped cream, it melts in your mouth.

½ **pound (2 sticks) unsalted butter**
8 **ounces unsweetened chocolate, chopped**
4 **ounces semisweet chocolate, chopped**
5 **large eggs, at room temperature**
½ **cup plus ½ cup sugar**
⅓ **cup light corn syrup**
1 **recipe Creamy Vanilla Sauce (see page 217) OR 1½ cups whipping cream softly whipped with 4 tablespoons powdered sugar**

BAKING PAN
9 x 3-inch or 9½ x 2-inch springform pan

Preheat oven to 350°. Butter springform. Cut a circle of wax paper or parchment to fit in bottom and butter paper. Wrap outside of pan in foil to keep batter from seeping out as it bakes.

Place butter and the unsweetened and semisweet chocolate in a medium-size heavy saucepan. Stir over low heat until melted. Set aside.

Beat eggs and ½ cup sugar in a large bowl with electric mixer on high speed, until very light and fluffy, about 5 minutes. Meanwhile, combine corn syrup and ½ cup sugar in a small saucepan. Bring to a full boil over moderate heat, stirring constantly. Transfer to heatproof glass measuring cup. With mixer on medium speed, slowly pour sugar syrup in a thin, steady stream into eggs. Stir a small amount of the egg mixture into the chocolate mixture to lighten it. Then fold the chocolate back into the eggs. Pour into prepared springform pan.

Place a shallow baking pan in the 350° oven. Place springform pan in baking pan and fill with about 1 inch hot water. Bake for 45 minutes or until cake tester inserted in center comes out clean. The center will not spring back. Do not overbake as cake will firm up as it cools. Remove cake from water and cool on rack for 30 minutes. Invert onto serving plate, remove paper and cool completely. (*) If desired, the torte may be covered with plastic wrap or foil and kept at room temperature overnight, or it may be refrigerated up to 3 days. Bring to room temperature before serving.

Make Creamy Vanilla Sauce, if using. Refrigerate until ready to serve. Serve torte at room temperature. It is easiest to cut this light, fudgy-textured cake if you wipe the blade of a sharp knife clean and dip it in hot water before each slice. Spoon Creamy Vanilla Sauce or whipped cream over each slice.

Serves 8 to 10.

Chocolate Nut Torte

This European-style torte, reminiscent of Old World elegance, is rich with nuts and fudgy chocolate. It's hard to believe anything this simple to prepare can be so sensational, but the use of a food processor makes it so.

4 squares (4 ounces) semisweet
  chocolate
1¾ cups shelled pecans or walnuts
  (about 7 ounces)
2 tablespoons plus ½ cup sugar
¼ pound (1 stick) unsalted butter,
  at room temperature
3 large eggs, at room temperature
1 tablespoon Grand Marnier OR
  rum

CHOCOLATE GLAZE AND
GARNISH

6 squares (6 ounces) semisweet
  chocolate, chopped
6 tablespoons unsalted butter
20 to 22 pecan or walnut halves,
  for garnish

BAKING PAN

8 x 1½-inch or 8 x 2-inch round
  layer-cake pan

Preheat oven to 375°. Grease cake pan. Cut circle of parchment or wax paper to fit in bottom and grease paper.

Melt chocolate in top of double boiler over hot water. Cool slightly. Place nuts and 2 tablespoons of the sugar in food processor fitted with a metal blade. Pulse on and off until nuts are ground. Remove to bowl. Place butter and ½ cup sugar in food processor. Mix until well blended. Pour in melted chocolate and process until smooth. Add eggs and Grand Marnier or rum and mix until incorporated. Scrape down sides of bowl and add nuts. Pulse on and off once or twice until nuts are incorporated.

Pour chocolate mixture into prepared cake pan. Bake in the 375° oven for 25 minutes. The cake will be soft, but will firm up as it cools. Remove from oven and cool 20 minutes on wire rack. Invert cake onto rack. Remove paper and cool completely.

(*) If desired, the unglazed torte may be kept covered at room temperature up to 2 days, or it may be frozen, tightly wrapped in aluminum foil. Defrost wrapped cake at room temperature.

GLAZE AND GARNISH

Up to 1 day or several hours before serving, preheat oven to 350°. Bake pecans or walnuts on baking sheet for 10 to 15 minutes, stirring occasionally until browned. Line a small baking sheet with wax paper. Place cake on rack set over a baking pan. Melt the chocolate and butter in small, heavy saucepan, stirring until smooth. Dip half of each nut into the glaze and place on paper-lined pan, as pictured. Refrigerate until set. Set the glaze aside until thickened slightly. The glaze should be soft enough to pour, but thick enough to coat the cake. Pour glaze onto middle of cake, tilting the cake so the glaze runs down the sides. Use a knife dipped in hot water to help smooth the sides, if necessary. Do not try to touch up the top once it is frosted or knife marks will show. Decorate top with a border of chocolate-dipped pecan or walnut halves. (*) The glazed torte may be held at room temperature, uncovered, overnight, if desired.

Serves 8.

1 *Dip half of each nut into Chocolate Glaze and place on wax-paper lined baking sheet. Refrigerate until set.*

2 *Place cake on rack on baking sheet and pour over remaining glaze.*

3 *Distribute chocolate by tilting the rack, allowing glaze to drip down the sides. Use a knife dipped in hot water to smooth the sides, if necessary. Don't touch the top once the glaze is poured over or it will not be smooth.*

4 *Completed torte decorated with a circle of chocolate coated nuts.*

Mocha Fudge Torte

The taste and texture of this incredible dessert are beyond description. Bound together by pure chocolate, with a dash of coffee and a thin layer of currant jelly, this torte is so unbelievably dense and undeniably fudgy, it has to be the ultimate chocolate dessert.

12 ounces semisweet chocolate, chopped
1½ cups sugar
¾ pound (3 sticks) unsalted butter
¾ cup water
1½ tablespoons instant coffee crystals or powder
6 large eggs, at room temperature

FROSTING AND GARNISH
⅓ cup currant jelly
1½ cups whipping cream
⅓ cup powdered sugar
½ teaspoon vanilla
Chocolate Curls or Chocolate Triangles (see page 227), for garnish (optional)

BAKING PAN
9 x 3-inch or 9½ x 2-inch springform pan

Preheat oven to 350°. Butter the pan. Cut a circle of wax paper or parchment to fit in bottom and butter paper. Wrap outside of pan in foil to keep batter from seeping out as it bakes.

Combine chocolate, sugar, butter, water and coffee in a medium-size heavy saucepan. Cook over low heat, stirring constantly, until chocolate and butter are melted. Set aside to cool slightly. Meanwhile, beat eggs in large bowl with electric mixer on high speed until frothy, about 1 minute. Reduce speed to low and slowly beat in chocolate mixture until incorporated. The batter will be thin.

Pour into prepared springform pan. Place on baking sheet. Bake in the 350° oven for 40 minutes, or until a crust forms around the top edges of the cake. It will be soft in the center, look underdone and will not test clean with a cake tester. Remove from the oven and cool completely on wire rack. It will sink as it cools. Bring to room temperature, cover with foil and refrigerate overnight or until firm.

To remove cake from pan, run a sharp knife around sides of torte. Remove sides of springform. Invert cake onto serving platter or onto a sheet of foil if you wish to freeze it. To remove bottom of pan, insert knife and run between bottom of springform and torte and pry loose. Lift to remove bottom. Don't worry about appearance since torte will be frosted. (*) If desired, the torte may be refrigerated up to 3 days, or it may be frozen wrapped in foil. Defrost wrapped cake in refrigerator overnight.

FROSTING

Several hours before serving, melt jelly in small saucepan. Spread over top of torte. Return to refrigerator for 15 minutes for jelly to set. Whip cream in large bowl with electric mixer on low speed until slightly thickened. Gradually add powdered sugar and vanilla and beat on medium speed until spreading consistency. Frost top and sides of torte with three-quarters of the whipped cream. If desired, spoon remaining cream into a pastry bag fitted with a ¾- to 1-inch rosette or star tip and pipe a border of rosettes around top. Or spoon cream in dollops around torte. Decorate with chocolate curls or triangles, if desired. Refrigerate until serving time.

Serves 8 to 10.

Lemon Meringue Spiral

If you like the taste of lemon meringue pie, than you will love this contemporary update. A classic lemon filling is rolled up in a light sponge cake and blanketed with a snowy baked meringue. This beautiful cake roll will bring forth raves from your guests.

CAKE

3 large eggs, at room temperature
½ cup sugar
1 teaspoon vanilla
⅔ cup all-purpose flour
1 teaspoon baking powder
Dash of salt
Grated peel of 1 lemon

LEMON FILLING

¾ cup sugar
Dash of salt
5 tablespoons cornstarch
1½ cups boiling water
3 large egg yolks, at room
*   temperature*
½ cup fresh lemon juice
2 tablespoons grated lemon peel

MERINGUE

5 large egg whites, at room
*   temperature*
¼ teaspoon cream of tartar
¾ cup sugar

BAKING PAN

15½ x 10½ x 1-inch jelly-roll pan
Ovenproof platter or board

Preheat oven to 375°. Grease jelly-roll pan. Line with parchment or wax paper, leaving a 2-inch overlap on each narrow end. Grease bottom and sides of paper.

CAKE

Beat eggs, sugar and vanilla in small bowl with electric mixer on high speed until mixture is very thick and pale, about 5 minutes. Sprinkle flour, baking powder, salt, and lemon peel over top. Gently fold together until incorporated.

Pour batter into prepared pan and smooth top evenly with a spatula. Bake in the 375° oven for 8 to 12 minutes or until top is pale golden and springs back when lightly pressed with fingertips and the cake pulls away from the sides of pan. While cake bakes, place a clean dish towel on counter. Spray with vegetable cooking spray or dust with sifted powdered sugar. Invert cake onto towel. Remove pan and gently pull off paper. Beginning at narrow end, roll cake and towel together as tightly as possible. (See pictures page 30 on making jelly roll.) Set aside seam-side down and cool completely. (*) The

continued

LEMON MERINGUE SPIRAL, CONTINUED

towel-wrapped roll may be held at room temperature overnight, if desired.

FILLING

Stir together ¾ cup sugar, salt and cornstarch in medium-size saucepan. Whisking constantly, slowly add boiling water. Cook over moderate heat, stirring constantly, until mixture comes to a full boil and is thick and clear. Remove from heat. Beat the yolks in a small bowl with a whisk until frothy. Mix in about ½ cup of the hot mixture. Return to saucepan. Stir in lemon juice and peel. Cook for 2 more minutes, whisking constantly. Remove to a bowl, place a piece of plastic wrap directly over the top and refrigerate until cold and thick enough to spread.

Unroll cake and spread with filling, leaving a 1-inch border. Roll up tightly, trim ends and place seam-side down.

(*) If desired, the filled roll may be refrigerated, wrapped in foil, overnight, or it may be frozen. Defrost wrapped cake in refrigerator overnight.

MERINGUE

Several hours before serving, preheat oven to 400°. Beat egg whites in medium-size bowl with electric mixer on low speed until frothy. Add cream of tartar and beat on high speed until soft peaks form. Slowly beat in ¾ cup sugar, 1 tablespoon at a time, until mixture forms stiff, glossy peaks. Place cake seam-side down on ovenproof platter or board. Spread a ½-inch layer of meringue smoothly over the roll, taking care to cover it completely. Spoon the remaining meringue into a pastry bag fitted with a ¾- to 1-inch rosette or star tip and pipe decoratively over the roll. Or use a spatula to swirl the meringue into peaks. Bake in the 400° oven for 10 to 12 minutes or until peaks are golden brown. Refrigerate until ready to serve, up to 6 hours.

Serves 8.

Strawberry Shortcake Roll

Coffee and strawberry? When my students read this recipe they invariably express surprise over the unlikely combination. When they taste this cake roll, however, they're always delighted. Think of it as enjoying a cup of coffee and a piece of strawberry shortcake, rolled up in one.

CAKE

4 large eggs, separated and at room temperature
¼ cup plus ¼ cup sugar
¼ teaspoon salt
Dash of cream of tartar
1 teaspoon vanilla
¼ cup all-purpose flour
½ cup finely chopped nuts (walnuts or pecans)

FILLING

1 cup whipping cream
1 pint box fresh strawberries, hulled and sliced (about 1½ cups)
2 teaspoons instant coffee powder or crystals

4 to 6 teaspoons milk
1 cup powdered sugar
¼ teaspoon vanilla

FROSTING AND GARNISH

½ cup whipping cream
¼ cup strawberries, mashed with a fork
½ cup whipping cream (optional)
4 to 6 fresh whole strawberries, sliced
Coffee candy beans, for garnish (optional)

BAKING PAN

15½ x 10½ x 1-inch jelly-roll pan

Preheat oven to 375°. Grease jelly-roll pan. Line with parchment or wax paper, leaving a 2-inch overlap on each narrow end, as pictured. Grease bottom and sides of the paper.

CAKE

Beat egg yolks and ¼ cup sugar in small mixing bowl with electric mixer on high speed until thick and lemon-colored, about 5 minutes. Beat egg whites in separate large bowl with mixer on low speed until frothy. Add salt and cream of tartar and beat on high speed until soft peaks begin to form. Beat in remaining ¼ cup sugar, 1 tablespoon at a time, until mixture forms stiff but moist peaks. Beat in vanilla. Pour yolks, flour and nuts over whites. Gently fold together until incorporated. Pour batter into prepared pan, smoothing top evenly with a spatula. Bake in 375° oven for 8 to 12 minutes or until top is lightly browned and springs back when pressed with fingertips and cake pulls away from sides of pan. While cake bakes, place a clean dish towel on counter. Spray with vegetable cooking spray, or dust with sifted powdered sugar. Remove cake from oven and invert onto towel. Remove pan and gently pull off the paper. Starting at narrow end, roll cake and towel together as tightly as possible. Set aside seam-side down and cool completely. (*) The towel-wrapped roll may be held at room temperature overnight.

FILLING

As close to serving as possible, but no more than 4 hours ahead, beat cream in large bowl with electric mixer on low speed until thick. Increase speed to high and beat until stiff peaks form. Fold in the sliced strawberries. In a small saucepan, bring coffee and 4 teaspoons

continued

1 *Pour batter into pan lined with greased paper and spread evenly.*

2 *Invert baked cake onto towel, remove pan and paper, and roll cake up in the towel.*

3 *Spread unrolled cake with coffee icing and strawberry cream filling. Reroll cake, using the towel to help you roll.*

4 *Completed roll decorated with sliced strawberries and coffee candy beans.*

STRAWBERRY SHORTCAKE ROLL,
CONTINUED

milk to a boil, stirring until coffee is dissolved. Stir into powdered sugar in a medium-size bowl. Slowly stir in enough additional milk to obtain a spreading consistency. Stir in vanilla.

Unroll cooled cake. Spread coffee icing over cake to the edges. (If icing is too firm, thin with additional drop or two of milk.) Spread cream mixture evenly over icing, leaving a 1-inch border all around. Reroll cake, trim ends and place seam-side down on serving platter.

FROSTING AND GARNISH

Beat ½ cup cream in medium bowl with electric mixer on medium speed until spreading consistency. Fold in mashed strawberries. Spread over entire cake. To match picture, beat remaining ½ cup cream and pipe onto top and sides of cake. Garnish with strawberry slices and coffee candy beans, if desired. Refrigerate until serving.

Serves 8.

Sherbet Alaska Roll

A light, pretty dessert that's ideal for luncheons, Easter dinner, and baby and bridal showers. An airy sponge cake is rolled around two sherbet layers and topped with meringue. I suggest lime and raspberry, but let your taste and imagination be your guide. The beauty of this roll is the blend of pastel colors —cotton-candy pink and pale lime green—topped with a brilliant ruby-red raspberry sauce. If you prefer to use ice cream, you may want to substitute a complementary-flavored sauce.

BAKING PAN
15½ x 10½ x 1-inch jelly-roll pan
Ovenproof serving platter or board

CAKE
3 large eggs, separated and at room temperature
¼ cup plus ¼ cup sugar
⅛ teaspoon cream of tartar
¼ teaspoon salt
½ teaspoon vanilla
⅓ cup all-purpose flour
1 pint raspberry sherbet
1 pint lime sherbet
1 recipe Ruby-Red Raspberry Sauce for serving (page 218)

Fresh raspberries, lime slices and mint leaves for garnish (optional)

MERINGUE
4 large egg whites, at room temperature
¼ teaspoon cream of tartar
¾ cup granulated sugar
1 teaspoon vanilla

Preheat oven to 375°. Grease jelly-roll pan. Line with parchment or wax paper, leaving a 2-inch overlap on narrow ends. Grease bottom and sides of paper; set aside.

CAKE

Beat egg yolks and ¼ cup sugar in small mixing bowl with electric mixer on high speed until very thick and lemon-colored, about 5 minutes. Beat egg whites in separate large mixing bowl with mixer on low speed, until frothy. Add cream of tartar and salt and beat on high speed until soft peaks form. Gradually add ¼ cup sugar, 1 tablespoon at a time, beating until mixture forms stiff but moist peaks. Beat in vanilla. Pour yolks and flour over whites. Gently fold together until incorporated.

Pour into prepared pan and smooth top evenly with a spatula. Bake in the 375° oven for 8 to 12 minutes or until top springs back when

continued

lightly pressed with fingertips and cake begins to pull away from sides of pan. While cake bakes, place a clean dish towel on counter. Spray towel with vegetable cooking spray, or dust with sifted powdered sugar. Remove cake from oven. Invert cake onto towel. Remove pan and gently pull off paper. Beginning at narrow end, roll cake and towel together as tightly as possible. (See pictures page 30 on making jelly roll.) Set aside seam-side down and cool completely. (*) The towel-wrapped roll may be held at room temperature overnight.

Stir sherbets to soften slightly. Unroll cake and spread with raspberry sherbet, leaving a 1-inch border all around. Spread lime sherbet over the raspberry. Roll up tightly and clean up sides. Wrap in foil and freeze overnight. (*) The filled roll may be frozen up to 1 month.

Make Raspberry Sauce as directed. Refrigerate until ready to use.

MERINGUE
Preheat oven to 500°.

Beat egg whites in medium-size bowl with mixer on low speed until frothy. Add cream of tartar and beat on high speed until soft peaks form. Add ¾ cup sugar, 1 tablespoon at a time, beating until mixture forms stiff, glossy peaks. Beat in vanilla. Place roll seam-side down on ovenproof platter. Spread a ½-inch layer of meringue smoothly over roll, taking care to cover it completely. Spoon remaining meringue into a pastry bag fitted with a ¾- to 1-inch rosette or star tip and pipe decoratively over roll. Or use a spatula to swirl meringue into peaks. (*) The meringue-covered roll may be returned to freezer for several hours, if desired. Bake roll in the 500° oven for 2 to 4 minutes or until golden. Garnish with fresh raspberries, lime slices and mint leaves, if desired. Serve with Ruby-Red Raspberry Sauce.

Serves 8.

Espresso Chocolate Soufflé Roll

This rich, soufflé-like cake is rolled with a softly whipped, slightly sweetened coffee cream. It's almost like eating air.

6 squares (6 ounces) semisweet chocolate, chopped
2 teaspoons instant espresso (OR 1 tablespoon instant coffee powder or crystals) dissolved in 6 tablespoons boiling water
6 large eggs, separated and at room temperature
¾ cup sugar
⅛ teaspoon cream of tartar
2 tablespoons unsweetened cocoa powder

1¼ cups plus 1 cup whipping cream
3 tablespoons powdered sugar
1 teaspoon vanilla
Chocolate Curls or Chocolate Triangles (page 227) OR cocoa powder for garnish

BAKING PAN
15½ x 10½ x 1-inch jelly-roll pan

Preheat oven to 350°. Grease jelly-roll pan. Line with parchment or wax paper, leaving 2-inch overlap on each narrow end. Grease paper.

Heat chocolate and 3 tablespoons of the coffee in top of double boiler over simmering water until melted, stirring. Set aside to cool slightly.

Beat egg yolks and sugar in small bowl with electric mixer on high speed until thick and light colored, about 3 minutes. Reduce speed to low and gradually beat in melted chocolate mixture. Beat egg whites in large mixing bowl with electric mixer on low speed, until foamy. Add cream of tartar and beat on high speed until soft peaks form. Stir a dollop of whites into the chocolate to lighten it. Then fold the chocolate into the whites.

Pour batter into prepared pan; spread evenly with spatula. Bake in the 350° oven for 15 minutes or until top forms a crust. Remove from oven and place a slightly damp dish towel directly on the top. Cool to room temperature. Remove towel and sift 2 tablespoons cocoa over the top.

On a flat surface, overlap 2 sheets of wax paper 16 inches long. Go around edges of cake with a small knife and invert cake onto wax paper. Remove pan and gently peel off paper.

Beat 1¼ cups whipping cream in large mixing bowl with electric mixer on low speed until thick. Add powdered sugar and vanilla. Mix in remaining 3 tablespoons room-temperature coffee. Beat on medium speed until stiff. Spread whipped cream over top of cake. Beginning with one long end, gently roll the cake up, using the wax paper to help turn the roll. The cake may crack slightly as you roll; push it gently together with your hands. Do not be concerned with the cracks as they will be covered. Wrap cake tightly in wax paper and foil. Refrigerate until chilled. (*) If desired, the filled cake may be wrapped and refrigerated overnight, or frozen. Defrost wrapped cake in refrigerator overnight.

Several hours before serving, whip remaining 1 cup cream in medium-size bowl with electric mixer on low speed until spreading consistency. Place cake, seam-side down, on serving platter. Spread cream over top and sides of cake, or spoon into pastry bag fitted with ¾- to 1-inch rosette or star tip and pipe cream. Decorate with Chocolate Curls or Chocolate Triangles, or dust the top lightly with cocoa. Refrigerate until serving time.

Serves 8.

Hot Apple Cake with Caramel Pecan Sauce

Hot Apple Cake with Caramel Pecan Sauce

This moist, chunky apple cake is served topped with vanilla ice cream and a warm, toasted-pecan caramel topping. The combination of creamy, cold ice cream with hot, crunchy caramel sauce and fresh-baked, fruity cake is sensational.

½ pound (2 sticks) unsalted butter, at room temperature
1 cup sugar
2 large eggs, at room temperature
1½ cups all-purpose flour
¼ teaspoon ground nutmeg
1½ teaspoons ground cinnamon
1 teaspoon baking soda
¼ teaspoon salt
3 medium-size tart apples (about 1¼ pounds), peeled, cored and finely chopped
¾ cup chopped pecans (about 3 ounces)
1 teaspoon vanilla

1 quart vanilla ice cream, for serving

CARAMEL PECAN SAUCE
4 tablespoons unsalted butter
½ cup pecan halves
1 cup firmly packed dark brown sugar
1 cup whipping cream

BAKING PAN
9 x 2-inch cake pan

Preheat oven to 350°. Grease cake pan and set aside.

Beat butter and sugar in large bowl with electric mixer on high speed until light and fluffy, about 2 minutes. Beat in eggs on low speed, one at a time, until well blended. Add flour, spices, baking soda and salt, beating just until incorporated. Mix in apples, nuts and the vanilla.

Spoon batter into prepared pan. Bake in the 350° oven for 35 to 45 minutes or until top is golden and cake tester inserted near center comes out clean. Remove to rack and cool. Turn cake out of pan by inverting onto rack after 10 minutes. (*) If desired, the cake may be stored at room temperature, well wrapped, overnight, or it may be frozen. Defrost at room temperature for several hours or overnight. Reheat in 350° oven for 10 minutes or until warm.

CARAMEL PECAN SAUCE
Melt butter in medium-size saucepan. Add nuts. Cook, stirring constantly, over moderately high heat, until nuts are toasted and butter is lightly browned. Add brown sugar and cream and continue to cook, stirring constantly, until sauce boils and sugar dissolves and turns deep golden brown. Remove from heat. Sauce will thicken slightly as it cools. (*) The sauce may be refrigerated several days. Reheat before serving.

To serve, place a wedge of warm cake on dessert plate. Serve with a scoop of vanilla ice cream and spoon hot Caramel Pecan Sauce over all.

Serves 6 to 8.

Apricot Upside-Down Ginger Cake

This amazingly easy recipe combines the homey, old-fashioned goodness of both gingerbread and upside-down cake. Because it is superb served warm, place it in the oven when you sit down to dinner. The wonderful aroma wafting from the kitchen will entice everyone to hurry through their meal.

3 tablespoons plus 4 tablespoons unsalted butter, at room temperature
⅓ cup golden brown sugar, firmly packed
1 can (1 pound, 14 ounces) apricot halves, drained and patted dry on paper towels
½ cup granulated sugar
1 large egg, at room temperature
½ cup light molasses
½ cup milk
1½ cups all-purpose flour
1 teaspoon baking soda
1 teaspoon ground cinnamon
1 teaspoon ground ginger
¼ teaspoon salt
Maraschino or candied cherries cut in half for garnishing (optional)
1 cup lightly whipped cream OR vanilla ice cream for serving (optional)

BAKING PAN
9 x 1½- or 9 x 2-inch round layer-cake pan

Preheat oven to 325°. Place 3 tablespoons butter in cake pan. Place in oven until melted. Remove pan from oven, swirl butter to coat pan, and immediately sprinkle brown sugar evenly over bottom of pan. Arrange apricot halves cut-side down in single layer over the brown sugar.

Beat together 4 tablespoons butter and granulated sugar in medium-size bowl with an electric mixer on high speed until creamy. Beat in egg, molasses and milk until well blended. Stir together flour, baking soda, cinnamon, ginger and salt in medium-size bowl. Beat into batter on low speed, mixing until incorporated. Spoon evenly over the apricots. (*) The cake may be held at room temperature up to 1 hour before baking, if desired.

Bake in the 325° oven for 60 minutes or until cake tester inserted near center comes out clean. Remove from oven and immediately turn out onto serving platter. Garnish the center of each apricot with a cherry half, if desired. Serve warm with whipped cream or ice cream, if desired.

Serves 8.

Strawberry Cream Sponge Tart

It may resemble a tart, but it tastes so much lighter—a sponge cake replaces the traditional crust. The cake shell is layered with cookie crumbs and Kirsch-scented cream and topped with glazed fresh berries.

NUT LAYER

¼ cup whole or chopped walnuts or pecans (about 3 tablespoons ground nuts)

8 vanilla wafers (about 3 tablespoons crumbs)

2 tablespoons unsalted butter, at room temperature

¼ cup golden brown sugar, packed

CAKE LAYER

2 large eggs, at room temperature

1 cup sugar

1 teaspoon vanilla

1 cup all-purpose flour

½ cup milk

1 tablespoon unsalted butter

CREAM FILLING

3 ounces cream cheese, at room temperature

2 tablespoons sugar

1 tablespoon plus 2 tablespoons Kirsch

⅓ cup whipping cream

FRUIT TOPPING

2 cups fresh strawberries, hulled

1 teaspoon unflavored gelatin

2 tablespoons cold water

1 package (10 ounces) frozen sliced strawberries in syrup, thawed slightly

3 tablespoons sugar

1 teaspoon fresh lemon juice

1 tablespoon Kirsch (optional)

BAKING PAN

10- to 11-inch tart pan with indented ridge, sometimes called Mary Ann pan

NUT LAYER

Spray tart pan well with vegetable cooking spray. Process nuts and wafers in food processor fitted with metal blade until ground. Add butter and brown sugar and mix until blended. Or, stir together ground nuts, crumbs, butter and brown sugar in a bowl. Press into flat center of pan only.

CAKE

Place oven rack in lower third of oven. Preheat oven to 350°.

Beat eggs in mixing bowl with electric mixer on high speed until foamy. Add sugar and vanilla, beating until mixture is very thick and creamy, about 5 minutes. Stir in flour. Heat milk and 1 tablespoon butter in small saucepan to a simmer. Beat hot milk into batter on low speed, mixing just until incorporated.

Pour into tart pan. Bake in the 350° oven for 20 to 25 minutes or until edges are golden and cake springs back when lightly pressed with fingertips. Cool in pan 5 minutes. Ease edges free with the tip of small knife and invert onto serving plate. If a few crumbs stay in pan, spread them with a knife onto the cake. Cool cake completely.

FILLING

Beat cheese and sugar in small bowl with electric mixer on medium speed until blended. Scrape down sides. Beating at high speed, mix in 1 tablespoon Kirsch and slowly pour in cream. Beat until mixture is consistency of whipped cream. Brush cake with remaining 2 tablespoons Kirsch. Spread cream filling evenly over indented area of rimmed sponge cake. (*) The cake may be refrigerated overnight. Cover very tightly with plastic wrap so edges of cake do not dry out.

continued

STRAWBERRY CREAM SPONGE TART,
CONTINUED

TOPPING

Several hours before serving, arrange fresh strawberries over top of tart. Make glaze by sprinkling unflavored gelatin over the cold water in a small saucepan. Let soften for 5 minutes. Meanwhile, in food processor fitted with metal blade or in blender, purée thawed strawberries with their syrup until smooth. Transfer to saucepan with gelatin. Stir in sugar and lemon juice. Cook, stirring, until mixture comes to a boil. Remove from heat and stir in Kirsch, if using. Place in refrigerator or in a bowl of ice water and chill, stirring occasionally, until thick enough to spread. Spoon as much glaze as needed over strawberries to thickly cover them. You may have some glaze left. Refrigerate until serving or up to 6 hours.

Serves 8.

Glazed Almond Date Cake

The honey-like date topping poured over the warm cake makes it so moist and flavorful it could almost be called a pudding. If you chop whole dates, rather than buying them already chopped, you will ensure a better textured and tastier cake.

BAKING PAN

9 x 3-inch or 9½ x 2-inch springform pan

½ pound whole pitted dates, chopped into small pieces
1 cup boiling water
1½ cups all-purpose flour
1 teaspoon baking soda
1 cup sugar
1 teaspoon baking powder
1 tablespoon unsalted butter, melted
1 large egg, lightly beaten
¼ cup almonds, coarsely chopped

1 tablespoon grated orange peel
1 cup whipping cream, softly whipped for serving (optional)

GLAZE

⅔ cup fresh orange juice
⅓ cup sugar
½ pound whole pitted dates, chopped into small pieces
¼ cup almonds, coarsely chopped

Preheat oven to 350°. Grease springform pan. Place dates in a large bowl. Pour boiling water over and set aside to cool completely.

Stir together the flour, baking soda, sugar and baking powder in a medium-size bowl. Add to cooled dates, stirring with a wooden spoon. Stir in melted butter, egg, nuts and orange peel. Pour batter into springform pan. Bake in the 350° oven for 30 to 35 minutes or until cake tester inserted near center comes out clean.

GLAZE

Meanwhile, combine orange juice and sugar in a medium-size saucepan. Bring to a boil, stirring until sugar is dissolved. Stir in dates. When cake comes out of the oven, stir almonds into glaze and immediately pour warm glaze over hot cake while still in pan. (*) The cake may be held at room temperature overnight, or it may be frozen, wrapped tightly in foil. Defrost wrapped cake at room temperature. To serve warm, reheat in 350° oven for 10 to 15 minutes.

Before serving, remove sides of springform. Serve warm or at room temperature with softly whipped cream, if desired.

Serves 8.

Bourbon Street Fudge Cake

The moist texture of this jet black cake comes from baking it in a very slow oven. Jazzed with bourbon to heighten the flavors, it is a perfect dessert for dark chocolate lovers.

2 teaspoons unsweetened cocoa powder
1¾ cups water
2 teaspoons instant coffee powder or crystals
¼ cup bourbon
5 ounces unsweetened chocolate, chopped
½ pound (2 sticks) unsalted butter, cut into small pieces and at room temperature
2 cups sugar
2 cups all-purpose flour
1 teaspoon baking soda
Dash of salt
2 large eggs, at room temperature
1 teaspoon vanilla

BAKING PAN
12-cup Bundt pan (see notes on Bundt pans, page 6)

Preheat oven to 275°. Grease Bundt pan and dust with the unsweetened cocoa. Rap pan sharply to remove excess cocoa. Set aside.

Combine water, instant coffee and bourbon in medium-size heavy saucepan. Simmer for 3 minutes. Add chocolate and butter and cook over moderate heat, stirring until mixture is melted and smooth. Remove from heat and stir in sugar until well blended. Let cool 3 minutes.

Transfer chocolate mixture to large bowl of electric mixer. Stir together flour, baking soda and salt in small bowl. Beating at medium speed, add the flour mixture, ½ cup at a time. When all the flour has been added, continue to beat for 1 minute. Beat in eggs one at a time. Add vanilla and mix until smooth. Batter will be thin.

Pour into prepared pan. Bake in the 275° oven for 1 hour and 20 to 30 minutes or until cake tester inserted in cake comes out clean and cake pulls away from the sides of pan. Cool in pan on rack 20 minutes. Invert cake onto rack, remove pan, and cool completely. (*) If desired, the cake may be stored at room temperature, covered, up to 3 days. Do not refrigerate. Or, it may be frozen, tightly wrapped in aluminum foil. Defrost wrapped cake at room temperature.

Serve at room temperature.

Serves 12.

Persimmon Spice Cake

Perfect for the holidays, this is a classic spice cake with a bright new look and taste, thanks to the persimmons. Since the persimmon season is so short, you may want to purée fresh ones and freeze them so that you can make this delicious cake more often.

2 large or 3 small persimmons (about 1½ pounds)
1 teaspoon baking soda
2 tablespoons fresh orange juice
⅔ cup vegetable oil
1½ cups sugar
3 large eggs, at room temperature
2 tablespoons fresh lemon juice
1¾ cups all-purpose flour
2 teaspoons baking powder
¼ teaspoon salt
1¼ teaspoons ground cinnamon
¾ teaspoon ground allspice
1 tablespoon grated orange peel

½ cup raisins, chopped
½ cup shelled pecans, chopped

ORANGE GLAZE

1 cup powdered sugar
2 to 3 tablespoons fresh orange juice
2 teaspoons grated orange peel

BAKING PAN

12-cup Bundt pan (see notes on Bundt pans, page 6)

Preheat oven to 350°. Grease pan. Sprinkle with flour and shake out the excess.

Cut persimmons in half. Cut out center core. Using a teaspoon, scoop out pulp and place it in a food processor fitted with a metal blade. Process on and off until persimmons are puréed. Measure 1¼ cups. Stir baking soda and orange juice into persimmon purée. Set aside until mixture thickens.

Beat vegetable oil and sugar in large bowl with electric mixer on high speed until well blended; scrape down sides. Add eggs one at a time, beating well after each addition. Stir the persimmon mixture with a fork and add to the batter, mixing well. Mix in lemon juice. Stir together the flour, baking powder, salt, cinnamon, and allspice in a medium-size bowl. On low speed, gradually add to the batter, mixing until incorporated. Scrape down sides and mix in orange peel, raisins and pecans.

Pour batter into prepared pan. Bake in the 350° oven for 50 to 55 minutes or until a cake tester comes out clean and the cake pulls away from sides of pan. Remove to rack and cool in pan 10 minutes. Invert cake onto rack set over a rimmed baking sheet, and remove pan. Cool 10 more minutes while preparing the glaze.

GLAZE

Stir together the powdered sugar and 2 tablespoons orange juice in a medium-size bowl. Stir in additional orange juice, if needed, a teaspoon at a time. Glaze should be thick enough to coat the cake, but thin enough to drip down the sides. Stir in the orange peel. Drizzle over warm cake. (*) If desired, the cake may be kept at room temperature, well covered, up to 3 days, or it may be frozen, wrapped in aluminum foil. Defrost wrapped cake at room temperature.

Serves 12.

Holiday Egg Nog Cake

Real egg nog baked into a luscious pound cake, soaked in a buttery rum-brandy glaze makes perfect holiday cheer.

½ pound (2 sticks) unsalted butter, at room temperature
1½ cups sugar
4 large eggs, separated and at room temperature
3 cups all-purpose flour
1 tablespoon baking powder
2 teaspoons ground nutmeg
1 cup egg nog

GLAZE
1 cup sugar
¼ pound (1 stick) unsalted butter
¼ cup water
¾ teaspoon ground nutmeg
¼ cup dark rum
¼ cup brandy

BAKING PAN
12-cup Bundt pan OR Angel-food cake pan (see notes on Bundt pans, page 6)

Preheat oven to 325°. Grease pan. Dust with flour and shake out excess. Beat butter and sugar in large mixing bowl with electric mixer on high speed until light and fluffy, about 3 minutes. Beat in egg yolks.

Stir together the flour, baking powder and nutmeg in medium-size bowl. With mixer on low speed, alternately add flour mixture in fourths and egg nog in thirds to batter, beginning and ending with flour. Mix until combined.

Beat egg whites in separate mixing bowl with an electric mixer on high speed until soft peaks form. Gently fold into batter.

Spoon into prepared pan, smoothing top with a spatula. Bake in the 325° oven for 50 to 55 minutes or until cake tester comes out clean. The top of the cake will be golden brown and will develop a crack. Remove to a rack and cool in pan 10 minutes.

GLAZE
While cake cools, combine sugar, butter, water and nutmeg in a small saucepan. Bring to a boil and boil 5 minutes, stirring constantly. Remove from heat and stir in rum and brandy. Glaze will be thin. Invert cake onto rack, remove pan and place on a small rimmed baking sheet or rimmed plate. Prick top of cake with a long fork or skewer at 1-inch intervals. Slowly pour and brush hot glaze over top and sides of hot cake, tilting the baking sheet or plate so the glaze soaks into the sides. Lift cake slightly with spatula allowing glaze to run underneath. Continue spooning glaze over cake until it is all used up. Let cake sit 1 to 2 hours at room temperature before serving. (*) If desired, the cake may be kept at room temperature for several days, well wrapped, or it may be frozen tightly wrapped in aluminum foil. Defrost wrapped cake at room temperature.

Serves 12.

Orange-Apricot Bundt Cake

This dried fruit fruitcake is drizzled with a fresh orange syrup made with grated orange peel. When the glaze is spooned over the cake, the peel doesn't sink in. Instead, it creates a shimmery halo to crown the cake. This cake is pictured on page 10 filled with dried fruit and nuts.

1 cup sugar
¼ pound (1 stick) unsalted butter, at room temperature
2 large eggs, at room temperature
2 teaspoons vanilla
1 cup pitted dates, chopped (about 6 ounces)
½ cup dried apricots, chopped (about 3 ounces)
½ cup chopped walnuts (about 2 ounces)
1 tablespoon grated orange peel
2 cups all-purpose flour
½ teaspoon baking soda
¼ teaspoon salt
¾ cup buttermilk

SYRUP

½ cup sugar
1 tablespoon grated orange peel
⅓ cup fresh orange juice
1 tablespoon fresh lemon juice

BAKING PAN

6-cup Bundt pan or ring mold or loaf pan (see notes on Bundt pans, page 6)

Preheat oven to 325°. Grease baking pan. Dust with flour and shake out excess.

Beat sugar and butter in large mixing bowl with electric mixer on high speed until light and fluffy, about 5 minutes. Add eggs, one at a time, beating well after each. Scrape down sides of bowl. On low speed, mix in vanilla, dates, apricots, walnuts and orange peel until incorporated.

Stir together the flour, baking soda and salt in a medium-size bowl. With mixer on low speed, alternately beat the flour in fourths and buttermilk in thirds into the batter, beginning and ending with the flour. Mix until incorporated.

Turn into prepared pan. Bake in the 325° oven for 45 to 55 minutes or until cake tester comes out clean and cake begins to pull away from sides of pan. Cool in pan on rack for 10 minutes while preparing the syrup.

SYRUP

Stir together the sugar, orange peel, orange juice and lemon juice in small saucepan. Bring to a boil and cook 3 minutes, stirring constantly, until mixture thickens slightly and orange peel is lightly glazed. Invert cake onto rack placed over rimmed baking sheet. Remove pan and prick top with a long fork or skewer at 1-inch intervals. Spoon hot orange syrup slowly over cake. Repeat spooning with any syrup which has fallen onto the baking sheet. Cool completely. (*) If desired, the cake may be stored, tightly covered, at room temperature up to 3 days, or it may be frozen, tightly wrapped in aluminum foil. Defrost wrapped cake at room temperature.

Serves 8 to 10.

Grand Marnier Nut Cake

This buttery-flavored Grand Marnier-soaked nut cake is great for coffees and meetings, or to take to friends' homes.

½ pound (2 sticks) unsalted butter, at room temperature
1 cup plus ¼ cup sugar
3 large eggs, separated and at room temperature
2 tablespoons Grand Marnier
2 teaspoons orange extract
2 cups all-purpose flour
1 teaspoon baking powder
1 teaspoon baking soda
1¼ cups sour cream
1 tablespoon grated orange peel

1 cup chopped walnuts or pecans (about 4 ounces)

SYRUP
½ cup sugar
1 cup fresh orange juice
½ cup Grand Marnier

BAKING PAN
12-cup Bundt pan (see notes on Bundt pans, page 6)

Preheat oven to 350°. Grease pan. Dust with flour and shake out excess.

Beat butter and 1 cup sugar in large mixing bowl with electric mixer on high speed until light and fluffy, about 2 minutes. Add egg yolks one at a time, beating well after each addition. Mix in Grand Marnier and orange extract.

Stir together flour, baking powder and soda in medium-size bowl. With mixer on low speed, alternately add flour mixture in fourths and sour cream in thirds to batter, beginning and ending with flour. Mix in the orange peel and nuts. The batter will be thick.

Beat egg whites in separate mixing bowl with electric mixer on high speed until soft peaks form. Slowly add the remaining ¼ cup sugar, beating until mixture forms stiff but moist peaks. Stir a small portion of whites into batter to lighten it, then gently fold in the rest.

Pour into prepared pan. Bake in the 350° oven for 40 to 50 minutes or until cake tester inserted in center comes out clean. Remove to rack and cool in pan 15 minutes.

SYRUP
While cake cools, combine sugar and orange juice in medium-size saucepan. Bring to a boil and boil gently, stirring occasionally, for 15 minutes or until thickened slightly. Remove from heat and stir in Grand Marnier. Invert cake onto cooling rack placed over a rimmed baking sheet. Remove pan and prick top with a long fork or skewer at 1-inch intervals. Slowly pour and brush hot syrup over cake. Spoon syrup which falls into the baking sheet back into bowl and pour over cake again. Repeat until all the syrup is used. Cool to room temperature. (*) If desired, the cake may be stored at room temperature, tightly wrapped, for several days, or it may be frozen. Defrost wrapped, at room temperature.

Serves 12.

Cheesecakes

According to my own private poll, cheesecakes are second in popularity only to chocolate desserts. They are a wonderful choice to make for parties, as one cake will serve a crowd. They can be refrigerated for several days before serving or, as indicated in the following recipes, many can be successfully frozen.

Cheesecakes are, however, somewhat tricky and unpredictable to make. Each recipe has its own individual personality, so no one rule applies to them all. Cheesecakes never appear to be fully cooked when they're removed from the oven. They confuse home cooks because they usually jiggle in their pans. But once they cool, they solidify. If you melt cream cheese, for example, it will again become firm when it cools. The same principle applies to baking cheesecakes.

I have developed my own baking technique for cheesecakes that diminishes those dreaded cracks running across their tops. I stumbled across the answer when testing the Chocolate Truffle Cheesecake some 20 times. It looked and tasted wonderful, but the San Andreas Fault was always running down its center.

When I began to experiment with the cooking time, I discovered that the best baking method for this and many other cheesecakes is to begin by baking them in a 400° to 425° oven for 10 to 15 minutes, and then reduce the temperature to 225° to 250° and bake them an additional 45 to 60 minutes. This technique results in incredibly creamy cakes with a very smooth top. I heartily recommend that you try this baking technique for your own favorite cheesecakes, if they are developing cracks. To help keep the top smooth, be sure to let the cake cool completely in a draft-free spot when you take it from the oven. If cheesecakes cool too quickly, they have a tendency to crack.

You will note that all my recipes are made with a cream cheese base rather than yogurt or cottage cheese. I created them this way because I believe that cream cheese produces the richest, creamiest cakes. For taste variations, the recipes feature out-of-the-ordinary flavorings, toppings, or crusts.

TIPS

- Most of these recipes are made in a springform pan. To remove the sides easily, place the pan on a bowl that is smaller than the diameter of the springform. Release the spring and carefully pull down the sides of the pan. This is shown on page 51.
- When pressing a crumb crust up the sides of a springform, it is not necessary to make the top edges even.
- When cutting a cheesecake, if it is so creamy that it sticks to the knife, dip the knife in a glass of hot water before cutting each slice.

CLOCKWISE FROM TOP: *Piña Colada Cheesecake with Pineapple Glaze, page 55; Banana Fudge Cheesecake, page 57; My Favorite Cheesecake, page 58.*

White Chocolate Cheesecake

I must admit the combination of white chocolate and cream cheese sounds almost too rich to eat, but I implore you to try this recipe. The elusive flavor and creamy texture of white chocolate turns this beautiful, ivory cheesecake into one of the lushest, most elegant desserts you've ever tasted. I use Tobler Narcisse white chocolate bars which are available in most supermarkets.

CRUST
1¾ cup graham cracker crumbs
    (about 16 crackers)
6 tablespoons (¾ stick) unsalted
    butter, melted
1 tablespoon sugar

FILLING
10 ounces white chocolate, broken
    up
½ cup whipping cream, at room
    temperature
2 packages (8 ounces each) cream
    cheese, at room temperature
4 large eggs, separated and at
    room temperature

4 teaspoons vanilla
Dash salt

TOPPING
6 ounces white chocolate,
    broken up
¼ cup whipping cream, at
    room temperature
2 tablespoons light crème de cacao

BAKING PAN
9 x 3-inch or 9½ x 2-inch
    springform pan

CRUST
Butter springform pan. Combine graham cracker crumbs, butter and sugar in food processor fitted with metal blade. Process until well blended. Or, combine crumbs, butter and sugar in a bowl. Press evenly over bottom and two thirds up sides of springform pan.

FILLING
Preheat oven to 300°.

Melt chocolate in top of double boiler over simmering water. Slowly stir in cream, stirring until smooth. Remove from heat and cool slightly. Beat cream cheese in large bowl with electric mixer on medium speed until smooth. Add egg yolks one at a time, blending well after each addition, stopping to scrape down sides of bowl and beaters once or twice. Add white chocolate, vanilla and salt. Beat at medium speed for 2 minutes. Beat egg whites in separate mixing bowl with electric mixer on low speed until foamy. Beat on high speed until soft, rounded peaks form. Fold whites into chocolate mixture. Pour into crust.

Place pan on baking sheet. Bake in the 300° oven for 55 minutes. The cake will rise and the top will jiggle slightly when shaken. Turn off oven. Let cake stand in oven for 1 hour. It will sink. Remove to wire rack in draft-free place and cool to room temperature.

TOPPING
Melt chocolate in top of double boiler over simmering water. Slowly stir in cream, stirring until mixture is smooth. Stir in crème de cacao. Pour topping over cool cake. Cover with plastic wrap and refrigerate several hours or overnight. (*) If desired, the cake may be tightly

covered and refrigerated up to 3 days, or it may be frozen, in springform tightly covered with plastic wrap and foil. Defrost wrapped cake in refrigerator overnight.

At least 2 hours before serving, remove cake from refrigerator and remove sides of springform. It is important to serve this cake at room temperature.

Serves 10 to 12.

Triple Cheese Flan

This is the only savory, or not sweet, recipe in this book. It is a smooth, creamy, crustless cheesecake which captures either the distinctive flavor of Roquefort or the tangy taste of goat cheese, depending on which you use. Although I love offering it with slices of fresh fruit as an after-dinner cheese course, it also serves as an excellent appetizer with bread or crackers.

12 ounces cream cheese, at room temperature
6 ounces (¾ cup) ricotta cheese, at room temperature
8 ounces Roquefort or goat cheese (chèvre) such as Montrachet, at room temperature
3 large eggs, at room temperature
½ cup plus ¾ cup sour cream
⅛ teaspoon ground black pepper
Pears, apples or other fruit for serving

BAKING PAN
9 x 3-inch or 9½ x 2-inch springform pan

Preheat oven to 350°. Butter springform pan.

Beat cream cheese, ricotta cheese and Roquefort or goat cheese in large bowl with electric mixer on medium speed until well blended, stopping to scrape down the bowl and beaters. The mixture will be slightly lumpy. While beating continuously, add eggs one at a time, mixing well after each. Mix in ½ cup sour cream and pepper. Pour into springform pan.

Place pan on baking sheet and bake in the 350° oven for 45 minutes or until top is golden.

Remove from oven and spread remaining ¾ cup sour cream over top; it will be thin. Return to oven and bake for an additional 10 minutes or until sour cream is set. Remove to wire rack and cool completely. (*) The cake may be refrigerated overnight, covered with plastic wrap, if desired. Bring to room temperature 1 hour before serving.

Before serving, remove sides of springform pan. Slice into wedges and serve at room temperature with desired fruit.

Serves 8.

Classic New York Cheesecake with Choice of Toppings

There's an excellent reason why this cheesecake is the traditional favorite: it's very high, super rich and extra dense, and sensational unadorned or with any of the suggested toppings.

CRUST

1 recipe Cookie Pastry for single crust pie (see page 88)
1 teaspoon grated lemon peel

FILLING

5 packages (8 ounces each) cream cheese, at room temperature
1¾ cups sugar
3 tablespoons all-purpose flour
1 teaspoon grated lemon peel
¼ teaspoon salt

¼ teaspoon vanilla
5 large eggs, at room temperature
2 large egg yolks, at room temperature
¼ cup sour cream
1 recipe Strawberry Glaze, Apricot Glaze, or Blueberry Glaze

BAKING PAN

9 x 3-inch or 10½ x 2-inch springform pan (see notes on springform pans, page 6)

Preheat oven to 400°.

CRUST

Make pastry as directed, adding lemon peel with the flour. Remove sides from springform pan and press one third of the pastry evenly over bottom.

Place on baking sheet and bake in the 400° oven for 6 minutes or until golden. Cool. Increase oven temperature to 500°.

Butter sides of pan and attach to bottom. Press remaining pastry about two thirds up sides.

FILLING

Beat cream cheese in large mixing bowl with electric mixer on medium speed until smooth and fluffy, stopping to scrape down sides of bowl occasionally. Gradually add sugar, flour, lemon peel, salt and vanilla, beating constantly. Add eggs and yolks one at a time, beating well after each addition. Scrape down sides once or twice. Mix in sour cream; the mixture will be thin. Pour into pastry lined pan.

Place on baking sheet. Bake in the 500° oven for 8 minutes or until top is golden. Reduce oven temperature to 200° and continue to bake for 1 hour or until center jiggles slightly. Remove to wire rack and cool in draft-free place at room temperature for 3 hours. Cover with plastic wrap and refrigerate for several hours or overnight. (*) If desired, the cake may be refrigerated up to 4 days, or it may be frozen in the springform, tightly covered with plastic wrap and foil. Defrost wrapped cake in refrigerator overnight.

Remove sides of springform. Make desired glaze and spread evenly over top of cheesecake as directed. Refrigerate until serving time.

Serves 10 to 12.

STRAWBERRY GLAZE	*2 pint boxes fresh strawberries* *1 cup water* *½ cup sugar* *1½ tablespoons cornstarch* *3 drops red food coloring (optional)*

Slice 1 cup of the berries and place in medium-size saucepan with the water. Bring to a boil over moderate heat and cook 2 minutes. Push berries with a spoon through a strainer placed over small bowl; scrape bottom of strainer to remove all pulp. Return berries to saucepan and stir in sugar and cornstarch. Bring to a boil over moderate heat, stirring constantly, until mixture thickens. Stir in food coloring, if using. Cool to lukewarm.

Slice remaining berries in half and arrange in concentric circles over top of cake. Spoon warm glaze over berries, letting some of the glaze drip down sides of cake. Refrigerate until set, about 1 hour, but not more than 4.

Yields topping for one cheesecake.

APRICOT GLAZE	*1¼ cups dried apricots (about 6*
	   ounces)
	1 cup boiling water plus ½ cup
	   water
	1 tablespoon lemon juice
	2 teaspoons cornstarch
	½ cup sugar

Place apricots in medium-size heatproof bowl. Pour over 1 cup boiling water and set aside to soften overnight. Transfer mixture to food processor fitted with metal blade; process until puréed. Pour mixture into medium-size saucepan and add lemon juice, the ½ cup water, cornstarch and sugar. Cook over moderate heat, stirring constantly, until mixture comes to a boil and thickens, about 10 minutes. Cool to room temperature. Spread over top of cheesecake.

Yields topping for one cheesecake.

BLUEBERRY GLAZE	*1 pint blueberries (2 cups)* *⅓ cup sugar* *4 teaspoons cornstarch* *2 tablespoons lemon juice*

Combine blueberries, sugar, cornstarch and lemon juice in medium-size saucepan. Bring to a boil over high heat and cook until mixture thickens and berries are glazed and glossy, about 3 to 4 minutes. Remove from heat and cool slightly. Pour over top of cheesecake; spread evenly. Refrigerate until serving time.

Yields topping for one cheesecake.

1 *Press the crumbs into the sides of pan, and into the inside edge of pan, using a spoon.*

2 *Pour in half the batter.*

3 *Sprinkle with cookies and top with remaining batter.*

Oreo Cheesecake

Imagine an incredibly smooth cheesecake that's encased in a delectable, buttery, crushed-Oreo crust. Hiding beneath a rich sour cream topping are more crumbled Oreos. Even if you're not Oreo-obsessed, you'll become a fan after just one bite of this sublime cheesecake.

CRUST
**25 Oreo creme sandwich cookies
(about 2½ cups crumbs)**
**4 tablespoons (½ stick) unsalted
butter, melted**

FILLING
**4 packages (8 ounces each) cream
cheese, at room temperature**
1¼ cups plus ¼ cup sugar
2 tablespoons all-purpose flour
4 large eggs, at room temperature
**3 large egg yolks, at room
temperature**
⅓ cup whipping cream
1 teaspoon plus 1 teaspoon vanilla

**1¾ cups coarsely chopped Oreo
creme sandwich cookies
(about 15 cookies)**
2 cups sour cream

BAKING PAN
**9 x 3-inch or 10½ x 2-inch
springform pan (see notes on
springforms, page 6)**

Preheat oven to 425°. Butter springform pan.

CRUST
Break up cookies and place in food processor fitted with metal blade; process until crumbs. Add butter and mix until blended. Or, mix cookie crumbs and butter together in bowl. Pour into springform pan. Press evenly over bottom and two thirds up sides of springform. Refrigerate while preparing filling.

4 *Place springform pan on a bowl that is smaller than the diameter of the pan. Release spring and carefully pull down sides of pan. Serve cake on springform bottom.*

FILLING

Beat cream cheese in large bowl with electric mixer on medium speed until smooth. Scrape down sides. Add 1¼ cups sugar, beating until mixture is light and fluffy, about 3 minutes, scraping down sides of bowl occasionally. Mix in flour. While beating continuously, add eggs and yolks; mix until smooth. Beat in whipping cream and 1 teaspoon vanilla until well blended.

Pour half the batter into prepared crust. Sprinkle with chopped Oreos. Pour remaining batter over and smooth top with a spatula. Some of the Oreos may rise to the top.

Place pan on baking sheet. Bake in the 425° oven for 15 minutes. Reduce oven temperature to 225° and bake for an additional 50 minutes or until set.

Remove cake from oven and increase oven temperature to 350°. Stir together sour cream, remaining ¼ cup sugar, and 1 teaspoon vanilla in small bowl. Spread sour cream mixture evenly over cake. Return to the 350° oven and bake 7 minutes or until sour cream begins to set. Remove from oven and cool in draft-free place to room temperature. Cover and refrigerate several hours or overnight. (*) The cake may be refrigerated up to 3 days.

Before serving, remove sides of springform. Serve chilled.

Serves 10 to 12.

Chocolate Truffle Cheesecake

How do you describe a chocolate lover's fantasy? Take one buttery, chocolate pastry and top it with a layer of dark chocolate truffle and creamy chocolate cheesecake filling. The result is a melt-in-your-mouth dessert that's too moist to be a cheesecake, and too dense to be a mousse. It's positively paradise.

BAKING PAN

9 x 3-inch or 9½ x 2-inch springform pan

1 recipe Chocolate Pastry (see page 89)
6 squares (6 ounces) plus 12 squares (12 ounces) semisweet chocolate, chopped
3 tablespoons plus 1 cup whipping cream
3 packages (8 ounces each) cream cheese, at room temperature
1¼ cups sugar
5 large eggs, at room temperature
2 teaspoons vanilla

Make the Chocolate Pastry as directed.

Preheat oven to 400°. Butter bottom and sides of springform. Remove sides of springform and pat half of the pastry evenly onto the bottom. Place bottom on baking sheet and bake for 6 minutes. Remove from oven and cool. Attach sides and pat remaining pastry three quarters up the sides; set aside. Increase oven temperature to 425°.

Melt 6 squares chocolate in top of double boiler over simmering water. Slowly add 3 tablespoons cream. Stir until smooth and chocolate is melted. Pour into pastry-lined pan and spread to within ½ inch of sides.

In same double boiler, melt 12 squares chocolate over simmering water. Set aside to cool slightly. Meanwhile, beat cream cheese and sugar in large mixing bowl with electric mixer on medium speed until light and fluffy, about 3 minutes. Add eggs one at a time, beating constantly, stopping to scrape down sides of bowl and beaters as needed. Mix in 1 cup cream, vanilla and melted chocolate. Pour into crust.

Place pan on baking sheet and bake in the 425° oven for 10 minutes. Reduce oven temperature to 225°. Bake for 45 minutes or until center jiggles slightly. Turn off heat and allow cake to stand in oven for at least 2 hours with oven door closed. Remove from oven and cool on wire rack in draft-free place to room temperature. Cover and refrigerate for several hours or until chilled. (*) If desired, the cake may be refrigerated, covered, up to 1 week, or it may be frozen in the springform, covered with plastic wrap and foil. Defrost wrapped cake in refrigerator overnight.

Before serving, remove sides of springform pan. Serve cake chilled.

Serves 12.

Lemonade Chiffon Cheesecake

The refreshingly sweet-tart flavor of lemonade is captured in this irresistible cheesecake. The filling is not baked, but set with gelatin which gives it a feather-light and airy texture. It's a great choice for any meal, anytime— from the most elegant dinner to an informal luncheon.

BAKING PAN

9 x 3-inch or 9½ x 2-inch springform pan

CRUST

1¾ cups graham cracker crumbs (about 16 crackers)
6 tablespoons (¾ stick) unsalted butter, melted
2 teaspoons grated lemon peel

FILLING

1 envelope unflavored gelatin
¼ cup cold water

5 large eggs, separated and at room temperature
¾ cup sugar plus ½ cup sugar
⅛ teaspoon salt
⅓ cup milk, heated until hot
3 packages (8 ounces each) cream cheese, at room temperature
1 can (6 ounces) lemonade concentrate, thawed
1 teaspoon lemon extract

Preheat oven to 350°. Butter springform pan.

CRUST

Mix graham cracker crumbs, butter and lemon peel in food processor fitted with metal blade until blended. Or, mix crumbs, butter and lemon peel in a bowl. Press evenly over bottom and two thirds up sides of springform pan.

Place on baking sheet. Bake in the 350° oven for 12 to 14 minutes or until firm. Cool completely.

FILLING

Meanwhile, sprinkle gelatin over water in small bowl; set aside for 5 minutes to soften. Whisk egg yolks, ¾ cup sugar and salt in top of double boiler off heat until well blended. Set over simmering water and gradually stir in hot milk. Stir constantly until it is very hot and thick enough to leave a path on a wooden spoon when you run your finger along it, about 7 minutes. Stir in softened gelatin until dissolved. Remove from heat and cool to lukewarm, about 15 minutes.

Beat cream cheese in large mixing bowl with electric mixer on medium speed until smooth. Gradually add the egg yolk mixture, lemonade and lemon extract, beating constantly. Scrape down sides of bowl and mix on low speed until smooth and blended. Beat egg whites in separate mixing bowl with electric mixer on low speed until frothy. Increase speed to high and beat until soft peaks form. Gradually add ½ cup sugar, beating until stiff but moist peaks form. Stir small amount of egg whites into lemon mixture, then fold in the rest. Pour into crust, smoothing top evenly with a spatula. Cover with plastic wrap and refrigerate for several hours or until set. (*) The cake may be refrigerated up to 2 days, if desired.

Before serving, remove sides of springform. Serve chilled.

Serves 12.

Miniature Fruit-Glazed Cheesecakes

These charming, individual cakes are baked in muffin tins and then topped and glazed with assorted fresh fruit. I love to serve them beautifully presented on a platter, each with its own fruit design on top.

CRUST
1 recipe Cookie Pastry for single
   crust pie (see page 88)
Grated peel of 1 lemon

FILLING AND TOPPING
1 package (8 ounces) cream cheese,
   at room temperature
½ cup sugar
½ teaspoon vanilla

2 large eggs, at room temperature
1½ teaspoons lemon juice
¼ cup sour cream
Assorted fruit such as raspberries,
   blueberries, bananas, grapes,
   kiwi, mandarin oranges
½ cup strawberry jelly

BAKING PAN
Twelve 2-inch muffin cups

CRUST

Make Cookie Pastry as directed, adding lemon peel with the flour.

Preheat oven to 400°. Place rack in lower third of oven.

Break off small pieces of dough and press into bottom and up sides of muffin cups, forming a very thin shell which you can almost see through. You will have some pastry left over.

Bake in the 400° oven for 5 to 6 minutes or until very pale golden. Remove from oven and cool. Reduce oven temperature to 350°.

FILLING AND TOPPING

Beat cream cheese until smooth in large bowl with electric mixer on medium speed. Scrape down sides of bowl. Add sugar, vanilla, eggs, lemon juice and sour cream. Beat until very smooth, about 2 minutes, stopping to scrape down sides of bowl and beaters once or twice. Pour into pastry cups, filling each three quarters full.

Bake in lower third of the 400° oven for 10 minutes. Sides will begin to set but center will jiggle. Remove from oven and cool in draft-free place to room temperature. Cover with plastic wrap and refrigerate for several hours or until well chilled. (*) If desired, the cakes may be refrigerated overnight, or frozen tightly covered with plastic wrap and foil. Defrost wrapped cakes in refrigerator overnight.

To remove from pans, loosen edges of cakes with small sharp knife and lift them out of pans. As close to serving as possible, arrange desired fruit over the tops. Stir jelly in small saucepan over low heat until melted. Carefully drizzle and brush as much jelly as needed to cover fruit, making sure bananas are well coated, if using. Refrigerate until ready to serve, but not more than 2 to 3 hours.

Makes 12 miniature cakes.

Piña Colada Cheesecake with Pineapple Glaze

One taste of this lovely, creamy cake will transport you to a tropical island. It's hard to believe a cheesecake can duplicate the lush flavors of that ever-popular drink—you'll have to taste it to believe it! This is pictured on page 44.

BAKING PAN

9 x 3-inch or 9½ x 2-inch springform pan

CRUST

1¾ cups graham cracker crumbs (about 16 crackers)
6 tablespoons (¾ stick) unsalted butter, melted
1 tablespoon sugar

FILLING

3 packages (8 ounces each) cream cheese, at room temperature
½ cup sugar
5 large eggs, at room temperature
1 can (8½ ounces) cream of coconut
1 can (8 ounces) crushed pineapple, drained
1 cup sour cream
4 teaspoons coconut extract
⅓ cup light rum

GLAZE

1 can (8 ounces) crushed pineapple
2 tablespoons lemon juice
¼ cup sugar
1 tablespoon cornstarch
1 tablespoon water
Shredded fresh coconut for garnishing (optional)

Preheat oven to 325°.

CRUST

To make crust, mix graham cracker crumbs, butter and sugar in food processor until well blended. Or, mix crumbs, butter and sugar in a bowl. Press evenly over bottom and two thirds up sides of pan.

FILLING

Beat cream cheese and sugar in large bowl with electric mixer on medium speed until light and fluffy, about 3 minutes, stopping to scrape down sides of bowl and beaters several times. Add eggs one at a time, beating well after each. Scrape down sides. Mix in cream of coconut, pineapple, sour cream, extract and rum. Pour into crust.

Place pan on baking sheet. Bake in the 325° oven for 55 minutes or until edges are brown and center jiggles slightly. Turn oven off and leave cake in oven for 1 hour with oven door closed. Remove from oven to wire rack in draft-free place and cool to room temperature.

GLAZE

Purée pineapple and its syrup in food processor fitted with metal blade. Pineapple will still be slightly chunky. Transfer to small saucepan and add lemon juice and sugar. Dissolve cornstarch in the water in a small bowl. Add to the saucepan. Cook over medium heat, stirring constantly until glaze comes to a boil and thickens. Cool thoroughly. Spread evenly over top of cake. Cover with plastic wrap and refrigerate for several hours. (*) The cake may be refrigerated up to 2 days, if desired.

Before serving, remove sides of springform. Garnish with fresh coconut if desired. Serve cake chilled.

Serves 10 to 12.

Peanut Butter Chocolate Chip Cheesecake

The consensus on this cake is unanimous. It tastes exactly like a Reese's Peanut Butter Cup—only better. A sinfully rich peanut butter filling is generously sprinkled throughout with chocolate chips and then topped with chocolate fudge. Isn't decadence fun?

BAKING PAN

9 x 3-inch or 9½ x 2-inch springform pan

CRUST
30 chocolate wafer cookies (2 cups crumbs)
1 stick unsalted butter, melted
OR
25 Oreo cookies (2½ cups crumbs)
½ stick unsalted butter, melted

FILLING
12 ounces cream cheese, at room temperature

1 cup sugar
1 cup creamy peanut butter
5 large eggs, at room temperature
½ cup sour cream
2 teaspoons lemon juice
1 cup mini or regular chocolate chips

TOPPING
¾ cup chocolate chips
1 cup sour cream
½ cup sugar

Preheat oven to 325°. Butter bottom and sides of springform pan.

CRUST
Place cookies in food processor fitted with metal blade and process into uniform crumbs. Add butter and mix until well combined. Or, mix crumbs and butter in bowl until blended. Pour into springform. Press evenly over bottom and about two thirds up sides of pan. Refrigerate while preparing filling.

FILLING
Beat cream cheese and sugar in large bowl with electric mixer on medium speed until mixture is light and fluffy, about 3 minutes, stopping to scrape down sides of bowl and beaters once or twice. Add peanut butter and mix until incorporated. Beat in eggs one at a time, stopping to scrape down sides of bowl and beaters several times. Add sour cream, lemon juice and chocolate chips and mix until incorporated. Pour into prepared pan.

Place on baking sheet. Bake in 325° oven 55 to 65 minutes or until sides are firm and center jiggles slightly. Remove to wire rack and cool in draft-free place 15 minutes. Increase oven temperature to 350°.

TOPPING
While cake cools, melt chocolate chips in top of double boiler over simmering water. Remove from heat. Add sour cream and sugar, stirring until smooth. Spread evenly over top of cake. Bake in the 350° oven for 10 minutes. Cool to room temperature. Cover with plastic wrap. Refrigerate at least 6 hours or until chilled. (*) If desired, the cake may be refrigerated up to 3 days, or frozen in springform, covered with plastic wrap and foil. Defrost wrapped cake in refrigerator overnight.

Before serving, remove sides of springform. Serve chilled.

Serves 10 to 12.

Banana Fudge Cheesecake

While I was testing cakes for this chapter, my son Kenny, who loves chocolate-covered bananas, asked me to create a cheesecake with those flavors. Although I succeeded in making the cake, he deserves the credit for the idea. A chocolate cookie pastry encases a lofty, creamy banana filling which surrounds a deep, dark tunnel of fudge. Be sure to use over-ripe bananas for an intense banana flavor. This is pictured on page 44.

1 recipe Chocolate Pastry (see page 89)
5 packages (8 ounces each) cream cheese, at room temperature
1½ cups sugar
½ teaspoon salt
2 teaspoons vanilla
5 large eggs, at room temperature
1 cup sour cream
4 squares (4 ounces) semisweet chocolate, melted over hot water and cooled
3 very ripe bananas

1 tablespoon lemon juice
Unsweetened cocoa powder for sprinkling on top, or Chocolate Triangles (see page 227), banana slices and whipped cream for garnishing

BAKING PAN

9 x 3-inch or 10½ x 2-inch springform pan (see notes on springform pans, page 6)

Make Chocolate Pastry as directed.

Preheat oven to 400°. Butter bottom and sides of springform pan. Remove sides. Press half of the pastry onto bottom.

Place on baking sheet and bake in the 400° oven for 6 minutes. Remove from oven and cool. Attach sides and pat remaining pastry three quarters up sides. Increase oven temperature to 425°.

Beat cream cheese and sugar in large mixing bowl with electric mixer on medium speed until smooth and fluffy, about 3 minutes, stopping to scrape down sides of bowl and beaters several times. Beat in salt and vanilla, mixing until well blended. Add eggs one at a time, beating well after each. Scrape down sides. Mix in sour cream. Remove 1¼ cups of the cheese mixture to medium-size bowl. Stir in melted chocolate.

Mash bananas; measure 1½ cups. Add mashed bananas and lemon juice to nonchocolate cheese mixture, mixing until well blended. Pour approximately two-thirds of the banana mixture into pastry lined pan. Spoon chocolate mixture in a ring over the banana, 1 inch from sides of pan. Cover with remaining banana mixture.

Place cake on baking sheet. Bake in the 425° oven for 15 minutes. Reduce oven temperature to 225°. Bake for 60 to 65 minutes longer. The cake will jiggle and not look set. Turn off oven and let cool in oven for at least 2 hours with oven door closed. Remove from oven to wire rack in draft-free place and cool to room temperature. Cover and refrigerate overnight. (*) If desired, the cake may be refrigerated up to 3 days, or it may be frozen covered with plastic wrap and foil. Defrost wrapped cake in refrigerator overnight.

continued

BANANA FUDGE CHEESECAKE,
CONTINUED

Before serving, remove sides of springform. If desired, decorate by placing a doily over top of cake. Place cocoa in a strainer and dust thickly over doily. Carefully lift up doily. Or, decorate with chocolate triangles, whipped cream and banana slices, as pictured on page 44. Serve cake chilled.

Serves 10 to 12.

My Favorite Cheesecake

This was my favorite cheesecake recipe until I began writing this book. After creating so many new ones that I really love, I have to say that this is now one of my favorite cheesecakes. I've never tasted any other that is as light and creamy. You're going to flip over the flavor of the crunchy amaretti crust, the mellow, cheesey filling and the shimmering raspberry topping. This is pictured on page 44.

CRUST

*1 cup Amaretti cookie crumbs
(6 ounces cookies)
1½ cups graham cracker crumbs
(about 14 crackers)
¼ pound (1 stick) plus 2
tablespoons unsalted butter,
melted*

FILLING

*2 packages (8 ounces each) plus 1
small package (3 ounces) cream
cheese, at room temperature
1¼ cups sugar
5 large eggs, at room temperature
1½ tablespoons lemon juice
Finely grated peel of 1 small lemon
2 teaspoons vanilla
Pinch salt*

TOPPING

*1½ pints (3 cups) sour cream
¾ cup sugar
Finely grated peel of 1 lemon
1 teaspoon vanilla
Pinch salt
½ cup good quality seedless
raspberry jam
Sliced almonds for garnish
(optional)*

BAKING PAN

*9 x 3-inch or 10½ x 2-inch
springform pan (see notes on
springform pans, page 6)*

Preheat oven to 350°.

CRUST

Mix cookie crumbs and graham cracker crumbs in food processor fitted with metal blade. Mix in butter until well blended. Or, mix cookie crumbs and graham cracker crumbs in medium-size bowl. Stir in butter. Press evenly over bottom and three quarters up sides of springform pan. (It is not important that the top edges be even.) Refrigerate while preparing filling.

FILLING

Beat all the cream cheese and sugar in large bowl with electric mixer on medium speed until light and fluffy, about 3 minutes, stopping several times to scrape down sides of bowl and beaters. Beat in eggs one at a time. Scrape down sides of bowl and beaters. Add lemon juice, peel, vanilla and salt. Mix until smooth and creamy. The mixture will be thin. Pour into prepared crust. Do not be concerned if it does not come to top of crumbs.

Place pan on baking sheet. Bake in the 350° oven for 45 to 50 minutes or until center 4 inches of cake jiggle when cake is lightly shaken and cake feels bouncy and rebounds slightly when lightly pressed with fingertips. It will look underdone, but will firm up as it cools. Remove from oven and cool on baking sheet in draft-free place for 45 minutes. Heat oven to 450°.

TOPPING

Whisk together sour cream, sugar, lemon peel, vanilla and salt in medium-size bowl. After cake has cooled 45 minutes, pour topping over cake.

Bake in 450° oven for 10 minutes. Remove from oven and cool on baking sheet in draft-free place until it reaches room temperature. The crust will weep slightly as it cools. Cover top with foil and let stand at room temperature at least 8 hours or overnight before serving. (*) The cake may be refrigerated up to 5 days, if desired. Bring to room temperature several hours before serving.

Before serving, melt jam in small saucepan over low heat, stirring until smooth. Spread evenly over top of cake. Remove cake from springform. Garnish with sliced almonds, if desired. Serve at room temperature.

Serves 10 to 12.

VARIATION

Amaretti cookies may be omitted from the crust. Make graham cracker crust by mixing together 2½ cups graham cracker crumbs with ¼ pound (1 stick) melted butter.

Hazelnut Praline Cheesecake

I love the sweet nutty taste of hazelnut praline blended with a cheesecake filling. There's an outrageous amount of cheese packed into this lofty, amber-colored cake, but baking it in a pan of water produces a creamy, custard-like texture that keeps it very light, but incredibly rich.

BAKING PAN

8 x 3-inch or 8½ x 2-inch springform pan
Baking sheet

CRUST
⅓ cup graham cracker crumbs

HAZELNUT PRALINE PASTE
⅓ cup sugar
½ cup whole hazelnuts, toasted at 350° for 10 to 12 minutes or until lightly browned

FILLING
4 packages (8 ounces each) cream cheese, at room temperature
½ cup whipping cream
4 large eggs, at room temperature
1¾ cups sugar
1 teaspoon vanilla

Preheat oven to 300°. Butter springform pan. Cover outside of pan with foil. This is to keep the water the cake bakes in from seeping into pan. Sprinkle bottom and sides of pan with graham cracker crumbs.

HAZELNUT PRALINE PASTE
Grease baking sheet. Melt ⅓ cup sugar in small saucepan over moderate heat, stirring once to help dissolve sugar. Bring to a boil, swirling and rotating the pan without stirring, until sugar turns mahogany. Immediately remove from heat, stir in hazelnuts and pour onto greased baking sheet. Allow to stand until cool and hard. Break into pieces and place in food processor fitted with metal blade. Pulse on and off until fine crumbs form. Continue processing until smooth paste, about 3 minutes.

FILLING
Beat cream cheese in large bowl with electric mixer on medium speed until light and fluffy, about 3 minutes. Scrape down sides of bowl. Add cream, eggs, sugar and vanilla, mixing until well blended. Scrape down sides of bowl and continue beating until smooth, about 3 minutes. Add praline paste and beat on high speed until thoroughly blended. Pour batter into prepared pan, smoothing top with a spatula.

Place pan in shallow baking pan or skillet with heatproof handle and place in oven. Fill pan half full of hot water. Bake cake in the 300° oven for 2 hours or until top is slightly cracked and golden brown. Turn off heat and let cake stand in oven for 1 hour with oven door closed. Lift cake out of water bath and place on wire rack in draft-free place. Cool to room temperature. (*) If desired, the cake may be held at room temperature, covered with plastic wrap, overnight or refrigerated up to 4 days. Or, it may be frozen in springform, covered with plastic wrap and foil. Defrost wrapped cake in refrigerator overnight or at room temperature. Remove sides of springform before serving at room temperature.

Serves 12.

Apricot Cheesecake

This easy food processor recipe was featured in Pleasures of Cooking, *a superlative culinary magazine published by Cuisinart. Cooked dried apricots are puréed and then whisked into cream cheese, creating a refreshingly tart-tasting cake with a beautiful golden-orange hue.*

CRUST
½ cup graham cracker crumbs (about 5 graham crackers)
1 tablespoon unsalted butter, melted

FILLING AND GLAZE
1 cup dried apricots (about 5 ounces)
1¼ cups water
Grated peel of ½ lemon

3 packages (8 ounces each) cream cheese, at room temperature and cut into quarters
4 large eggs, at room temperature
1 cup sugar
½ cup sour cream
½ cup apricot preserves
1 tablespoon brandy

BAKING PAN
8 x 3-inch or 8½ x 2-inch springform pan

CRUST
Butter bottom and sides of pan. Mix graham cracker crumbs and butter in food processor fitted with metal blade until combined. Or, combine crumbs and butter in a bowl. Press evenly over bottom of springform pan.

FILLING AND GLAZE
Place dried apricots and water in medium-size saucepan. Bring to a boil and boil gently, uncovered, until liquid has evaporated and apricots are tender, about 20 minutes.

Preheat oven to 325°.

Purée apricots with grated lemon peel in food processor fitted with metal blade for 15 seconds. Add 1 package cream cheese and 2 eggs and process until smooth, stopping to scrape down sides of work bowl. Repeat 2 more times, adding 1 package of cream cheese and 1 egg each time. Add sugar and sour cream. Process 5 seconds. Scrape down sides of bowl. Process 10 seconds more. Pour batter into pan.

Place pan on baking sheet. Bake in the 325° oven for 55 minutes or until center of cake is just firm. Remove to wire rack and cool to room temperature in draft-free place. Cover pan and refrigerate several hours or overnight. (*) If desired, the cake may be refrigerated up to 3 days, or it may be frozen in springform covered with plastic wrap and foil. Defrost wrapped cake in refrigerator.

Several hours before serving, make apricot glaze by heating preserves in small saucepan. Stir in brandy. Strain the mixture through metal strainer into small bowl. Spoon warm glaze over cake. Refrigerate for at least 15 minutes for glaze to set. Before serving, remove sides of springform. Serve chilled or at room temperature.

Serves 8 to 10.

Puddings and Old-Fashioned Fruit Desserts

With the advent of packaged convenience foods such as "instant" puddings and pie fillings, puddings are rarely thought of as baked or steamed, but rather as thick mixtures cooked in a saucepan on top of the stove. Although steamed puddings admittedly cook for a long time, they are very easy to prepare and can be made ahead. And they are so warm and comforting that it's time they were rediscovered.

Steamed puddings are much coarser and more cake-like than other varieties. Cooked in the moist heat of a water bath, they are usually made on top of a stove, although they can be baked, if you prefer. Traditionally, steamed puddings are served with a sauce to complement the pudding's density and provide an interesting taste contrast.

Bread pudding is probably the homiest and heartiest of the pudding family. All three bread puddings included in this chapter are custard-based, yet offer a range of tastes and textures from cinnamon-spiced Mexican to a traditional, rich English cream. Cobblers are upside-down, deep-dish pies utilizing the freshest of summer's fruits and berries. They are baked in a large shallow baking dish. Originally the pastry which covered the fruit was cut into rounds and arranged over the top, thereby creating a cobbled effect. My recipes offer you several different types of toppings, from tender biscuit to flaky pastry, along with a variety of presentations.

TIPS	• Steamed puddings may be made in any type of heat-resistant mold or bowl, not just in a traditional steamed pudding mold. If the mold does not have a lid, cover the top tightly with a double thickness of foil.
	• Do not fill a steamed pudding mold over three quarters full, in order to allow room for expansion.
	• Steamed puddings should be cooked in a steamer or pot which is large enough to allow good circulation. In order to keep the mold from cracking or rattling around, do not place it directly on the bottom of the pot or steamer. Set it on a rack, trivet or a folded dish towel.
	• If you don't have any stale bread for bread puddings, leave some fresh slices on the kitchen counter overnight and lightly toast them before you begin the recipe. This is an important step, because fresh bread will absorb the custard and then not rise to the top of the pudding and become toasted.
CLOCKWISE FROM TOP: Christmas Cranberry Pudding, page 70; Steamed Chocolate Pudding, page 67; Olde English Bread Pudding, page 72; Rhubarb-Peach Cobbler with Lattice Biscuit, page 78.	• For cobblers, mix the fruit with the sugar and other ingredients as close to baking time as possible. The fruit will hold its shape and retain its flavor better if not allowed to sit at room temperature too long.
	• Techniques and photos showing how to make pastry are on page 86.

1 First spoon orange-flavored batter into mold, then add dark batter.

2 Place covered mold on a rack or folded towel in a deep saucepan, half filled with water. Cover pan and simmer pudding.

3 Wrap pudding in brandy-soaked cheesecloth.

4 Finished pudding with Brandy Cream Sauce served on the side.

Light and Dark Steamed Pudding with Brandy Cream Sauce

One-half the batter is flavored with orange and pecans, while the other is fragrant with Kahlúa, dried fruit and cocoa. You may bake the batter in any size or shape molds, from custard cups or soufflé dishes to fluted Jello or brioche molds. After the puddings bake, they are wrapped and soaked for at least 2 weeks in brandy-drenched cheesecloth for additional flavor and moistness. They make a wonderful holiday gift when accompanied by a jar of Brandy Cream Sauce.

BAKING PAN

Three 2½- to 3-cup heatproof molds
OR
Two 4- to 5-cup heatproof molds
OR
One 8-cup heatproof mold

¾ cup (1½ sticks) unsalted butter, at room temperature
1¼ cups sugar
4 large eggs, at room temperature
2 cups all-purpose flour
4 teaspoons baking powder
1½ teaspoons salt
2¼ cups soft fresh white bread crumbs (5 slices with crusts removed)
2 heaping teaspoons grated orange peel
½ cup chopped pecans or walnuts
3 tablespoons brandy
2 tablespoons orange juice
6 tablespoons Kahlúa
1 cup dark raisins
1 cup chopped dates
1 tablespoon unsweetened cocoa powder
½ teaspoon ground cinnamon
¼ teaspoon ground nutmeg
¼ teaspoon ground allspice
Cheesecloth and brandy for wrapping puddings
1 recipe Brandy Cream Sauce (see page 222)

Oil mold(s) or spray with nonstick vegetable cooking spray and set aside. Beat butter and sugar in large bowl with electric mixer on medium speed until light and fluffy, about 2 minutes. Mix in eggs one at a time, beating constantly. Add flour, baking powder, salt and bread crumbs, mixing until incorporated. Remove 2¾ cups batter and set aside.

To original batter in large bowl add orange peel, nuts, brandy and orange juice. Mix until blended. Spoon batter into greased mold(s), smoothing tops evenly with a spatula. Return remaining 2¾ cups batter to bowl and mix in Kahlúa, raisins, dates, cocoa, cinnamon, nutmeg and allspice until blended. Spoon over light-colored layer. Mold(s) should be no more than two-thirds full. Cover with lid(s) or foil. Place mold(s) on a rack or towel in deep pot. Pour in enough boiling water to come halfway up the mold(s). Place lid on pot and simmer at a low boil for the following times: 2½- to 3-cup molds will take from 1½ to 1¾ hours; 4- to 5-cup molds from 1¾ to 2 hours; and an 8-cup mold, 2 to 2½ hours. Add water as needed to keep the level halfway up the mold. Pudding is done when cake tester inserted in center comes out clean. Remove mold(s) from water and let cool on wire rack for 15 minutes. Run tip of sharp knife around edge and invert onto racks. Cool completely.

Soak 2 layers of cheesecloth per pudding in brandy. Wrap each pudding in cheesecloth, then in foil. Refrigerate for at least 2 weeks before serving. (*) The pudding(s) may be refrigerated for several months, if desired. Resprinkle cheesecloth with brandy every month. Or, they may be frozen after they have been soaked in the cheesecloth for one month. Wrap foil over the cheesecloth. Defrost wrapped pudding at room temperature. Make Brandy Cream Sauce as directed. Serve pudding at room temperature topped with sauce.

Serves 8 to 10.

Steamed Blueberry Pudding with Lemon Sauce

Elegant but homey, this coarse-crumbed pudding is rich with whole, juicy blueberries that retain their plump shape and pure flavor. Served warm from the oven and topped with Lemon Sauce, this dessert takes you straight to blueberry heaven.

1 recipe Lemon Sauce (page 220)
1 pint fresh blueberries (2 cups)
½ cup plus 2 cups all-purpose flour
2½ teaspoons baking powder
¼ teaspoon salt
¼ pound (1 stick) unsalted butter, at room temperature
¾ cup sugar
2 large eggs, at room temperature
1 cup milk

BAKING PAN

8-cup (2 quart) soufflé dish, round glass baking dish or steamed pudding mold

Make Lemon Sauce as directed. Refrigerate until ready to serve. Oil mold or spray with nonstick vegetable cooking spray.

Wash blueberries and pat dry on paper towels. Put into a bowl and toss lightly with ½ cup flour. In another bowl, stir together 2 cups flour, baking powder and salt. Beat butter and sugar in large bowl with electric mixer on medium speed until light and fluffy, about 2 minutes. Scrape down sides of bowl and beat in eggs one at a time, mixing well after each.

Alternately add milk and flour mixture in thirds, stirring with a wooden spoon until incorporated. Fold in blueberries.

Pour batter into baking dish or mold. Cover tightly with lid or foil. Place mold on rack or towel in deep pot. Pour in enough boiling water to come halfway up the mold. Place lid on pot and simmer at a low boil for 1½ hours. Add more water as needed to keep the level halfway up the mold. Remove mold from water and immediately invert pudding onto rack. (*) If desired, the pudding may be kept tightly wrapped at room temperature overnight. To reheat, unwrap and return to mold and steam until heated through, about 30 minutes. Or wrap in foil and bake in a preheated 325° oven for 20 minutes or until heated through.

Serve warm topped with Lemon Sauce.

Serves 8.

Steamed Chocolate Pudding with Creamy Vanilla Sauce

A steamed pudding is quite different from other puddings. Its consistency is similar to a moist, light, airy cake. This one is very chocolatey and tastes like a cross between a brownie and a pudding. Serve it warm with a cool Creamy Vanilla Sauce for a super-moist dessert. This is pictured on page 62. Garnish with green chocolate leaves (see page 228).

1 recipe Creamy Vanilla Sauce
   (see page 217)
3 squares (3 ounces) unsweetened
   chocolate, chopped
¼ pound (1 stick) unsalted butter,
   at room temperature
1 cup sugar
2 large eggs, separated and at room
   temperature
1 teaspoon vanilla

1¼ cups all-purpose flour
1 teaspoon baking powder
Dash salt
¾ cup milk

BAKING PAN

8-cup steamed pudding mold,
   soufflé dish or heatproof mold

Oil mold generously or spray with nonstick vegetable cooking spray. Make Creamy Vanilla Sauce as directed. Refrigerate until serving time. Melt chocolate in top of double boiler over simmering water. Set aside to cool. Beat butter and sugar in large bowl with electric mixer on medium speed until light and fluffy, about 2 minutes. Scrape down sides of bowl. Beat in egg yolks and vanilla, mixing until well combined. Stir together flour, baking powder and salt in small bowl. Alternately mix in flour and milk on low speed, beginning and ending with the flour. Scrape down sides of bowl. Mix in chocolate.

Beat egg whites in small mixing bowl with electric mixer on low speed until frothy. Increase speed to high and beat until soft, rounded peaks form. Fold small amount of whites into chocolate mixture to lighten it. Then gently fold in remaining whites until thoroughly incorporated. Pour into prepared mold, smoothing top with a spatula; batter will only fill half the mold. Cover mold tightly with lid or foil.

Place mold on rack or towel in deep pot. Fill pot with enough boiling water to come halfway up the mold. Place the lid on the pot and simmer the pudding for 3 hours. The water should maintain a low boil. Add more water as needed to keep the level halfway up the pudding. Remove mold from pot and let cool on wire rack for 30 minutes. Run small knife around sides and invert pudding onto rack or serving plate. (*) If desired, the pudding may be well wrapped and kept at room temperature, covered, overnight, or, it may be refrigerated up to 2 days or frozen. Defrost wrapped, at room temperature. To reheat, unwrap and return to mold and steam until heated through, about 30 minutes.

To serve, slice warm pudding onto dessert plates and top with spoonfuls of Creamy Vanilla Sauce.

Serves 8 to 10.

Orange Sponge Pudding

If an Orange Julius was baked into a pudding, it would taste like this one. Made with concentrate instead of fresh orange juice, this pudding practically bursts in your mouth. Simple to prepare, one batter magically separates into two while baking. The top layer becomes a sponge-like cake, and the bottom transforms itself into a creamy custard.

3 large eggs, separated and at room temperature
½ cup plus ¼ cup sugar
Half of 6-ounce can frozen orange juice concentrate, thawed and undiluted
1 tablespoon grated orange peel
2 tablespoons melted unsalted butter
1½ cups milk
½ cup all-purpose flour
½ teaspoon baking powder
¼ teaspoon salt

BAKING DISH
1½- or 2-quart (6 to 8 cup) soufflé dish or round glass baking dish

Preheat oven to 350°. Butter baking dish.

Mix egg yolks and ½ cup sugar in medium-size bowl with electric mixer on medium speed or in food processor fitted with metal blade, until creamy and light in color. Mix in orange juice, peel, melted butter and milk until blended. Mix in flour, baking powder and salt just until flour is incorporated.

Beat egg whites in medium-size bowl with electric mixer on low speed until frothy. Increase speed to high and beat until soft peaks form. Gradually add ¼ cup sugar, beating until stiff but not dry peaks form. Fold orange mixture into whites.

Pour batter into baking dish. Place dish into shallow baking pan. Place on oven rack and pour in about 1 inch of boiling water. Bake in the 350° oven for 25 to 30 minutes or until top is puffed and golden. Remove from the water and cool completely. Cover with plastic wrap and refrigerate until chilled. (*) The pudding may be refrigerated overnight, if desired.

To serve, spoon chilled sponge pudding into shallow bowls or plates, topping each serving with some of the sauce from the bottom of the dish.

Serves 6.

Caramel Pumpkin Pudding

Here's a new way to present the traditional flavors of pumpkin pie. Baked into a custard, it's cloaked with a chestnut-brown caramel sauce that forms a shimmering pool around its base.

1 cup granulated sugar
3 tablespoons water
3 large eggs
1 can (16 ounces) mashed pumpkin
½ cup firmly packed golden brown
    sugar
1 tablespoon molasses
1½ teaspoons ground cinnamon
1½ teaspoons ground ginger
Dash ground nutmeg
2 tablespoons all-purpose flour
1 teaspoon salt

1 tablespoon unsalted butter,
    melted
1 tablespoon brandy
2 cups whipping cream
1 cup softly whipped cream for
    serving (optional)

BAKING DISH

2-quart (8 cup) round glass baking
    dish or soufflé dish

Preheat oven to 350°.

Melt sugar and water in a small heavy saucepan or skillet over moderate heat, stirring once to help dissolve the sugar. Bring to a boil over moderately high heat, swirling or rotating pan, without stirring, until sugar turns mahogany, about 5 minutes. Watch carefully, as it goes from mahogany to burnt very quickly. Pick up baking dish with pot holder and immediately pour sugar into dish, swirling to coat dish with the caramelized sugar. Set aside to cool and harden.

Beat eggs in large bowl with electric mixer on low speed, or whisk, until frothy. Mix in pumpkin, brown sugar, molasses, cinnamon, ginger, nutmeg, flour, salt, butter and brandy until blended. On low speed, slowly beat in 2 cups whipping cream. Pour pumpkin mixture into caramel-coated dish.

Place shallow baking pan or skillet with ovenproof handle into which the pudding fits comfortably on oven rack. Place pudding in pan and fill pan half full with boiling water. Bake, uncovered, in the 350° oven for 1 hour and 40 to 45 minutes or until cake tester inserted near center comes out almost clean. A little custard adhering to tester will ensure a creamy consistency. The pudding will jiggle slightly and the top will be puffed. Remove from water and cool to room temperature. (*) The pudding, covered with plastic wrap, may be refrigerated up to 2 days, if desired.

Before serving, run a small knife around edges of pudding and invert onto rimmed platter. Do not be concerned if some of the caramelized sugar stays in the dish. Serve pudding at room temperature with softly whipped cream, if desired.

Serves 8.

Christmas Cranberry Pudding

Served warm with sweetened whipped cream, this cranberry-laden pudding is baked with a Christmas-red, shimmering cranberry glaze. The pudding not only tastes terrific, it positively glistens. It's guaranteed to brighten any holiday table. This is pictured on page 62.

PUDDING

1 cup firmly packed golden brown sugar
½ cup whipping cream
2 large eggs, separated and at room temperature
2 teaspoons vanilla
½ teaspoon ground nutmeg
1 teaspoon ground cinnamon
1½ cups all-purpose flour
1 teaspoon baking powder
¼ teaspoon plus ¼ teaspoon cream of tartar
Grated peel of 1 orange
3 cups (12 ounces) cranberries, coarsely chopped in food processor or by hand
¼ cup (½ stick) unsalted butter, melted
⅛ teaspoon salt

CRANBERRY GLAZE

1½ cups granulated sugar
½ cup orange juice
2½ cups (10 ounces) whole cranberries

Powdered sugar for garnishing
1 cup whipping cream, softly whipped with 3 tablespoons powdered sugar, for serving

BAKING PAN

9 x 3-inch or 9½ x 2-inch springform pan

Preheat oven to 350°. Grease the springform.

PUDDING

Whisk together brown sugar, whipping cream, egg yolks, vanilla, nutmeg and cinnamon in small bowl until combined; set aside.

Stir together flour, baking powder, ¼ teaspoon cream of tartar and orange peel in large bowl. Stir in chopped cranberries, and toss until well coated. Add brown sugar mixture and melted butter, stirring until well combined. Batter will be stiff. In separate bowl, beat egg whites with electric mixer on low speed until foamy. Add ¼ teaspoon cream of tartar and salt and beat on high speed until soft, rounded peaks form. Fold into batter. Turn into pan.

Place on baking sheet and bake in the 350° oven for 30 to 35 minutes or until pudding is set and top springs back when pressed with fingertips.

GLAZE

About 10 minutes before the pudding is done, combine sugar and orange juice in medium-size saucepan. Boil over moderate heat, stirring constantly, until the sugar is melted and the mixture is foamy, about 5 minutes. Stir in cranberries. Cook over low heat, stirring until cranberries are coated and most of the berries have popped, about 5 minutes.

Remove pudding from oven when it is set. Pour hot glaze over top of pudding, distributing syrup and berries as evenly as possible. Bake in the 350° oven for an additional 10 minutes. The top will still look liquid and a cake tester will not test clean. Remove from oven and cool at least 1 hour before serving. (*) The pudding may be held, covered with foil, at room temperature overnight, if desired. Reheat, uncovered, in a preheated 350° oven for 10 to 15 minutes or until warm.

Before serving, sprinkle top with powdered sugar. Remove sides of springform pan. Slice and serve with sweetened whipped cream.

Serves 8 to 10.

Cinnamon Apple Bread Pudding

This earthy, homespun pudding is created by sprinkling golden bread crumbs in a pie dish and topping them with buttery, sautéed apples and a soft, creamy custard.

2 slices stale or toasted egg bread, crusts removed
3 tablespoons plus 3 tablespoons unsalted butter
2 large tart green apples (about 1 pound)
¼ teaspoon ground cinnamon
2 large eggs
½ cup milk
½ cup whipping cream
⅓ cup sugar

BAKING PAN
9-inch pie dish

Preheat oven to 325°. Butter pie dish.

Process bread in food processor fitted with metal blade into crumbs; you should have about 1¼ cups. Melt 3 tablespoons butter in medium-size skillet. Sauté bread crumbs over low heat until golden and very crisp. Sprinkle crumbs over bottom of buttered pie dish.

Peel, core and slice apples into ¼-inch slices by hand or with medium (4 mm) slicing blade of food processor. Melt remaining 3 tablespoons butter in same skillet. Sauté apples until tender, about 10 to 15 minutes, tossing gently occasionally. Arrange apple slices over crumbs. Sprinkle with cinnamon. Whisk eggs in medium-size bowl until frothy. Whisk in milk, cream and sugar until blended. Carefully pour mixture over apples.

Bake in the 325° oven for 25 to 30 minutes or until knife inserted in center comes out clean. Serve warm.

Serves 6.

Olde English Bread Pudding

This beautiful, creamy pudding, shimmering in its apricot-Grand Marnier glaze and dotted with tiny currants, is homey enough for the family, yet elegant enough for your most important guests. Like most puddings of this kind, the bread is layered on the bottom and rises during baking to form a toasty top. This is pictured on page 62.

¼ loaf day-old French bread
1 tablespoon plus 1 tablespoon
    unsalted butter, at room
    temperature
3 large eggs, at room temperature
½ cup sugar
2 cups whipping cream
½ cup milk
1 tablespoon vanilla
Pinch salt
3 tablespoons currants
¼ cup apricot jam
1 tablespoon Grand Marnier

BAKING PAN
4- to 5-cup soufflé dish or
    1½-quart glass baking dish

Preheat oven to 350°. Butter baking dish.

Cut bread into ¼- to ⅓-inch thick slices. Remove crusts. Spread one side of the bread with 1 tablespoon of the butter. Cut bread into 1½ -inch triangles or squares. Overlap the pieces buttered-side up in bottom of baking dish. Set aside.

Whisk eggs and sugar in medium-size bowl until blended. Bring cream, milk, vanilla and salt to a boil in medium-size saucepan. Remove from heat and gradually pour in eggs, whisking constantly. Carefully pour through strainer over bread. Dot with remaining 1 tablespoon butter and currants.

Place in roasting pan or shallow baking pan on oven rack. Pour in enough hot water to half fill the pan. Bake in the 350° oven for 35 to 40 minutes or until cake tester or toothpick inserted in center comes out almost clean and the bread is toasted; a little custard clinging to tester ensures a creamy consistency.

Bring jam to a full boil in small, heavy saucepan, stirring constantly. Press through strainer set over small bowl to remove all large pieces. Stir in Grand Marnier. Remove pudding from oven and brush jam evenly over top. Serve warm or at room temperature. (*) The pudding may be held at room temperature for several hours, if desired.

Serves 4 to 6.

Mexican Bread and Cheese Pudding

This unique, versatile dish is equally at home following spicy Spanish dinners, for midday brunches or by the fireside after the theater. Warm melted cheese adds moistness and creaminess to this delicious pudding.

1 cup sugar
1½ cups warm water
½ teaspoon vanilla
¾ teaspoon ground cinnamon
10 slices firm white bread, crusts removed
4 tablespoons unsalted butter, at room temperature
½ cup golden raisins
2 cups shredded Monterey Jack cheese (about 8 ounces)

BAKING DISH

9-inch glass or porcelain quiche dish or pie dish

Preheat oven to 350°. Butter the baking dish.

Melt sugar in deep, heavy saucepan over moderately high heat, stirring once to dissolve sugar. Bring to a boil, swirling and rotating the pan, without stirring, until sugar turns mahogany, about 5 minutes. Watch carefully, as it goes from mahogany to burnt very quickly. Immediately remove pan from heat and slowly and carefully stir in warm water in steady stream. Place mixture over moderately low heat and stir until sugar is completely dissolved. The sugar will harden initially, but will dissolve as it is stirred. Stir in vanilla and cinnamon and simmer 1 minute. Remove from heat.

Toast bread and spread with butter. Place 2 layers of bread buttered-side down, one on top of the other, in buttered baking dish, cutting to fit as necessary. Sprinkle bread with raisins and top with cheese. Pour syrup over all; press down on cheese to moisten it.

Bake in the 350° oven for 15 minutes or until top is browned and puffed and cheese is melted. Serve warm.

Serves 6.

Mixed Fruit Cobbler

Mixed Fruit Cobbler

You aren't limited to choosing just one sumptuous fruit when making this recipe, as this cobbler offers you the opportunity to combine the best of summer's bounty.

BAKING DISH

11 x 7-inch glass baking dish or 4- to 5-cup gratin dish

BISCUIT TOPPING

2 cups all-purpose flour
3 tablespoons sugar
1 tablespoon baking powder
½ teaspoon salt
6 tablespoons (¾ stick) unsalted butter, cut into 6 pieces
2 large egg yolks, at room temperature
⅓ cup half and half
1 egg beaten with 1 teaspoon water for wash

FILLING

6 nectarines or peaches (about 2 pounds)
1 cup blueberries
6 yellow or red plums (about 1½ pounds)
⅓ cup sugar
1 tablespoon cornstarch
2 tablespoons lemon juice
Grated peel of 1 lemon
2 tablespoons unsalted butter

BISCUIT TOPPING

Combine flour, sugar, baking powder and salt in food processor fitted with metal blade or in medium-size bowl with pastry blender or fingertips. Add butter and pulse on and off or mix until mixture resembles coarse meal. Whisk yolks with half and half in small bowl. Add to flour mixture all at once. Mix only until mixture is thoroughly moistened and dough holds together when pinched between your fingers. Do not form a ball. Shape dough into a flat disc. Wrap in plastic wrap and refrigerate for at least 30 minutes. (*) Dough may be refrigerated up to 3 days, or it may be frozen, well wrapped, if desired.

Preheat oven to 400°. Butter baking dish.

FILLING

Peel nectarines or peaches by plunging them into pot of boiling water to cover for 20 seconds. Remove with slotted spoon and run under cold water. When cool enough to handle, slip off peels, pit and slice into about ½-inch slices. Slice plums. Place fruit in large bowl. Add sugar, cornstarch, lemon juice and peel. Toss with hands or large spoon until well combined. Pour into baking dish and dot top with small pieces of butter.

Roll out dough on lightly floured surface into rectangle or oval that is 1 inch smaller than diameter of dish, and about ½ inch thick. Flute edges, if desired. Place over fruit. Cut 2 slashes in pastry approximately 2 inches long to allow steam to escape. Decorate with remaining dough, as pictured, if desired. Brush with egg wash, using only enough to cover pastry and decorations.

Bake in the 400° oven for 30 to 35 minutes or until pastry is lightly browned and fruit is bubbling around edges. Remove from oven and cool 15 minutes before serving. Serve warm.

Serves 6.

Fresh Peach Cobbler

A cobbler is really an upside-down pie. This one features sliced peaches immersed in a brown sugar syrup and baked under rich, flaky pastry.

PASTRY

1¾ cups all-purpose flour
½ teaspoon salt
⅓ cup vegetable shortening, chilled in freezer
5 tablespoons unsalted butter, cold and cut into 5 pieces
4 tablespoons ice water

BAKING DISH

11 x 7-inch glass baking dish or 4- to 5-cup gratin dish

FILLING

6 to 7 ripe peaches (about 2 pounds)
⅔ cup loosely packed golden brown sugar
¼ teaspoon ground nutmeg
2 tablespoons all-purpose flour
Dash salt
¼ cup (½ stick) unsalted butter, at room temperature
Vanilla ice cream for serving (optional)

PASTRY

Combine flour and salt in food processor fitted with metal blade or in medium-size bowl with pastry blender or fingertips. Add shortening and butter and pulse on and off or mix until the mixture resembles coarse meal. Sprinkle ice water over and mix just until pastry holds together when pinched between your fingers. Do not form into ball. Flatten pastry into disc, wrap in plastic wrap and refrigerate for 30 minutes or until firm enough to roll. (*) The pastry may be refrigerated up to 5 days, if desired.

FILLING

Peel peaches by plunging them into boiling water to cover in large pot for 20 seconds. Run under cold water and when cool enough to handle, slip off peel. Slice into about ½-inch-thick slices, discarding pits, and place in large bowl; you should have about 5 cups. Add sugar, nutmeg, flour and salt and toss with your hands until well combined. Pour into buttered baking dish. Dot top with butter.

Preheat oven to 400°. Roll out pastry on lightly floured board into rectangle about 1 inch larger than baking dish and approximately ⅓ inch thick; it should be slightly thicker than a pie crust. Place over top of fruit and press pastry against sides of dish, forming a border and sealing the edges. Cut 4 to 6 slits in top to allow steam to escape.

Bake in the 400° oven for 35 minutes or until pastry is golden and fruit is bubbling. Cool 15 minutes before serving. The cobbler is best served warm. Serve with vanilla ice cream, if desired.

Serves 6 to 8.

VARIATIONS

To make Nectarine Cobbler, substitute nectarines for the peaches.

To make Apricot Cobbler, substitute 2½ pounds (about 17) unpeeled apricots, pitted and cut into quarters, for the peaches. Add ¼ teaspoon allspice and 1 tablespoon lemon juice to the apricots. Everything else remains the same.

Fresh Blackberry Cobbler

This lovely, old-fashioned cobbler, reminiscent of the cottage puddings grandmother used to make, is topped with a delicious golden pastry that is between a pie crust and a biscuit. If this homey dessert doesn't make you nostalgic, it's not too late to begin a tradition. You'll be glad you did!

BAKING PAN

11 x 7-inch glass baking dish or 4- to 5-cup gratin dish

PASTRY

¼ pound (1 stick) unsalted butter, cut into 8 pieces and at room temperature
½ cup sugar
1 cup all-purpose flour
2 teaspoons baking powder
¼ teaspoon salt
½ cup milk

FILLING

1 recipe Crème Fraîche Sauce (see page 219) or vanilla ice cream, for serving with cobbler (optional)
3 pints fresh blackberries (6 cups)
½ cup sugar
1½ tablespoons cornstarch
2 tablespoons lemon juice
2 tablespoons unsalted butter

At least one day before serving, make Crème Fraîche Sauce, if desired.

Preheat oven to 350°. Butter baking dish.

PASTRY

Mix butter and sugar in food processor fitted with metal blade or in medium-size bowl with electric mixer on medium speed until light and fluffy, about 2 minutes. Add flour, baking powder, salt and milk. Pulse on and off or mix just until combined. Batter will be stiff.

FILLING

Gently toss berries with sugar, cornstarch and lemon juice in large bowl. Pour into baking dish. Dot top with butter. Spoon batter over top of berries, covering them as much as possible; they will not be completely covered.

Bake in the 350° oven for 40 minutes or until pastry is light golden and berries are bubbling along sides. Serve warm with Crème Fraîche Sauce or vanilla ice cream, if desired.

Serves 6.

VARIATION

To make Boysenberry Cobbler, substitute boysenberries for the blackberries.

Rhubarb-Peach Cobbler with Lattice Biscuit

Tart, pink rhubarb and sweet, golden peaches enhanced by a sumptuous woven biscuit topping elevate this cobbler from the farmhouse kitchen to the dining room. This is pictured on page 62.

BISCUIT TOPPING
2 cups all-purpose flour
1 tablespoon baking powder
1 tablespoon sugar
1 teaspoon salt
¼ cup (½ stick) unsalted butter, cold and cut into 4 pieces
1 cup whipping cream

FILLING
6 to 8 peaches (about 2 to 2½ pounds)
3 to 4 stalks fresh rhubarb
1¼ cups sugar
1 large egg, lightly beaten
⅓ cup all-purpose flour
Juice and grated peel of 1 lemon
3 tablespoons unsalted butter

BAKING PAN
11 x 7-inch glass baking dish

Preheat oven to 400°.

BISCUIT TOPPING

Combine flour, baking powder, sugar and salt in food processor fitted with metal blade or in mixing bowl with pastry blender or fingertips. Add butter and pulse on and off or mix until mixture resembles coarse meal. Add cream all at once and mix just until blended. Dough will not form a ball. Press into flat disc, wrap in plastic wrap and refrigerate while preparing fruit.

FILLING

Peel peaches by dropping them into boiling water to cover in large pot for 20 seconds. Run under cold water and when cool enough to handle, slip off peel. Slice into ½-inch-thick slices, discarding pits; you should have about 5 cups. Wash rhubarb and cut into ½-inch segments; you should have about 3 cups. Combine peaches, rhubarb, sugar, egg, flour, lemon juice and peel in large bowl. Toss to mix well with large spoon. Pour fruit into ungreased baking dish. Dot with butter.

Roll out dough on lightly floured surface into 14 x 9-inch rectangle, approximately ½ inch thick. Cut dough lengthwise into 1-inch-wide strips, making 8 strips. Place 4 of these strips lengthwise across the fruit. Weave remaining 4 strips over the top across the width. Press edges of dough into sides of dish, trimming to fit as needed.

Bake in the 400° oven for 20 to 25 minutes or until crust is golden brown. Cool 10 to 15 minutes before serving. Serve warm.

Serves 8.

Warm Blueberry Puff

A great combination of hot pancake, cold cream, and fresh sweet berries makes a fabulous last minute dessert or brunch dish.

2 large eggs
¼ cup plus 3 tablespoons plus ¼ cup powdered sugar
½ cup all-purpose flour
1½ cups milk
2 tablespoons unsalted butter, melted

1 pint fresh blueberries (2 cups)
1 cup whipping cream
2 tablespoons brandy (optional)

BAKING DISH

9-inch porcelain or glass quiche dish or pie dish

Preheat oven to 450°. Butter the baking dish.

Beat eggs in medium-size bowl with electric mixer on low speed until frothy. Gradually mix in ¼ cup powdered sugar and the flour; mixture will be stiff. Pour in milk and melted butter and mix until well blended. Pour into baking dish. Bake in the 450° oven for 20 to 25 minutes or until well puffed and golden brown.

Meanwhile, rinse blueberries and pat dry with paper towels. Beat cream in medium-size bowl with electric mixer on low speed until thick. Add 3 tablespoons powdered sugar and brandy, if using. Beat on high speed until soft peaks form.

Remove pancake from oven and immediately top with blueberries and sprinkle with ¼ cup powdered sugar. Spread whipping cream over all. Serve immediately.

Serves 6.

Blueberry Fritters

Fresh blueberries release their juices when you bite into these delectable, crisp-fried fritters. To make banana fritters, *substitute two bananas, chopped, for the blueberries.*

1 cup all-purpose flour
2 tablespoons sugar
1 teaspoon baking powder
¼ teaspoon ground nutmeg
⅛ teaspoon ground cinnamon
¼ teaspoon salt
½ cup milk

1 large egg, lightly beaten
1 cup fresh blueberries, rinsed and patted dry
1 cup vegetable shortening or oil for frying
Powdered sugar for sprinkling on top

Stir together flour, sugar, baking powder, nutmeg, cinnamon and salt in medium-size bowl. Stir in milk and beaten egg until combined. Gently fold in berries. Heat shortening or oil in deep fryer or 10-inch skillet to 375° on a deep-fat frying thermometer or until small piece of bread browns in 20 seconds. Drop batter by rounded teaspoon into oil and fry for 3 minutes or until golden brown, turning once with slotted spoon. Transfer fritters to paper towels to drain. Dust tops with powdered sugar and serve immediately.

Makes 16 to 20.

Chocolate Strawberry Shortcake

Strawberry shortcake has been a classic dessert for decades. In this original version, a chocolate buttermilk biscuit is smothered with juicy, ripe berries, softly whipped cream and gobs of chocolatey hot fudge sauce. Yum!

SHORTCAKE
1⅔ cups all-purpose flour
1½ teaspoons baking powder
3 tablespoons unsweetened cocoa powder
¼ teaspoon salt
⅓ cup granulated sugar
½ teaspoon baking soda
¼ cup (½ stick) unsalted butter, cold and cut into 4 pieces
½ cup chocolate chips (about 3 ounces)
¾ cup buttermilk

FILLING
2 pint boxes fresh strawberries
½ cup granulated sugar
2 cups whipping cream
4 tablespoons powdered sugar
1 to 2 recipes Hot Bittersweet Fudge Sauce (see page 221) or Hot Chocolate Fudge Sauce (see page 220)

BAKING PAN
Baking sheet

Preheat oven to 450°.

SHORTCAKE

Combine flour, baking powder, cocoa, salt, sugar and soda in food processor fitted with metal blade or in medium-size bowl with pastry blender or fingertips until well blended. Add butter and process on and off or mix until mixture is consistency of coarse meal. Add chocolate chips and buttermilk and mix just until dry ingredients are moistened and dough begins to hold together. Do not process into a ball. Turn out onto well floured board; dough will be sticky. Knead about 10 times and pat into 7-inch circle, ¾ inch thick. Dough should feel moist.

Cut out 7 to 8 biscuits with floured 2-inch round biscuit cutter. Place biscuits on ungreased baking sheet. Lightly flour board. Combine leftover pieces of dough and pat them into ¾-inch-thick circle. Cut out 4 more biscuits. Place on ungreased baking sheet.

Bake in the 450° oven for 12 minutes only. They should have risen slightly and look dry on top. (*) The biscuits may be kept in airtight container at room temperature overnight, or they may be frozen, if desired. Do not refrigerate or they will dry out. Defrost in airtight container at room temperature.

FILLING

Hull and quarter strawberries. Place in a bowl and toss with sugar. Let stand at least 30 minutes or up to 4 hours. Make sauce.

Whip cream with electric mixer on low speed until thick. Add powdered sugar and beat on high speed until soft peaks form.

To assemble, cut biscuits in half horizontally and place 2 to 3 halves on each plate. Top with spoonfuls of strawberries, a heaping tablespoon of fudge sauce, whipped cream, and drizzle more sauce over all.

Serves 8 to 12.

1 Mix until dough is moist enough to hold together when pinched between your fingers.

2 Pat into a 7-inch x ¾-inch circle.

3 Using lightly floured cutter, cut out biscuits and place on a baking sheet.

4 Chocolate shortcakes with Hot Fudge Sauce.

Pies, Tarts and Tartlets

Let's begin with the difference between a pie, a tart, and a tartlet. In general, a pie is made in a pastry crust and served in a dish, with or without a top crust. A tart is generally not as deep and is customarily removed from its baking pan before being served. Tarts are made in springform pans or tart pans with a removable bottom, rather than in pie plates. A tartlet is simply a small tart.

PASTRY CRUSTS

Short Crust Pastry   Pastry used for pies and tarts is usually referred to as "short crust pastry." Crisp, flaky and tender, it is made by combining fat—either shortening, butter or lard—with flour, so that the fat coats the particles of flour. Different fats possess different qualities. For example, butter adds flavor to pastry dough, but shortening makes it flakier. When deciding upon which fat to use, remember that you can combine the two to get the benefits of both, as in my Rich All-Purpose Pastry (see page 85). When moisture—usually water—is added, the fat prevents the moisture from activating the flour's gluten. The result is a sturdy yet tender and flaky crust.

Cookie Pastry   Sweetened short crust, such as my Cookie Pastry (see page 88), has less gluten or protein development because it is moistened with egg rather than water. The result is a more fragile, crumbly crust that works well as a bottom crust, but not for a top. Because it contains egg, this pastry shrinks less than a basic short crust. Water tends to evaporate from the oven heat and turns to steam, thereby shrinking the pastry. The egg acts much like glue, holding the dough in place. It is important to roll a cookie pastry slightly thicker than you would any other. Otherwise, the sugar in the pastry will burn before the pastry browns. As this pastry tastes like a cookie, the thickness will not detract from the pie's flavor.

Crumb Crusts   I have included two chocolate cookie crusts in this chapter. One is made with Oreo creme sandwich cookies and the other with chocolate wafers. Either cookie will work well. Chocolate wafers, however, are sometimes very difficult to obtain, while Oreos are readily available.

Rolling Pastry   It is very important that pastry is chilled and firm when you roll it out, or it will stick to your work surface and rolling pin. If the dough gets too warm, the butter or fat melts and makes the pastry very difficult to work with. Lightly flour a smooth counter top, chopping board or pastry slab. (Although marble makes a good surface because it remains cool, it is not necessary if your dough is cold.) Place a flattened disc of pastry in the center and lightly flour the rolling pin. Roll from the center out, turning the pastry a quarter of a turn after each roll. Use a pastry scraper (not your fingers, as the heat from them will cause the pastry to get too

CLOCKWISE FROM TOP: *Cranberry Pear Pie, page 101; Amaretti Fruit Tartlets, page 117; Brandy and Ginger Peach Tart, page 99.*

warm), to help lift up the pastry. If it sticks to the surface, reflour it lightly, as needed.

Blind Baking   Blind baking is a term applied to crusts that are baked without a filling. As there is nothing to hold the crust in place, it must be weighted down during cooking so it won't shrink or puff up too much. Crusts are prebaked for several reasons: (1) They will be filled with a filling that is already cooked or doesn't need to be cooked, such as fresh fruit; (2) The filling is so moist that unless the pastry is at least partially baked, it will become too wet and soggy. (3) The filling does not bake long enough for the pastry to cook through.

To blind bake, line the pastry with parchment, foil or wax paper. (I find there are advantages and disadvantages to each type of paper. Parchment and foil sometimes crease or gouge the pastry. Parchment should be crumpled up or folded and then smoothed out to soften. Foil should be the lightest type available. Wax paper is soft, but the edges burn in the oven, making it a little difficult to remove.) Fill the lined crust with commercially packaged aluminum pie weights, dried beans or rice. They should come up even with the top of the pastry to ensure that the sides do not fall or shrink as they bake. The weights may be saved and reused.

Freezing   A disc of unbaked pastry should be wrapped in a heavy plastic bag for freezing. The pastry can be defrosted in the refrigerator or at room temperature just until the pastry is softened enough to roll but is still very cold. Baked crusts should be frozen in the tart pan or pie dish, tightly wrapped in heavy-duty aluminum foil. Defrost the crust, covered, at room temperature.

To blind bake, line the pastry with wax paper or foil. Fill to the top of the tart pan with pie weights, as pictured, or dried beans.

TIPS

- It's best to make pastry when the ingredients are cold. If the weather is warm, freeze the shortening and flour for several hours or overnight before using them. If you're using butter, there's no need to freeze it; simply remove it from the refrigerator immediately before using. Make sure the liquid is cold so it won't melt the fat.
- Once the pie crust is in the baking dish, refrigerate it for a minimum of 30 minutes or even overnight before baking to minimize shrinking and cracking.
- If pastry is difficult to roll, try rolling it between 2 sheets of lightly floured wax paper. Roll until smooth and even, lifting the paper often to make sure it doesn't stick.
- To obtain an extra shiny glaze on pastry, lightly mix 1 egg with 1 teaspoon water. Brush as much as is needed to evenly cover the pastry. Refrigerate the pastry for 10 minutes and then brush it again.
- When blind baking, it's best to completely cook the crust, even if it will be baked again with the filling in it. Some cooks tend to bake it only until it's pale, believing that it will finish cooking when it's baking with the filling. But for the best results—a crisp, flaky pastry—the crust should be completely prebaked and then continue to be cooked with the filling. If the edges of the crust brown too quickly, cover with foil.

Rich All-Purpose Pastry

This is my favorite basic pie crust. It is buttery, flaky, tender, extremely versatile and always reliable. The combination of butter and shortening is a good one—the butter adds flavor, the shortening, flakiness. See photos on page 86.

1¼ cups all-purpose flour, chilled in
   freezer
¼ teaspoon salt
¼ pound (1 stick) unsalted butter,
   cold and cut into 16 pieces
2 tablespoons vegetable shortening,
   chilled in freezer
3 to 5 tablespoons ice water

FOOD PROCESSOR METHOD
Place flour and salt in work bowl with metal blade; mix with 1 pulse. Add butter and shortening and pulse on and off 6 or 8 times or until pieces are size of peas. Turn off machine and add 3 tablespoons ice water. Pulse only until dough is thoroughly moistened. Do not process until dough forms a ball. The dough should hold together when you pinch it between your fingers. If it is too crumbly, add additional water a teaspoon at a time until dough holds together. Remove metal blade and place large plastic bag over top of work bowl. Invert bowl and turn pastry into bag. Shape pastry in the bag into a ball and flatten into a disc. Seal bag and refrigerate until pastry is cold enough to roll.

BY HAND
Stir flour and salt together in medium-size bowl with a fork. Mix in butter and shortening with the tips of your fingers, pastry blender or 2 knives until pieces are size of small peas. Add 3 tablespoons ice water and toss with a fork until flour is moistened and mixture starts to form a ball. If necessary, add additional water a teaspoon at a time until dough holds together. Gather dough in your hands and gently shape into a ball. Flatten into a disc. Wrap in plastic wrap or bag and refrigerate until cold enough to roll.

(*) Pastry may be refrigerated up to 3 days, or it may be frozen in a heavy plastic bag, if desired. Defrost in refrigerator or at room temperature. Before using, let stand at room temperature until softened just enough to roll, but still very cold.

Yields crust for one 9-inch pie or one 11-inch tart.

VARIATION
To make pastry for double-crust pie, follow directions, doubling the ingredients. Divide pastry into 2 equal discs.

Hand Method 1 *Cut butter into 8 pieces and add it and the shortening to flour.*

2 *Cut fat into flour until the mixture resembles the texture of coarse crumbs.*

3 *Add water and toss with a fork until flour is coated and mixture begins to hold together.*

Food Processor Method 1 *Add butter and shortening to flour and salt in the food processor.*

2 *Process until butter is the size of peas. It will not be uniform size. Some pieces will be larger, some smaller.*

3 *Add ice water and mix until pastry is moist enough to hold together when pinched between your fingers. Shape into a flat disc.*

To Roll and Shape into Pan 1 *Roll pastry out on a lightly floured board. Use a pastry scraper to help roll the pastry up over the rolling pin.*

2 *Unroll pastry over tart pan or pie plate.*

3 *Roll rolling pin across top of tart pan to trim the edges of the pastry.*

Shortening Pastry

Almost always used in double-crust pies, this pastry made with shortening is flakier, lighter and more subtly flavored than rich, firm, butter-based ones. The methods described are shown in the photographs opposite.

⅓ cup vegetable shortening
1 cup all-purpose flour, chilled in
* freezer*
¼ teaspoon salt
3 to 4 tablespoons ice water

Carefully measure shortening in a dry measure so you can level off the top. Spread shortening approximately ½-inch thick on sheet of waxed paper. Place in freezer and chill 15 minutes.

FOOD PROCESSOR METHOD
Place flour and salt in work bowl with metal blade. Mix with 1 pulse. Cut shortening into approximately ½-inch pieces. Process on and off 6 or 8 times with flour until pieces are about the size of peas. With machine off, add 3 tablespoons of the ice water. Pulse on and off until dough begins to hold together when you pinch it with your fingers. Do not let it form a ball. Unless it is very dry, you will not need the extra water. Remove metal blade and place large plastic bag over top of work bowl. Invert bowl and turn pastry into bag. Shape pastry in bag into a ball and flatten into a disc. The pastry may be used immediately or sealed in bag and refrigerated until ready to use.

BY HAND
Stir together flour and salt in medium-size bowl. Mix in shortening with the tips of your fingers, pastry blender or 2 knives until pieces are size of small peas. Add 3 tablespoons ice water and toss with a fork until all the flour is moistened and mixture begins to hold together. If necessary, add additional water to crumbs in the bottom of bowl. Gather dough in your hands and gently shape into a ball; flatten into a disc. The pastry may be used immediately or wrapped in plastic wrap or bag and refrigerated until ready to use.

(*) Pastry may be refrigerated up to 2 days, or it may be frozen in a heavy plastic bag, if desired. Defrost in refrigerator or at room temperature. Before using, let stand at room temperature until softened just enough to roll, but still very cold.

Yields pastry for one 9-inch pie.

VARIATION
To make pastry for a double-crust pie, follow recipe, doubling the ingredients. Divide into 2 equal discs.

Cookie Pastry

A wonderful, delicate pastry that tastes like a rich, buttery, firm cookie. The beauty of a cookie pastry is that it can be patted into a pan, rather than rolled, if desired. It can also be prebaked without the addition of pie weights or beans, and it doesn't shrink nearly as much as a traditional pie crust. It will not toughen if overmixed. How can you go wrong?

¼ pound (1 stick) unsalted butter, cold and cut into 8 pieces for food processor; at room temperature for mixer
¼ cup sugar
1 large egg
1½ cups all-purpose flour

FOOD PROCESSOR METHOD

Place butter and sugar in food processor with metal blade and pulse until mixture holds together. Add egg and pulse 5 or 6 times to blend. Add flour all at once and pulse several more times. Scrape down sides and pulse until all ingredients are incorporated and a cookie-like dough is formed. Remove metal blade and place plastic bag over top of work bowl. Invert bowl and turn dough into bag. Shape pastry in bag into a ball and flatten into a disc. If pressing pastry into dish with hands, it may be used immediately. If rolling out pastry, seal bag and refrigerate until firm.

ELECTRIC MIXER METHOD

Beat butter and sugar in medium-size bowl with electric mixer on medium speed until light and fluffy, about 2 minutes. Add egg and flour and mix until smooth dough is formed. With hands, shape into a ball and flatten into a disc. Wrap in plastic wrap or bag and refrigerate until chilled.

(*) Pastry may be refrigerated up to 5 days, wrapped in plastic wrap or sealed in heavy plastic bag, or it may be frozen, if desired. Before using, let stand at room temperature until softened just enough to roll, but still cold.

Yields pastry for one 9-inch pie or one 11-inch tart.

Chocolate Pastry

Although this dark chocolate pastry has a cookie-like texture, it's only subtly sweet. Rather than detract or compete with its filling, this pastry works as a flavor enhancer.

1 cup all-purpose flour
¼ cup sugar
¼ teaspoon salt
6 tablespoons (¾ stick) unsalted butter, cold and cut into 12 pieces
3 tablespoons unsweetened cocoa powder
½ teaspoon vanilla
2 tablespoons ice water
1 large egg yolk

FOOD PROCESSOR METHOD

Place flour, sugar, and salt in work bowl with metal blade and pulse once to combine. Add butter and pulse on and off 9 or 10 times or until mixture is consistency of small peas or coarse meal. Add cocoa powder and vanilla and pulse 2 to 3 times until incorporated. With machine off, add ice water and egg yolk; pulse until mixture is consistency of wet sand and holds together when pressed between fingers. Remove metal blade and place large plastic bag over top of work bowl. Invert bowl and turn pastry into bag. Shape pastry in bag into a ball and flatten into a disc. Use immediately or refrigerate until ready to use.

BY HAND

Stir together flour, sugar and salt in medium-size bowl. Cut in butter with pastry blender, 2 knives or fingertips until consistency of coarse meal. Add cocoa, vanilla, ice water and egg yolk. Mix with fork until dough is consistency of wet sand. Gather with hands into a ball and flatten into a disc. Use immediately or wrap in plastic wrap or bag and refrigerate until ready to use.

(*) Pastry may be refrigerated up to 2 days, or it may be frozen, if desired. Defrost in refrigerator or at room temperature. Before using, let stand at room temperature until just softened enough to roll, but still very cold.

Yields pastry for 9- or 10-inch pie or 9-inch springform pan.

Cream Cheese Pastry for Tartlets

It's flaky and foolproof—it won't crack when you press it into the pan. I've included a choice of four varied but equally superb fillings, Sour Cream Lime (see page 116), Honey Walnut (see page 118), Chocolate Truffle (see page 118), and Toasted Coconut Cream (see page 119). When served as part of a buffet, these mini-tartlets make a colorful and attractive addition to the table. They're also lovely served for dessert with fresh fruit, sherbet or ices.

¼ pound (1 stick) unsalted butter, cold and cut into 8 pieces for food processor; at room temperature for mixer

1 package (3 ounces) cream cheese, cold and cut into pieces for food processor; at room temperature for mixer

1 cup all-purpose flour

BAKING PAN

Two miniature muffin pans each with twelve 1½-inch muffin cups

Mix butter and cream cheese in food processor fitted with metal blade or in medium-size bowl with electric mixer on medium speed until blended. Add flour and continue mixing until incorporated. The pastry may be used immediately or wrapped in plastic wrap or bag and refrigerated until ready to use. (*) Pastry may be refrigerated up to 5 days, or it may be frozen, if desired. Defrost wrapped pastry at room temperature until soft enough to use.

Preheat oven to 350°.

Divide pastry into twenty-four 1-inch balls. Press into bottom and up sides of muffin cups, extending ¼ inch over top of rim. Bake in the 350° oven for 22 to 25 minutes or until golden. Remove to wire rack and cool completely. Remove from tins by inserting tip of small knife into an edge and lifting out. (*) The tartlet shells may be stored in airtight container at room temperature for up 2 days, or they may be frozen in a covered container, if desired. Defrost, covered, at room temperature.

Makes 24 tartlet shells.

Apple Lemon Tart

Apples and lemon are a fabulous combination that marry well because they are both refreshingly tart. Topping a buttery crust is a thin layer of ultra-smooth custard and lightly poached apple slices. The poaching liquid is reduced to a glaze and poured over the top of the tart to intensify the apple flavor.

BAKING PAN

11-inch tart pan with removable bottom

1 recipe Cookie Pastry for
   single-crust pie (see page 88)
4 large eggs, at room temperature
1 cup plus ⅔ cup sugar
5 tablespoons fresh lemon juice
Grated peel of 1 lemon

4 large tart green apples, Pippin
   or Granny Smith (about 2
   pounds)
3 tablespoons unsalted butter
1 teaspoon vanilla

Make pastry as directed. Roll out on a lightly floured board into 13-inch circle. Fit into tart pan and trim edges even with top of pan. Prick bottom of pastry with fork. Place on baking sheet and refrigerate for at least 30 minutes.

Place oven rack in lower third of oven. Preheat oven to 400°. Bake crust in the 400° oven for 10 minutes. Remove from oven and carefully reprick any areas which have puffed up. Continue baking for 7 to 10 minutes or until sides are golden and bottom is lightly browned. The pastry may shrink and crack slightly. Remove from oven and cool on wire rack.

To make lemon filling, whisk eggs in top of double boiler off the heat until frothy. Whisk in 1 cup sugar, lemon juice and peel. Place pan over simmering water. Stir constantly until mixture is very hot and thickens enough to hold its shape when dropped from a spoon, about 10 to 15 minutes. Do not allow to boil. Remove from heat. Refrigerate or stir over ice water until chilled. Spread evenly into cooled pie shell. (*) The tart, covered with plastic wrap, may be refrigerated overnight, if desired.

Peel and core apples. Melt butter in large skillet; stir in ⅔ cup sugar and vanilla. Remove pan from heat. Slice apples into ¼-inch-thick slices by hand or with medium (4 mm) slicing blade of food processor. Place apple slices in skillet and cook over moderate heat for 8 to 10 minutes or until they begin to turn transparent; move them around with a spatula to ensure even cooking. Taste; they should be soft but still retain a slight resistance. Remove apples with slotted spatula or spoon to a plate. Reserve juices.

Arrange apple slices overlapping in circles over lemon filling. Make a rose shape in center of tart by curving slices tightly together. Bring juices in skillet to a boil over moderate heat and cook until reduced to about ¼ cup. Spoon and brush juice over apples to glaze them. Refrigerate tart until chilled or up to 6 hours. Remove sides of pan. Serve chilled.

Serves 8 to 10.

Double-Crust Apple Pie with Custard

A traditional apple pie is made with two layers of flaky pastry encasing apple slices and fragrant spices. As the pie bakes, the apples fall slightly, leaving a pocket of empty space between the fruit and the top pastry layer. What a perfect place for a filling of creamy, slightly lemony custard. You might say this is apple pie with a built-in sauce. Certainly convenient and decidedly irresistible! If you prefer a classic apple pie, just omit the custard.

1 recipe Shortening Pastry for
   double-crust pie (see page 87)
¾ cup sugar
2 tablespoons all-purpose flour
Grated peel of 1 lemon
¾ teaspoon ground cinnamon
¼ teaspoon ground nutmeg
¼ teaspoon salt
2 pounds Golden Delicious apples
   (about 6 small or 5 large)
1 tablespoon lemon juice
2 tablespoons unsalted butter, at
   room temperature
1 egg mixed with 1 teaspoon
   water for glazing crust

CUSTARD
2 large eggs
¼ cup sugar
1 teaspoon cornstarch
3 tablespoons lemon juice
1 package (3 ounces) cream cheese,
   at room temperature cut into
   9 pieces
¾ cup sour cream, at room
   temperature
¼ cup milk

BAKING PAN
9-inch pie plate

Make pastry as directed. Roll out half the dough on lightly floured board into 11-inch circle. Fit into 9-inch pie plate. Trim to fit. Refrigerate while preparing filling.

Preheat oven to 450°. Stir together sugar, flour, lemon peel, cinnamon, nutmeg and salt in large bowl. Set aside. Peel, quarter and core apples. Slice into ¼-inch slices by hand or with medium (4 mm) slicing blade of food processor. Add to sugar mixture along with lemon juice. Toss with hands to coat apples evenly. Turn into prepared crust, distributing apples evenly. Cut butter into tiny pieces and sprinkle on top of filling.

Roll out remaining half of dough on lightly floured board into 10-inch circle. Moisten edges of bottom pastry with water. Carefully place pastry on top of pie. Press edges of bottom and top pastry together. With a scissors, trim even with edge of pie plate. Crimp edges decoratively. Brush pastry with enough egg wash to glaze.

Place pie on baking sheet. Bake in the 450° oven for 10 minutes. Reduce oven temperature to 375° and continue to bake for 35 to 45 minutes, or until crust is golden brown and filling is bubbling. If edges get too brown, cover them with foil. Remove pie from oven and cool on wire rack for at least 1 hour. As pie cools, the apples will fall, leaving a space for the custard.

CUSTARD
After the pie has cooled, make custard by whisking eggs lightly in medium-size saucepan. Whisk in sugar until well blended. Stir cornstarch into lemon juice in small bowl until dissolved. Whisk into eggs. Add cream cheese and cook, stirring constantly until mixture

1 *Flute edges with handle of a knife or your fingers.*

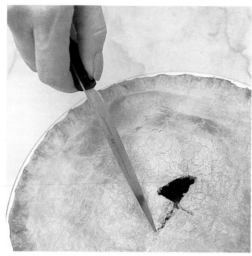

2 *After pie has cooled, cut an "X" in the center of the top crust. Cut an opening in the crust, using the "X" as a guide.*

3 *Pour custard into opening, shaking the pie gently to distribute the custard.*

thickens and comes just to a boil. Do not be concerned if mixture is slightly lumpy. Remove from heat and whisk in sour cream and milk. Transfer to glass measuring cup or small pitcher.

Cut an X about 2 inches long with a sharp knife in center of pie. Cut an opening, using the lines as a guide. Pour the warm custard into opening, slowly, shaking the pan gently to distribute the custard. Let pie stand at least 1 hour before serving for custard to set. (*) The pie may be held uncovered at room temperature for several hours, if desired.

Serves 6 to 8.

Apple Streusel Tart

This sky-high dessert makes apple pie seem passé. Layer upon layer of brown sugar and cinnamon-coated apples are laced with bourbon and raisins. Adding euphoria to ecstasy is a generous streusel topping of crunchy walnuts, oats, brown sugar and cinnamon.

CRUST
1 recipe Cookie Pastry for
    single-crust pie (see page 88)

APPLE FILLING
3 tablespoons bourbon
½ cup dark raisins
Juice of 1 lemon
3 pounds tart cooking apples,
    such as Pippin or Granny Smith
    (about 6 large apples)
½ cup firmly packed golden brown
    sugar
½ cup granulated sugar
1½ teaspoons ground cinnamon
¼ teaspoon ground nutmeg
¼ cup all-purpose flour
¼ cup (½ stick) unsalted butter,
    melted

STREUSEL
½ cup quick-cooking oats
½ cup firmly packed golden
    brown sugar
¼ cup all-purpose flour
½ teaspoon ground cinnamon
Dash salt
6 tablespoons unsalted butter,
    at room temperature
1 cup walnuts, chopped into
    medium-size pieces (about
    4 ounces)

BAKING PAN
9 x 3-inch or 9½ x 2-inch
    springform pan

Place oven rack in lower third of oven. Preheat oven to 450°.

CRUST
Make pastry as directed. Divide pastry in half and press half into bottom of springform. Press remaining pastry two thirds up sides of pan.

FILLING
Warm bourbon in small saucepan. Do not allow to boil. Add raisins, remove from heat and cover pan. Let stand for at least 10 minutes for raisins to soften.

Fill large bowl with water and the juice of one lemon. Peel and core apples. Drop them into the lemon water to prevent them from turning dark. Slice into ¼-inch slices by hand or with medium (4 mm) slicing blade of food processor. Transfer raisins and bourbon to a large bowl; stir in apple slices. Toss apples with hands to coat with bourbon.

Stir together sugars, cinnamon, nutmeg and flour; add to apples. Add butter and mix with hands until distributed. Place apple mixture in pastry-lined pan.

Place pan on baking sheet. Bake in the lower third of the 450° oven for 15 minutes.

STREUSEL

Meanwhile, mix oats, sugar, flour, cinnamon and salt in medium-size bowl. Cut in butter using fork, fingertips, or pastry blender until mixture is crumbly. Mix in nuts.

Remove tart from oven and reduce oven temperature to 350°. Sprinkle streusel evenly over top of apples. Press down lightly with hands. Bake in the 350° oven for an additional 60 to 70 minutes or until top is golden brown and edges are bubbling. Remove from oven and cool for 1 hour. Run knife around edges of tart to make sure tart does not stick to springform. Do not remove sides until ready to serve. (*) The tart may be covered with plastic wrap and foil and held at room temperature overnight, if desired. It may be reheated in a preheated 350° oven for 15 minutes, if desired.

Before serving, remove sides of springform. Serve warm or at room temperature.

Serves 8.

Pineapple Banana Pie

When dining on Oriental cuisine, it's difficult to conjure up an appropriate dessert. Never fear. This pie is filled with the wonderful flavors of the Far East: pineapple, banana, ginger and macadamia nuts.

CRUST

1 cup all-purpose flour
6 tablespoons unsalted butter, cold and cut into 6 pieces
¼ cup firmly packed golden brown sugar
¾ cup chopped macadamia nuts (about 3 ounces), toasted at 350° until golden, about 10 minutes, stirring occasionally
1 tablespoon ice water

FILLING AND TOPPING

1 can (1 pound 4 ounces) crushed pineapple in its own juice
¼ cup lemon juice
Grated peel of 1 lemon
½ cup sugar
1½ teaspoons finely minced fresh ginger or 1¼ teaspoons ground ginger
3 tablespoons cornstarch mixed with 3 tablespoons water
8 ounces apricot preserves
4 bananas

BAKING PAN

11-inch tart pan with removable bottom

CRUST

Mix flour and butter in food processor fitted with metal blade or in medium-size mixing bowl with pastry blender or fingertips until size of peas. Add sugar, nuts and ice water and mix until dough begins to hold together. Do not let dough form a ball (see technique and pictures on making pastry, page 86). With hands, press evenly over bottom and up sides of tart pan. Prick bottom lightly with fork. Place on baking sheet and refrigerate for at least 30 minutes.

Heat oven to 375° and bake for 12 to 15 minutes or until bottom is golden. Remove to wire rack and cool.

FILLING AND TOPPING

Place pineapple with juice, lemon juice and peel, sugar and ginger in medium-size saucepan. Stir in cornstarch and water mixture. Cook over moderate heat, stirring constantly, until mixture comes to a boil and thickens. Cool slightly and pour into baked crust. (*) The pie may be refrigerated, covered with plastic wrap, overnight, if desired.

Not more than 2 hours before serving, make topping by boiling preserves in small heavy saucepan over moderate heat for 1 minute, stirring constantly. Push through a strainer into bowl to remove all large pieces. Slice bananas diagonally and place them overlapping in rings on pineapple filling. Brush generously with hot apricot preserves. Make sure bananas are completely covered so they do not turn dark. Refrigerate until ready to serve. Remove sides of pan before serving.

Serves 8.

Berries and Cream Tart

With its white, creamy, cream cheese filling and luscious red and blue berry topping, this graham cracker-and-nut-crust pie positively sings of patriotism. Although perfect for a Fourth of July or Memorial Day party, it's an ideal dessert for any hot summer day since it's so easily assembled.

CRUST

2 cups graham cracker crumbs (about 20 crackers)
1 cup finely chopped pecans (4 ounces)
¼ cup granulated sugar
¼ pound (1 stick) unsalted butter, melted

FILLING AND TOPPING

1 package (8 ounces) cream cheese, at room temperature
⅓ cup powdered sugar, sifted
1 teaspoon vanilla
2 tablespoons orange liqueur, such as Grand Marnier
1 cup whipping cream
Approximately 4 cups assorted berries, such as strawberries, blueberries, raspberries, blackberries, boysenberries

BAKING PAN

11-inch tart pan with removable bottom

Preheat oven to 350°.

CRUST

Mix crumbs, nuts, sugar and butter in food processor fitted with metal blade or in medium-size bowl until combined. Press evenly over bottom and up sides of pan.

Place on baking sheet. Bake in the 350° oven for 10 minutes. Cool.

FILLING AND TOPPING

Mix cream cheese and sugar in small bowl with electric mixer on medium speed until light and fluffy, about 3 minutes. Scrape down sides of bowl and beat again. Mix in vanilla and liqueur. Beat whipping cream in separate mixing bowl until soft peaks form. Fold into cream cheese mixture and pour into cooled crust. Refrigerate several hours or until well chilled. (*) The tart may be refrigerated overnight covered with plastic wrap, if desired.

Before serving, arrange berries on top of tart. Beginning around outside edge, make a circle of blackberries or boysenberries. Arrange remaining berries, except strawberries, in 1 or 2 more circles, working towards the center and leaving a 6-inch circle in center uncovered. Cut stems off strawberries. Reserve one large strawberry for center. Cut remaining strawberries in half lengthwise. Arrange strawberries cut-side up in overlapping circles in center of tart. Place whole strawberry in center. Refrigerate until serving time. Before serving, remove sides of pan.

Serves 8.

Purple Plum Tart

A scrumptious, buttery, cinnamony streusel works as both the crust and topping, enveloping soft, ripe, sweetened plums.

FILLING

12 to 16 ripe red-meat plums (about 2 to 3 pounds)
¾ cup sugar
3 tablespoons quick-cooking tapioca

CRUST AND TOPPING

¼ pound (1 stick) unsalted butter, at room temperature
1 cup sugar
1¼ cups all-purpose flour
½ teaspoon salt
1 teaspoon ground cinnamon
¼ teaspoon baking powder

BAKING PAN

9 x 3-inch or 9½ x 2-inch springform pan

FILLING

Halve and pit plums. Toss plums in medium-size bowl with ¾ cup sugar and tapioca until well coated. Let the mixture stand for 30 minutes, tossing 2 or 3 times.

CRUST AND TOPPING

Preheat oven to 400°. Mix butter and sugar in food processor fitted with metal blade or in medium-size bowl with electric mixer on medium speed until blended. Add flour, salt, cinnamon and baking powder with on and off pulses. Mix until well combined; the mixture will be crumbly. Measure ½ cup of the pastry and set aside.

Press remaining pastry evenly over bottom and 1 inch up sides of springform. Tightly arrange layer of plums cut-side down over bottom of pastry. Make a second layer over the first. Spoon any remaining sugar mixture from plums over top. Sprinkle top evenly with reserved ½ cup pastry.

Place pan on baking sheet. Bake in the 400° oven for 45 minutes or until crust is golden brown and sides are bubbling. The tart will firm up as it cools. Remove from the oven. Run small sharp knife around edges of pastry to make sure pastry doesn't stick to pan as it cools. Cool to room temperature. The tart may be held several hours before serving.

Before serving, remove sides of springform. Serve at room temperature. Best served the same day.

Serves 8.

Brandy and Ginger Peach Tart

The essence of pure peach flavor is captured by not baking the fruit. Instead, the peaches are marinated in brandy and ginger and they retain a subtle hint of these flavorings. This is pictured on page 82, garnished with raspberries.

CRUST

1 recipe Cookie Pastry for single-crust pie (see page 88)
¼ teaspoon ground ginger
1 teaspoon grated lemon peel

BAKING PAN

11- or 12-inch round or square tart pan with removable bottom

FILLING

7 to 8 ripe peaches (about 3 pounds)
⅓ cup brandy
½ teaspoon grated lemon peel
¼ teaspoon ground ginger
1 jar (10 ounces) currant jelly
2 tablespoons plus 2 teaspoons cornstarch
¼ cup water

CRUST

Make pastry as directed, adding ground ginger and lemon peel with the flour. Roll out dough on lightly floured board into 13-inch circle or into a 14-inch square. Transfer to tart pan and press into bottom and up sides. Trim edges even with the top of pan. Prick bottom with fork. Place on baking sheet and refrigerate at least 30 minutes.

Place oven rack in lower third of oven. Preheat oven to 400°. Bake crust for 10 minutes and then carefully reprick any areas which have puffed up. Continue baking for 7 to 10 minutes or until sides are golden and bottom is lightly browned. Pastry will shrink slightly. Remove from oven and place on wire rack to cool. (*) The crust may be kept, covered, at room temperature overnight, or it may be frozen in the pan, tightly covered with heavy-duty foil. Defrost, covered, at room temperature.

FILLING

Peel peaches by plunging them into boiling water to cover for 20 seconds. Run under cold water and when cool enough to handle, peel off skin. Slice peaches, discarding pits. Stir together brandy, grated lemon peel, and ground ginger in large bowl. Add peach slices and toss to coat well. Marinate at room temperature for 30 minutes.

Pour marinade from peaches into measuring cup. Set peaches aside. Add enough water to marinade to make 1 cup. Pour into small saucepan. Stir in jelly. Cook over medium heat, stirring constantly until jelly is melted. Stir water and cornstarch together in small bowl; stir into jelly mixture. Cook over medium heat, stirring constantly until mixture thickens and comes to a boil. Boil 1 minute. Remove from heat and refrigerate 10 minutes while arranging peaches. Arrange peach slices overlapping on pastry. Spoon glaze evenly over top. (You may have some left over.) Refrigerate tart for 1½ to 2 hours or until set. The tart is best served within 4 hours. Before serving, remove sides of pan.

Serves 8 to 10.

Cherry Quiche

Baked in a quiche pan, this dessert boasts plump, burgundy red cherries interspersed in a creamy custard base that's sweetened with a splash of Kirsch.

1 recipe Cookie Pastry for single-crust pie (see page 88)
2 cans (16 ounces each) pitted dark sweet cherries
1 large egg
⅓ cup sugar
2 tablespoons all-purpose flour
⅓ cup whipping cream
1 tablespoon Kirsch
1 teaspoon vanilla

BAKING PAN
9-inch porcelain or glass quiche pan or tart pan with removable bottom

Make pastry as directed. Roll out pastry on lightly floured board, into 12-inch circle. Fit into tart pan and trim edges even with the top of pan. Prick bottom of pastry with fork. Place on baking sheet and refrigerate for at least 30 minutes.

Place oven rack in lower third of oven. Preheat oven to 400°. Bake crust 10 minutes or until pastry begins to brown but is still pale. Pastry will shrink slightly. Remove from oven and cool on wire rack. (*) The crust may be held, covered, at room temperature overnight, or may be frozen in the pan tightly wrapped with heavy-duty foil, if desired. Defrost, covered, at room temperature.

Reduce oven temperature to 350°. Drain cherries and pat dry on paper towels. Arrange cherries in single layer in pastry shell. (You may have a few cherries left over.) Whisk egg lightly in medium-size bowl. Add sugar and flour, whisking well to remove lumps. Whisk in cream, Kirsch and vanilla. Pour custard over cherries.

Place tart on baking sheet. Bake in the 350° oven for 30 to 35 minutes or until filling is set and top is golden.

Before serving, remove sides of pan. Serve tart warm or at room temperature.

Serves 6.

Cranberry Pear Pie

This pie is special. Ruby-red cranberries combined with golden, spiced pears make a tart, sweet, warm, winter pie. To match the picture on page 82, make extra pastry. Cut out leaves, glaze them with egg wash and bake on baking sheet at 375° until golden. Then place them around rim of the pie.

1 recipe Shortening Pastry for double-crust pie (see page 87) or Rich All-Purpose Pastry for double-crust pie (see page 85)
2½ cups fresh or frozen cranberries
1½ cups sugar
¼ cup water
2½ tablespoons cornstarch
¼ teaspoon ground allspice
⅛ teaspoon ground cardamom (optional)
2 large or 3 medium-size ripe pears (about 1¾ pounds)

1 tablespoon unsalted butter
1 egg beaten with 1 tablespoon milk for glaze
Whipped cream or vanilla ice cream for serving (optional)

BAKING PAN
9-inch pie plate

Make pastry as directed.

Place cranberries, sugar and water in medium-size saucepan. Bring to a boil and cook, stirring, until the skins pop, about 5 minutes. Combine cornstarch, allspice and cardamom, if using, in small bowl. Stir into hot cranberries and continue cooking, stirring constantly, until mixture comes to a full boil and thickens. Remove from heat. Peel, core and slice pears into ¼-inch-thick slices; measure 3 cups and stir into cranberries. Set aside to cool.

Preheat oven to 375°.

Roll out half the pastry on lightly floured board into 12-inch circle. Fit into pie plate. Trim pastry to ½ inch beyond edge of pie plate. Turn cranberry-pear filling into pastry. Dot with small pieces of butter. Roll out remaining pastry to 10 x 6-inch rectangle. With pastry cutter or sharp knife, cut 12 strips, each ½ inch wide and 10 inches long. Weave strips over filling to make lattice crust. Press edges of pastry together to form sealed rim. Flute edges, if desired. Carefully brush lattice strips and edges with as much egg-milk glaze as needed. To prevent overbrowning, cover edge of pastry with foil.

Place pie on baking sheet. Bake in the 375° oven for 30 minutes. Remove foil and bake 20 to 30 more minutes or until crust is golden. Remove to wire rack to cool. (*) The pie, covered with plastic wrap or foil, may be held at room temperature overnight. Reheat in preheated 350° oven for 10 minutes before serving, if desired.

Serve with whipped cream or vanilla ice cream, if desired.

Serves 6 to 8.

Pear and Cheddar Tart

Cheddar cheese and apples have been a team for decades, but this cheese is equally delicious with pears. In this recipe, the cheese is incorporated right into the crust and streusel-like topping.

CHEDDAR CHEESE CRUST

⅓ cup vegetable shortening
1 cup all purpose flour
⅛ teaspoon salt
⅛ teaspoon sugar
1 cup shredded sharp Cheddar cheese (about 4 ounces)
4 to 6 teaspoons ice water

FILLING AND TOPPING

1 stick unsalted butter, melted
1 cup all-purpose flour
½ cup sugar
¼ teaspoon salt
1 cup shredded sharp Cheddar cheese (about 4 ounces)

1¾ pounds firm but ripe pears (about 3 to 4 pears)
Juice of 1 lemon

BAKING PAN

9-or 10-inch tart pan with removable bottom

CRUST

Carefully measure shortening in a dry measure so you can level off the top. Spread shortening approximately ½ inch thick on sheet of waxed paper. Place in freezer and chill 15 minutes. Cut shortening into approximately ½-inch pieces. Place flour, shortening, salt, sugar and cheese in food processor fitted with metal blade or in mixing bowl. Pulse 6 or 8 times or mix with pastry blender until mixture is the size of peas. With machine off, add 4 teaspoons of the ice water. Pulse on and off or mix with fork until dough holds together. If too dry, add additional water a teaspoon at a time. Do not process into a ball. Press pastry into a disc. Refrigerate until cold enough to roll.

Place dough between 2 sheets of lightly floured waxed paper and roll into an 11- or 12-inch circle. Remove top paper and invert pastry onto tart pan. Peel off the paper. Fit into tart pan and trim the edges even with the top of the pan. Do not worry if you need to patch it. Preheat oven to 400°. Place oven rack in lowest position.

Line crust with waxed paper or foil. Fill to rim with pie weights or beans. Place on baking sheet in bottom of 400° oven for 10 minutes. Carefully remove paper and weights and return crust to oven. Bake for 13 to 15 minutes more or until sides are golden and crust is baked. Cool on rack. (*) Crust may be frozen or covered and kept at room temperature overnight. Defrost at room temperature.

FILLING AND TOPPING

Preheat oven to 400°. Mix together butter, flour, sugar, salt and cheese in medium-size bowl with pastry blender, fork, or fingertips until crumbly; set aside. Peel pears. As you work, drop them into a bowl of water to which the juice of 1 lemon has been added to keep them from turning dark. Cut pears in half, core and cut into ¾- to 1-inch-thick slices. Arrange slices overlapping very close together in single layer around inside of crust. Mound a swirl of slices in center. Sprinkle cheese mixture evenly over top. Place tart pan on baking sheet. Bake in the 400° oven for 35 to 40 minutes or until crumbs are golden brown and pears are tender. Before serving, remove sides of pan. Serve warm. The tart is best served within 4 hours.

Serves 6.

Pumpkin Praline Chiffon Pie

An airy mixture of pumpkin, spices and eggnog resting on a crunchy layer of brown sugar praline makes this pie a perfect harbinger of holiday joy. If desired, cut scraps of pastry into a pumpkin shape, bake and place on top of the pie for decoration.

BAKING PAN
10-or 10½-inch deep dish pie plate

1 or 1½ recipes Rich All-Purpose Pastry for single-crust pie (see page 85) or Shortening Pastry for single-crust pie (see page 87)
5 tablespoons unsalted butter, at room temperature
½ cup firmly packed golden brown sugar
¾ cup chopped walnuts or pecans (about 3 ounces)
½ cup plus ¼ cup sugar

1 tablespoon plus 1½ teaspoons unflavored gelatin (1½ envelopes)
1 teaspoon ground cinnamon
½ teaspoon ground ginger
¼ teaspoon ground nutmeg
3 large eggs, separated
1½ cups eggnog
1 can (16 ounces) mashed pumpkin
¼ teaspoon cream of tartar
1 cup whipping cream
Whipped cream for garnishing (optional)

Preheat oven to 450°. Make pastry as directed. Roll out pastry on a lightly floured board into circle at least 3 inches larger than pie dish. Fit pastry into dish and flute edges. Prick pastry with fork. To blind bake, line with wax paper. Fill to the rim with pie weights or beans. Bake crust in the 450° oven for 10 minutes. Remove paper and weights and return crust to oven. Bake 5 to 7 minutes longer or until pastry just begins to brown. Remove from oven; leave oven on 450°. Meanwhile, beat butter and brown sugar in medium-size bowl with electric mixer on medium speed until blended. Stir in nuts. Spread over bottom of partially baked pie shell. Bake in the 450° oven for 4 to 5 minutes or until sugar is bubbly and pastry is golden. Remove to wire rack and cool completely.

Stir together ½ cup sugar, gelatin, cinnamon, ginger and nutmeg in medium-size heavy saucepan. Whisk in egg yolks and eggnog. Cook over moderate heat, stirring constantly until mixture is very hot to the touch and is thick enough to leave a path on a wooden spoon when you run your finger along it. Do not bring to a boil. Remove from heat and stir in pumpkin. Transfer mixture to medium-size bowl. Place bowl in larger bowl of ice water and stir occasionally until mixture thickens enough to mound when dropped from spoon.

Meanwhile, beat egg whites until foamy in large mixing bowl with electric mixer on low speed. Add cream of tartar and beat on high speed until soft peaks form. Add remaining ¼ cup sugar, 1 tablespoon at a time, beating until whites form stiff but not dry peaks. Spoon whites over pumpkin. In same mixing bowl, beat cream until soft peaks form. Fold pumpkin mixture and whites into whipped cream until blended. Pour into prepared shell. Refrigerate for several hours or until set. (*) The pie may be refrigerated, covered, overnight. Before serving, decorate top with rosettes of whipping cream.

Serves 8.

White Chocolate Mousse Pie

White Chocolate Mousse Pie

This pie is sensuous, eye-catching and an absolute winner. Sweet, juicy red strawberries floating in clouds of white chocolate mousse make the most luxurious combination imaginable. I use two 3-ounce bars Toblerone Narcisse white chocolate.

CRUST

43 vanilla wafers (about 6 ounces, 1¼ cups crumbs)
¼ cup sliced or whole blanched almonds (¼ cup ground)
6 tablespoons unsalted butter, melted

BAKING PAN

9-inch pie plate

MOUSSE

6 ounces white chocolate (see notes on chocolate, pages 7–8)
⅓ cup milk
2 large egg whites, at room temperature
1 cup whipping cream
2 pint boxes fresh strawberries, hulled
White chocolate shavings for garnish, optional (see page 228)

CRUST

Preheat oven to 350°. Break up wafers and place with almonds in food processor fitted with metal blade. Process with pulses until finely ground. Add butter and process with pulses until incorporated. Or, mix crumbs, ground nuts and butter in medium-size bowl until blended. Press evenly over bottom and up sides of pie plate.

Bake in the 350° oven for 10 minutes or until lightly golden. Crust will puff up but will sink down as it cools. Remove from oven and cool completely.

MOUSSE

Melt chocolate in top of double boiler over simmering water. Add milk slowly, stirring until mixture is completely smooth. Remove from heat and cool to room temperature. Beat egg whites in medium-size bowl with electric mixer until foamy. Beat at high speed until soft, rounded peaks form. Spoon whites over chocolate; do not mix. In same mixing bowl, whip cream until soft peaks form. Fold chocolate mixture and whites into cream.

Place strawberries about ½ inch apart on bottom of crust. Save remaining berries for garnish. Spoon mousse over berries, mounding toward center. Refrigerate until chilled. (*) The pie may be refrigerated covered with plastic wrap overnight if desired.

Before serving, cut remaining berries in half lengthwise. Place border of berries cut-side down with tips pointing inward around top edge of pie. Sprinkle chocolate shavings over center of pie, if desired. Refrigerate until serving.

Serves 6.

Caramel Custard Fruit Tart

There is always a moment of total silence when my guests take their first bite of this sublime tart. The taste of crunchy, caramelized sugar hidden beneath a cool, creamy custard and sweet, fresh fruit is an unexpected, delightful surprise. Many thanks to Jacques Pépin for this unparalleled dessert.

CRUST

1 recipe Cookie Pastry for single-crust pie (see page 88)

CARAMEL

⅔ cup sugar
3 tablespoons water

CUSTARD AND TOPPING

6 large egg yolks
½ cup sugar
⅓ cup all-purpose flour
2 cups milk, heated until hot

1 teaspoon vanilla
¼ pound (1 stick) unsalted butter, at room temperature and cut into small pieces
Assorted fresh fruit such as kiwi slices, berries, orange slices, banana slices, peach slices, seedless grapes
½ cup apricot jam
2 tablespoons water

BAKING PAN

11-inch tart pan with removable bottom

CRUST

Make Cookie Pastry as directed. Roll out pastry on lightly floured board into 13-inch circle at least ¼ inch thick. Do not roll pastry too thin. Fit into tart pan and trim edges even with top of pan. Prick bottom well with a fork. Place on baking sheet and refrigerate for at least 30 minutes.

Place oven rack in lower third of oven. Preheat oven to 400°. Bake crust for 18 to 20 minutes or until bottom is lightly golden. The pastry will shrink slightly. Remove from oven and cool completely. (*) The crust may be wrapped and kept at room temperature overnight, or it may be frozen, if desired.

CARAMEL

Place sugar and water in small heavy skillet or saucepan. Heat over moderate heat until sugar is melted, stirring once to help dissolve the sugar. Increase heat to moderately high and bring to a boil, swirling and rotating pan but without stirring, until sugar turns mahogany. Watch carefully as it burns easily once it has turned mahogany. Working quickly, pour caramel onto cooled pastry and roll around until bottom is covered. It may be helpful to use the back of a wooden spoon. Set tart aside until caramel cools and hardens. (*) The crust may be held at room temperature up to 6 hours, if desired.

CUSTARD AND TOPPING

Whisk yolks in medium-size heavy saucepan. Add sugar and flour and mix until creamy. Slowly whisk in hot milk. Place over moderate heat and cook, stirring and whisking constantly until mixture comes to a boil. Lower heat slightly and continue cooking, stirring constantly for 2 minutes, or until thick and smooth. Custard may lump slightly as it comes to a boil, but whisking will smooth it out. Remove from heat and whisk in vanilla and butter a small amount at a time. If not using immediately, cover by placing piece of plastic wrap directly on custard.

(*) The custard may be refrigerated overnight, if desired. Stir well before using.

Not more than 6 hours before serving, spread custard over caramel. Arrange assorted fresh fruit in circles over custard. Make glaze by bringing jam and water to a boil in small saucepan. Lower heat and simmer, stirring occasionally, for 3 to 4 minutes. Press through strainer placed over small bowl. Brush as much warm glaze as needed over fruit to cover. Refrigerate until ready to serve, but not more than 6 hours, or the caramel will melt. Before serving, remove sides of pan.

Serves 8.

Zesty Lemon Custard Pie

One day while cooking with my friend Danny Kaye, he offered to make me the most lemony pie I'd ever eaten. True to his word, one bite of this pie and my whole mouth puckered. Although I've adapted it to my taste, it reflects Danny's passionate philosophy of infusing life with zest, fervor and gusto. There's nothing subtle about this pie.

CRUST

1 recipe Cookie pastry (page 88)

FILLING

¼ pound (1 stick) unsalted butter
4 large eggs
1 cup sugar
1 tablespoon grated lemon peel
    (1 large lemon)
⅔ cup fresh lemon juice
Powdered sugar for topping pie

BAKING PAN

9-inch porcelain or glass quiche dish or pie plate

CRUST

Place oven rack in lowest position. Preheat oven to 350°.

Make pastry as directed.

Roll or press dough evenly over bottom and up sides of dish. If using a quiche dish, trim edges even with top of dish. If using a pie dish, press edges of pastry evenly over rim of pan.

FILLING

Melt butter in small saucepan; set aside. Whisk eggs and sugar in medium-size bowl until blended. Add peel and slowly stir in butter and lemon juice until incorporated. Pour into crust.

Bake in the 350° oven for 30 to 40 minutes or until top of custard is lightly browned. It will not test clean and will look underdone, but will set as it cools. If using a pie dish, it may be necessary to cover edges of pastry with foil halfway through baking to prevent crust from becoming too brown. Remove to wire rack and cool completely. When cool, refrigerate until serving time. (*) The pie may be refrigerated, covered, overnight, or it may be frozen, covered with plastic wrap and foil, if desired. Defrost wrapped pie in refrigerator overnight.

Before serving, sprinkle top heavily with powdered sugar.

Serve chilled.

Serves 6.

Lemon Almond Tart

The contrasting tastes of this dessert will captivate your senses—sweet and crunchy almond meringue playing off smooth and tangy lemon custard.

BAKING PAN

9 x 3-inch or 9½ x 2-inch springform pan

CRUST

1 recipe Cookie Pastry (page 88)
1 teaspoon grated lemon peel

ALMOND FILLING

1¼ cups coarsely ground almonds
1 cup sugar
3 large egg whites, at room temperature
Dash cream of tartar

LEMON CUSTARD

5 large egg yolks
½ cup sugar
⅓ cup fresh lemon juice (2 to 3 lemons)
Grated peel of 1 lemon
¼ cup (½ stick) unsalted butter, at room temperature
8 to 10 sliced almonds for garnish (optional)

CRUST

Make pastry as directed, adding 1 teaspoon grated lemon peel with the flour. Press pastry evenly over bottom and 1 inch up sides of pan.

Set oven rack in lower third of oven. Preheat oven to 350°.

FILLING

Reserve 3 tablespoons ground almonds for garnish. To make filling, stir together remaining almonds and sugar in small bowl; set aside. Beat egg whites in large mixing bowl with electric mixer on low speed until frothy. Add cream of tartar and beat on high speed until stiff peaks form. Gently fold almond mixture into whites. Pour into prepared crust.

Bake in the 350° oven for 30 to 40 minutes or until the top is golden. Remove to wire rack and cool to room temperature.

CUSTARD

Meanwhile, to make custard, whisk egg yolks and sugar in top of double boiler until thick and creamy. Whisk in lemon juice and peel. Cook over simmering water, whisking constantly, until mixture becomes thick enough to hold its shape and mound when dropped from a spoon, about 10 to 15 minutes. Do not bring to a boil. Remove from heat and pour into bowl. Whisk in butter a small amount at a time. Cool to room temperature. Spread custard over filling in crust. (*) The tart may be refrigerated, covered, up to 2 days, or it may be frozen, covered with plastic wrap and foil, if desired. Defrost covered pie at room temperature.

Before serving, sprinkle reserved ground almonds around top of tart, making a 1-inch border. Place sliced almonds in center in daisy pattern, if desired. Remove sides of springform. Serve at room temperature.

Serves 8.

Regal Pecan Tart

This recipe elevates pecan pie from hearty fare to haute cuisine. While baking, pecan halves rise to the surface through a rich, dark, chestnut-brown custard, forming concentric rings of toasted nuts. Towering above all others in taste, size and appearance, this dessert is fit for royalty.

CRUST
1 cup all-purpose flour
⅓ cup powdered sugar
12 tablespoons (1½ sticks) unsalted butter, cold and cut into 12 pieces for food processor; at room temperature for mixer
Pinch salt

BAKING PAN
9 x 3-inch or 9½ x 2-inch springform pan

FILLING
¾ cup firmly packed dark brown sugar
3 tablespoons unsalted butter, at room temperature
3 large eggs, at room temperature
¾ cup dark corn syrup
2 teaspoons vanilla
⅛ teaspoon salt
2 cups chopped pecans (about 8 ounces)
1½ cups pecan halves (about 6 ounces)
Whipped cream or vanilla ice cream for serving (optional)

Preheat oven to 350°.

CRUST
Place flour, sugar, butter and salt in food processor fitted with metal blade or in medium-size bowl. Mix until dough holds together and forms a soft ball. Press pastry evenly over bottom and 1 inch up sides of springform. Prick crust with fork and set aside.

FILLING
Beat brown sugar and butter in large bowl with electric mixer on medium speed until fluffy, about 2 minutes. Add eggs, syrup, vanilla and salt. Mix thoroughly. Sprinkle chopped pecans over bottom of crust and cover with half the filling. Place pecan halves in concentric circles over entire top of pie. Pour remaining filling carefully over pecans.

Place pan on baking sheet. Bake in the 350° oven for 60 to 70 minutes or until knife inserted into middle comes out clean and pastry is golden. (*) The tart may be kept covered at room temperature or in the refrigerator overnight, or it may be frozen in springform covered with plastic wrap and foil, if desired. Defrost wrapped tart at room temperature.

Serve tart at room temperature, or reheat in 350° oven for 15 minutes and serve warm. Before serving, remove sides of springform. Serve with whipped cream or ice cream, if desired.

Serves 8.

Regal Pecan Tart

1

2

3

1 *Stir pecans into caramelized sugar.*

2 *Spread praline out slightly onto greased baking sheet with the back of a spoon.*

3 *Stir chopped praline into softened ice cream. Pie plate in background is lined with slices of pound cake.*

4 *With a large rosette or star tip, pipe meringue on top of pie.*

5 *Completed ice cream pie with rum sauce.*

4

5

Praline Ice Cream Pie

This spectacular pie is served at Fournous' Ovens, the renowned restaurant in San Francisco's Stanford Court Hotel. The filling for this pound cake-lined pie is vanilla ice cream flecked with pecan praline. A billowy meringue is spread over all, baked to a golden brown, and then the whole pie is frozen. The final touch is a golden rum sauce. I never feel a trip to the Stanford Court is complete until I've devoured a piece of this magnificent pie.

1 cup plus 1 cup sugar
3 tablespoons water
1½ cups pecan halves or pieces
8 ounces pound cake, cut into ¼-inch-thick slices, fresh or thawed frozen
3 pints good quality vanilla ice cream
1 recipe Rum Sauce (page 222)
6 large egg whites, at room temperature
⅛ teaspoon cream of tartar

BAKING PAN
9-inch pie plate
Baking sheet

Oil a baking sheet and set aside. Combine 1 cup sugar with the water in small saucepan over moderate heat, stirring once to help dissolve the sugar. Bring to a boil, swirling and rotating pan without stirring, until sugar turns mahogany. Watch carefully, as it goes from mahogany to burnt very quickly. Stir in pecans and immediately pour praline mixture onto prepared baking sheet. Set aside to cool and harden.

Meanwhile, line bottom of pie plate with slices of pound cake. Cut slices as necessary to fit bottom of plate, taking care to leave no gaps. Cut rectangles to fit around the sides and press them firmly against plate. Trim edges even with rim of plate. Set aside.

Break hardened praline into 1- to 2-inch pieces. Chop to medium coarseness in food processor fitted with metal blade, pulsing 10 to 15 times. Or, wrap praline in dish towel and crush with hammer or meat mallet.

Remove the ice cream from the freezer and let it soften slightly. Beat ice cream with electric mixer until soft and smooth but not melted. Fold in chopped praline. Fill pie shell with ice cream, smoothing top into slight dome. Cover with plastic wrap and foil and freeze until solid. (*) The pie may be frozen for several weeks, if desired.

Make Rum Sauce as directed and leave at room temperature until ready to use.

Preheat oven to 500°. Beat egg whites with electric mixer at low speed until frothy. Add the cream of tartar, increase speed to high and beat until soft peaks form. Add the 1 cup sugar, 1 tablespoon at a time, continuing to beat until mixture is stiff and shiny and the texture of marshmallow cream.

continued

Spread ½-inch layer of meringue with a spatula smoothly over pie, taking care to completely cover ice cream. Fit a large pastry bag with a ¾- to 1-inch rosette or star tip. Spoon remaining meringue into bag and pipe decoratively over pie. Or, if you prefer, use a spatula to shape meringue into swirls.

Bake in the 500° oven for 2 to 3 minutes or until meringue is lightly browned. Immediately return to freezer for several hours. (*) The pie may be frozen, uncovered, overnight, if desired.

Remove from freezer 5 to 10 minutes before serving. Spoon a couple of tablespoons of Rum Sauce on bottom of each dessert plate, swirling plate to cover bottom. Using a knife dipped in hot water, cut pie into slices. Place on rum sauce.

Serves 8.

Peanut Butter Ice Cream Pie with Hot Fudge Sauce

We're talking total decadence. How else can you describe a dessert made with peanut butter, ice cream and toasted cashews that's topped with hot fudge sauce? It combines the best flavors of childhood for every adult who has never grown up. It's a great dessert for large family gatherings.

CRUST
30 chocolate wafer cookies (about 2 cups crumbs)
¼ pound (1 stick) unsalted butter, melted

OR

25 Oreo cookies (about 2½ cups crumbs)
¼ cup (½ stick) unsalted butter, melted

FILLING
¾ cup unsalted cashews, coarsely chopped
3 pints vanilla ice cream, softened
1½ cups creamy peanut butter
¾ cup clover honey
1 or 2 recipes Hot Chocolate Fudge Sauce (see page 220) or Hot Bittersweet Fudge Sauce (see page 221)

BAKING PAN
9 x 3-inch or 9½ x 2-inch springform pan
Rimmed baking sheet

Preheat oven to 350°. Lightly oil bottom and sides of springform pan.

CRUST
Mix either chocolate wafers or Oreos and butter in food processor fitted with metal blade until they hold together. Or, mix crumbs and butter in medium-size bowl. Press evenly over bottom and two thirds up sides of pan.

FILLING

Place cashews on rimmed baking sheet. Bake in the 350° oven until lightly toasted, about 10 minutes, stirring occasionally. Cool completely. Mix ice cream, peanut butter, honey and cashews in large bowl, with electric mixer on low speed, until combined. Pour into prepared crust. Cover with plastic wrap and foil and freeze overnight or until solid. (*) The pie may be frozen up to one month, if desired.

Make 1 or 2 recipes of desired fudge sauce, depending on amount of people you will be serving. Remove pie from freezer 10 minutes before serving. Run sharp knife around edges and remove sides of springform. Place on serving platter and serve with sauce. Any leftovers may be refrozen.

Serves 12 to 14.

Coffee Fudge Ice Cream Torte

What an amazingly simple dessert to prepare. All you do is layer cookies, ice cream, fudge sauce and toffee candy. When you discover how much guests adore it, you may be tempted never to bake again.

1 package (10 ounces) coconut or almond macaroon cookies
1 pint chocolate ice cream, softened
1 recipe Hot Chocolate Fudge Sauce (see page 220), or Hot Bittersweet Fudge Sauce (see page 221), or 1 jar (10 ounces) hot fudge sauce
1 pint coffee ice cream, softened
½ pound Almond Roca or chocolate-coated English Toffee candy

BAKING DISH
8 x 3-inch or 8½ x 2-inch springform pan

Crush macaroons with rolling pin or in food processor fitted with metal blade. Place half the macaroons evenly over bottom of pan. Spread chocolate ice cream over with a spatula. Freeze until firm. Drizzle with half the fudge sauce. Sprinkle with remaining macaroons and spread coffee ice cream over with a spatula. Freeze until firm. Drizzle three quarters of the remaining fudge sauce over top. Chop candy into coarse pieces with a meat mallot, rolling pin or hammer. Sprinkle over the entire top. Drizzle remaining fudge sauce over the candy. Cover with foil and freeze until ready to serve. (*) The torte may be frozen for 1 month, if desired.

Remove from freezer 15 to 20 minutes before serving. Remove sides of springform.

Serves 8.

Ice Cream Cone Pie

Since it's so simple to make, this recipe is a treasure for children and novice cooks. The crust is prepared from crushed ice cream sugar cones, almonds and melted chocolate, rather than from pastry dough.

1 cup slivered almonds, coarsely
    chopped (about 4 ounces)
12 sugar cones (4-ounce box)
½ cup chocolate chips
5 tablespoons unsalted butter
1 quart ice cream, any flavor,
    softened

BAKING PAN
9-inch pie plate

Preheat oven to 350°. Place almonds on baking sheet and toast, stirring occasionally until lightly browned, about 10 to 12 minutes. Cool completely. With a rolling pin crush cones into small pieces between a dish towel or sheets of waxed paper. Do not chop in food processor. Place almonds and chopped cones in medium-size bowl.

Stir chocolate chips and butter in small heavy saucepan over low heat until melted. Pour over cones, stirring to coat evenly. Press one third of the crumb mixture evenly over bottom of pie dish. Spread half the ice cream over. Repeat with 2 more layers of crumbs and ice cream, ending with crumbs on top. Press down on crumbs with hands to help them adhere. Cover with foil and freeze until firm. (*) The pie may be frozen up to 1 month, if desired.

Serves 6.

Sour Cream Lime Tartlets

Cool, pale lime custard adds a perky citrus taste to these bite-size pastries.

1 recipe Cream Cheese Pastry for
    Tartlets (see page 90)
½ cup sugar
1 tablespoon cornstarch
½ cup whipping cream
3 tablespoons lime juice
Grated peel of 1 lime

2 tablespoons unsalted butter, at
    room temperature
⅓ cup sour cream
2 drops yellow food coloring
1 drop green food coloring
½ cup whipping cream, whipped
    for garnish (optional)

Make tartlet shells as directed. Stir together sugar and cornstarch in medium-size saucepan. Gradually stir in cream, lime juice and lime peel. Bring to a boil over medium-high heat, whisking constantly. Reduce heat to simmer and cook for 1 minute, stirring constantly, until thick and smooth. Remove from heat and stir in butter. Cool to room temperature, stirring occasionally. Stir in sour cream and food coloring. Spoon into tart shells. (*) Tartlets may be refrigerated in covered container overnight, or they may be frozen, if desired. Defrost at room temperature. Before serving, pipe a small rosette of whipped cream in the center of each tart, if desired.

Makes 24 tartlets.

Amaretti Fruit Tartlets

A most sophisticated dessert, these individual tartlets possess a distinct almond flavor both in the graham cracker–amaretti cookie crust and the super-smooth amaretto cream. The glazed fresh fruit adds vibrant color and a dash of elegance. See picture on page 82.

CRUST
½ cup amaretti cookie crumbs (about 2½ ounces)
1 cup graham cracker crumbs (16 crackers)
6 tablespoons (¾ stick) unsalted butter, melted

FILLING AND TOPPING
6 ounces cream cheese, at room temperature
⅓ cup sugar
2 tablespoons plus 1 tablespoon amaretto liqueur
¼ teaspoon almond extract
½ cup whipping cream
Assorted fresh fruit such as banana, peeled and sliced; kiwi, peeled and sliced; strawberries; raspberries; blueberries; grapes; peaches, peeled, pitted and sliced; oranges, peeled and sliced
½ cup apricot preserves

BAKING PAN
Four 4½ x ½-inch tartlet pans with removable bottoms

Preheat oven to 350°.

CRUST

Mix amaretti and graham cracker crumbs in food processor fitted with metal blade. Mix in butter. Or, mix amaretti crumbs, graham cracker crumbs and butter in medium-size bowl. Place about 3½ tablespoons crumbs into bottom of each tartlet pan. Press crumbs into bottom and up sides. Place pans on baking sheet. Bake in the 350° oven for 8 to 10 minutes or until crust is lightly browned. Cool to room temperature.

FILLING AND TOPPING

Mix cream cheese and sugar in food processor fitted with metal blade or in medium-size bowl with electric mixer on medium speed until light and fluffy, about 3 minutes. Scrape down sides and mix in 2 tablespoons amaretto and almond extract. Beat whipping cream in separate mixing bowl until soft peaks form; do not beat stiff. Fold into cheese mixture. Divide among tart pans, keeping filling a little lower than rim of pan. Refrigerate until ready to serve. (*) The tartlets may be refrigerated covered with plastic wrap and foil overnight, or they may be frozen, if desired. Defrost covered tartlets in refrigerator overnight.

As close to serving as possible, arrange assorted fruit over the top of the tarts. Bring apricot preserves and 1 tablespoon amaretto to a boil in small saucepan. Lower heat and simmer, stirring occasionally, for 3 to 4 minutes. Press through strainer placed over small bowl. Brush as much warm glaze as needed to cover fruit, being careful not to let glaze run down sides of pan. Be sure to cover the bananas completely so they will not turn dark. Refrigerate until ready to serve. Before serving, remove sides of tartlet pans.

Serves 4.

Chocolate Truffle Tartlets

Smooth and satiny chocolate truffle filling is piped or spooned into delicate miniature shells.

1 recipe Cream Cheese Pastry for Tartlets (see page 90)
2 squares (2 ounces) unsweetened chocolate
3 squares (3 ounces) semisweet chocolate

¼ cup water
4 tablespoons (½ stick) unsalted butter, at room temperature
1⅓ cups powdered sugar, sifted
1 large egg yolk
1½ tablespoons dark rum

Make tartlet shells as directed. Melt all the chocolate with the water in top of double boiler over simmering water, stirring until smooth. Remove from heat and cool slightly. Beat butter, sugar, egg yolk and rum in small bowl with electric mixer on medium speed until light and fluffy. Beat in chocolate. If not stiff enough to pipe or mound from a spoon, allow to sit at room temperature until slightly thickened. Fit a pastry bag with a ¾- to 1-inch rosette tip or star tip. Fill with chocolate mixture and pipe 1 large rosette into each shell. Or, spoon dollop into each shell. (*) Tartlets may be kept in covered container at room temperature up to 2 days. They are better when not refrigerated. Or, they may be frozen. Defrost at room temperature.

Serve at room temperature.

Makes 24 tartlets.

Honey Walnut Tartlets

With their creamy, crunchy texture, these tartlets have a similar consistency to pecan pie. Butter, honey and cream pack a lot of flavor into a little filling.

1 recipe Cream Cheese Pastry for Tartlets (see page 90)
1½ tablespoons honey
2½ tablespoons sugar
¼ cup firmly packed golden brown sugar

1½ tablespoons unsalted butter
⅛ teaspoon salt
1 cup coarsely chopped walnuts (about 4 ounces)
2½ tablespoons whipping cream

Make tartlet shells as directed. Stir together honey, sugar, brown sugar, butter and salt in small saucepan over moderate heat. Bring to a boil and cook for 3 minutes. Stir in nuts and cream; remove from heat. Cool 10 minutes and spoon into shells. (*) Tartlets may be kept in covered container at room temperature overnight, or they may be frozen, if desired. Defrost at room temperature.

Serve at room temperature.

Makes 24 tartlets.

Toasted Coconut Cream Tartlets

Toasted coconut mixed into the filling and sprinkled on top adds just enough flavor to the creamy vanilla custard.

1 recipe Cream Cheese Pastry for Tartlets (see page 90)
½ cup flaked coconut
1 tablespoon cornstarch
¼ cup sugar
⅛ teaspoon salt
1 cup milk
3 large egg yolks
1 tablespoon unsalted butter
1 teaspoon vanilla

Make tartlet shells as directed.

Preheat oven to 350°. Place coconut on baking sheet. Bake for 10 to 15 minutes, stirring occasionally, until golden. Stir together cornstarch, sugar and salt in medium-size saucepan. Whisk milk and egg yolks in medium-size bowl until blended. Stir into sugar mixture. Cook over moderate heat, whisking constantly, until mixture thickens and boils for a full minute. Remove from heat and stir in butter and vanilla. Reserve 2 tablespoons coconut for garnish. Stir the rest into custard. Place piece of plastic wrap directly on surface of cream to keep skin from forming. Cool to room temperature and then chill in refrigerator for at least 30 minutes. Spoon coconut cream into tart shells and sprinkle tops with reserved coconut. (*) Tartlets may be refrigerated in covered container overnight.

Bring to room temperature before serving.

Makes 24 tartlets.

Presentations in Pastry

This chapter explores the wonderful versatility of pastry. There are many different types with their own special uses, and they can be formed into a variety of shapes—lacy cups and saucers, rings, rolls, rectangles and puffs.

PUFF PASTRY

I do not use the classic puff pastry recipe—it is simply too much work and too time-consuming to prepare. My solution is to use Easy Puff Pastry (see page 122), which is equally flaky, tender and buttery. Unlike the traditional variety, Easy Puff Pastry can be made from beginning to end without pausing at intervals for the pastry to rest.

Frozen puff pastry, found in the freezer section of most supermarkets, can be substituted in all my recipes. It contains oil rather than butter which alters the flavor, but the result will still be flaky.

TIP

- Always work with puff pastry well chilled. After it is rolled and shaped, refrigerate it for at least 30 minutes before baking.

PHYLLO

Whenever possible, buy fresh phyllo. It can be purchased from specialty food stores and ethnic markets—Italian and Middle Eastern. Store-bought frozen phyllo sometimes becomes brittle and breaks when defrosted.

TIP

- When working with phyllo, remove the sheet(s) you need to work with and return the remainder to the package. Cover the sheets you will be using with plastic wrap and work on a lightly dampened towel. The towel should not be too wet or the phyllo will become soggy.

CREAM PUFF PASTRY

In French, cream puff pastry is called pâte à choux. In English the name is often confused with puff pastry, but the two are very different. Cream puff pastry contains more liquid and eggs than other pastries. When it bakes, the liquid becomes steam and expands and the eggs help hold it up, thereby creating a dough with large holes. It can be shaped in a variety of ways and freezes beautifully after it is baked.

TIPS

- To ensure success when making cream puff pastry, cut the butter into small pieces, so it will melt at the same time the water comes to a boil.
- If you wish to freeze cream puffs with ice cream in them, try substituting milk for the water called for in the recipe. The milk will not freeze as solid as water, thereby making a softer frozen puff which is easier to eat.

CLOCKWISE FROM TOP: *Chocolate Cream Puffs filled with Chocolate Mocha Mousse, page 136; Strawberry Phyllo Napoleon, page 133; Gorgonzola Pear Dumplings, page 135.*

Easy Puff Pastry

This incredible pastry was created by my friend, famed chef and culinary instructor Jacques Pépin. If you've hesitated to make puff pastry because it's so time consuming, or if you've never made it because you assumed it was too difficult, then you can rejoice over this wonderful pastry.

1 cup unbleached all-purpose flour, chilled in freezer for at least 4 hours

¾ cup cake flour, chilled in freezer for at least 4 hours

⅛ teaspoon salt

½ cup plus 1 tablespoon ice water

½ pound (2 sticks) unsalted butter, cold and cut into ⅛-inch slices

Place both flours, salt and ice water in food processor fitted with metal blade. Process until mixture begins to hold together, about 10 seconds. Or, mix with your fingertips or a pastry blender in a mixing bowl until pastry holds together. Transfer to lightly floured surface and roll mixture into a square about 10 inches across. Distribute the chilled butter evenly over top, leaving a 1-inch border on all sides (photo 1). Fold dough in half over butter and press the edges together (photo 2). Pat into rectangle about 10 x 6 inches. Fold dough in thirds from short ends, like a business letter (photo 3). Flour surface lightly and rotate dough so that short side is toward you.

Roll dough into rectangle about 12 x 6 inches and ½ inch thick (photo 4). Then fold short ends to meet in center (photo 5) and fold in half along line where edges meet (photo 6). This is one double turn.

Rotate dough so that a short side is toward you. Roll into rectangle 12 x ½ x 6 inches. Make second double turn.

Rotate dough again. Roll into 12 x ½ x 6-inch rectangle. Make third and final double turn. If dough is too elastic to roll, or the butter becomes too soft, chill for 30 minutes before making final turn.

Wrap pastry in plastic wrap and refrigerate for at least 2 hours before using. (*) Pastry may be refrigerated up to 5 days, or it may be frozen up to 3 months wrapped in a heavy plastic bag, if desired. Defrost wrapped pastry in the refrigerator or at room temperature just until softened enough to roll, but still very cold.

Makes 1½ pounds pastry.

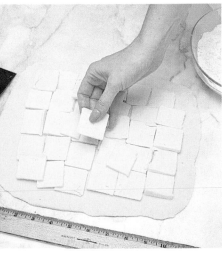

1 *Place chilled butter slices over the dough, leaving a 1-inch border all around.*

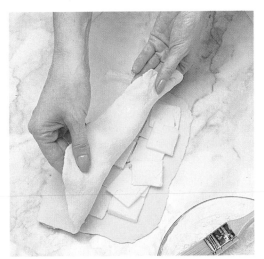

2 *Fold dough in half, enclosing the butter.*

3 *Fold dough in thirds, like a business letter.*

4 *Roll into a 6 x 12-inch rectangle.*

5 *Fold short edges to meet in the center.*

6 *Fold in half where the edges meet. This is one double turn. Repeat through step 4, making 2 more double turns.*

Open-Face Apple Tart

*This precious little tart is made
free-form by shaping Easy or frozen
puff pastry into the shape of an apple
and filling it with fresh apple slices.*

BAKING PAN
Rimmed baking sheet

¼ teaspoon ground cinnamon
3 tablespoons sugar
6 large or 7 small Golden
    Delicious apples
1 lemon, cut in half
½ recipe Easy Puff Pastry (see
    page 122) or ½ pound frozen
    puff pastry (½ package or

1 sheet), defrosted in
    refrigerator
2 tablespoons unsalted butter, at
    room temperature
1 large egg mixed with 1
    tablespoon water for egg wash
½ cup apricot jam
¼ cup water

Draw and cut out a pattern of an apple 10½ x 10½ inches.

Mix cinnamon and sugar in small bowl and set aside. Peel apples, cut
in half and core. Rub with lemon to prevent discoloring. Place flat
side of each apple half on cutting board. Slice apples into thin slices,
keeping slices in order.

Roll out puff pastry on lightly floured board into 12 x 12-inch
square, ¼ inch thick. Cut around pattern to form the shape of an
apple. Place pastry on rimmed baking sheet. Prick center of pastry
with fork, leaving a 1-inch border all around unpierced. Arrange
sliced apple halves, flat-side down, on pierced area of pastry. The
apples will fit better if you discard the first few small slices. It may
seem that all of the slices will not fit, but wedge them in very
tightly, as they will shrink when they bake. Sprinkle apples with
cinnamon-sugar mixture. Fold sides of pastry up over apples,
maintaining the shape as much as possible. Roll out remaining scraps
of dough and cut out stem and leaves. Place on baking sheet. Prop
leaves with foil to resemble curved leaf, as pictured.

Dot apples with butter cut into tiny pieces. Brush egg wash over
pastry using as much as needed, being careful not to let it run
underneath or it will keep pastry from puffing up. Brush leaves and
stem also. Refrigerate for 30 minutes.

Preheat oven to 375°. Bake tart for 30 to 35 minutes or until pastry
is golden brown. Pastry stem and leaves should be removed after 20
to 25 minutes, or when golden. Cool slightly and remove to serving
platter.

Bring jam and water to a boil in small saucepan, stirring. Press
through strainer over small bowl and discard all large pieces. Return
to saucepan and cook until reduced to a glaze consistency. Brush
warm glaze over pastry and apples, realigning any apples which may
have fallen over. Put stem and leaves in place. The tart is best served
within a few hours after baking.

Serves 6.

1 *Place pattern on pastry and cut around it with pastry cutter or small knife.*

2 *Keeping the sliced apples in their original shape, place them on the pastry, wedging them in as tightly as possible, leaving a 1-inch border all around.*

3 *Sprinkle apples with cinnamon and sugar and fold the pastry up around the apples. Place leaves over foil to bend them slightly.*

4 *Completed tart.*

Fresh Blueberry Turnovers

Although fresh blueberries are wonderful, any type of cooked fruit pie filling, jam or marmalade may be substituted when making these mouth-watering turnovers.

1 pint blueberries (2 cups)
⅓ cup sugar
4 teaspoons cornstarch
¼ teaspoon ground cinnamon
1 recipe Easy Puff Pastry (see page 122) or 1 pound frozen puff pastry, defrosted in refrigerator
1 egg beaten with 2 teaspoons water for egg wash

BAKING PAN
Rimmed baking sheet

Wash blueberries and remove any stems. Place berries, sugar, cornstarch and cinnamon in medium-size saucepan. Toss together until coated. Cook over medium-high heat for 3 to 4 minutes or until berries are dark and glossy and liquid in pan has thickened. Cool to room temperature.

Preheat oven to 450°.

If using Easy Puff Pastry, divide in half. Return half to refrigerator. Roll out pastry on lightly floured surface, into 10-inch square. Trim with knife to even edges. If using frozen pastry, remove 1 sheet; it is not necessary to roll it. Cut pastry into 4 equal squares, about 5 inches each. Place a heaping spoonful of filling in center of each square. Brush a 1-inch border of egg wash around edges. Fold 2 opposite corners to meet, forming a triangle. Press edges together firmly, sealing with tines of fork. Cut 1-inch slit in top. Place on rimmed baking sheet. Repeat with remaining pastry. You may have some filling left over.

Bake turnovers in the 450° oven for 10 to 15 minutes or until golden. Serve warm. (*) Turnovers may be held at room temperature overnight, or they may be frozen, tightly wrapped in foil, if desired. Defrost wrapped at room temperature. Reheat in 400° oven for 10 minutes.

Makes 8 turnovers.

Apricot Strudel

Dried apricots simmered in apricot nectar become a soft, thick purée that's mixed with crunchy walnuts, grated apples and raisins.

1 recipe Easy Puff Pastry (page 122) or 1 pound frozen puff pastry, defrosted in refrigerator
6 ounces dried apricots, coarsely chopped
1 cup apricot nectar
½ cup sugar
½ cup chopped walnuts
1 tablespoon lemon juice
1 tart green apple, peeled, cored and grated
⅓ cup raisins
1 egg mixed with 2 teaspoons water for egg wash

BAKING PAN
Rimmed baking sheet

Make Easy Puff Pastry, if using.

Place apricots, nectar and sugar in small saucepan; nectar should almost cover apricots. Bring to a boil. Reduce heat and simmer, covered, until the apricots are soft and most of the liquid is absorbed, about 15 minutes. The mixture should be a thick purée. Remove from heat and cool to room temperature.

Stir in walnuts, lemon juice, apple and raisins. Taste for sweetness or tartness and add additional sugar or lemon juice to taste.

If using Easy Puff Pastry, divide in half, and refrigerate half. Roll out half the pastry on lightly floured board into 15 x 10-inch rectangle with long side toward you. If using frozen pastry, it is not necessary to roll it. Spread half the cooled filling over bottom half of pastry, leaving 1½-inch border all around. Brush border with enough egg wash to moisten it. Fold top half over filling, press edges together and crimp with tines of fork to form approximately 15 x 5-inch strudel. Place on rimmed baking sheet. Repeat with remaining pastry and filling. (*) Unbaked strudel may be refrigerated, covered, overnight, or it may be frozen, if desired. Freeze uncovered until frozen. Then wrap tightly in foil. Defrost, wrapped, in the refrigerator overnight.

Preheat oven to 450°. Bake strudel for 20 to 25 minutes or until pastry is golden brown. Cut into 1½- to 2-inch slices and serve warm.

Makes 2 strudels, 6 to 8 slices each.

Almond Paste Chocolate Chip Strudel

Flaky, crisp layers of phyllo encase one of my favorite fillings—almond paste, strawberry jam and chocolate chips. Because it is easily eaten without a fork, this rich and delectable dessert makes a nice addition to a cake or cookie buffet platter.

1 cup finely chopped walnuts (about 4 ounces)
1 heaping teaspoon ground cinnamon
⅓ cup sugar
12 ounces almond paste
½ cup strawberry jam
½ cup chocolate chips
8 to 10 sheets phyllo pastry
12 tablespoons (1½ sticks) unsalted butter, melted

BAKING PAN
2 rimmed baking sheets

Preheat oven to 375°. Mix walnuts, cinnamon and sugar in small bowl; set aside. Beat almond paste in medium-size bowl with electric mixer on low speed until soft. Add jam and mix until well blended. Stir in chocolate chips.

Stack 4 to 5 sheets of phyllo on damp towel. Brush with butter and sprinkle each sheet evenly with small amount of cinnamon-nut mixture, as pictured. Place half of filling along one short end of phyllo, making rounded, narrow log, about 1½ inches from edge. Fold in sides over filling and roll up as for a jelly roll. Place on baking sheet. Repeat to make second strudel. Place on separate baking sheet. Brush top of each strudel with butter.

Bake strudels in the 375° oven for 10 minutes. Remove from oven and brush with butter. Cut each roll with serrated knife into 1-inch diagonal pieces, wiping knife clean between each cut. Leave rolls assembled and return to oven. Bake 10 to 15 minutes longer or until pastry is golden, brushing once with butter. (*) Strudel may be stored at room temperature in airtight container or tightly wrapped in foil for several days, or it may be frozen, if desired. Defrost at room temperature. Reheat in a preheated 350° oven for 10 minutes, if desired.

Makes 2 strudels, 8 pieces each.

1 Place a sheet of wax paper over the left half of pastry. Fold right half of pastry over the wax paper like a book. Working with right side of pastry, unfold one sheet. Brush it with butter.

2 Sprinkle with cinnamon/sugar/nut mixture. Continue with remaining half sheets, buttering and sprinkling each in the same manner. Do not butter or sprinkle the top sheet.

3 Move wax paper to right side of pastry and fold left half over. Repeat buttering and sprinkling in same manner.

4 Remove wax paper and brush top sheet with butter.

5 Using 2 spoons, drop filling into a log, leaving approximately a 1½-inch border on 3 sides.

6 Fold both sides over filling and then fold end over.

7 Gently roll up strudel and place on baking sheet seam side down.

8 Completed strudel cut into 1-inch diagonal pieces.

Viennese Apple Strudel

In Austria apples used in strudels are called "strudlers". They are tart green apples similar in taste and texture to our Golden Delicious, which work best in this recipe. Butter-brushed phyllo is filled with cinnamon-scented apple slices, crunchy walnuts and plump raisins. Use the method shown in the photos on the preceding page to butter the phyllo sheets.

2 slices lightly toasted or stale egg bread, crusts removed
2 pounds Golden Delicious apples (about 4 large apples)
2 tablespoons lemon juice
Grated peel from 1 lemon
½ cup chopped walnuts
¼ cup golden or dark raisins
¾ to 1 cup sugar
1½ teaspoons ground cinnamon
¼ teaspoon ground cardamom (optional)

¼ teaspoon ground cloves
¼ teaspoon ground ginger
6 sheets phyllo pastry
12 tablespoons (1½ sticks) unsalted butter, melted
Powdered sugar for sprinkling on top

BAKING PAN
Rimmed baking sheet

Preheat oven to 350°. Place bread in food processor fitted with metal blade. Process until fine crumbs form. Place on baking sheet and bake for 10 to 15 minutes or until dry and golden, stirring occasionally. Cool to room temperature. You will need about ¾ cup crumbs. (*) Bread crumbs may be frozen.

Preheat oven to 400°. Peel, core and slice apples into ⅛-inch-thick slices by hand or with thin (2 mm) slicing blade of food processor. Place in large bowl and stir in lemon juice and peel, nuts, raisins, ¾ cup sugar, cinnamon, cardamom, if using, cloves and ginger. Toss with hands or wooden spoon until well blended. Taste and if too tart, add more sugar.

Place a damp towel on counter. Stack phyllo sheets on towel, long side facing you, brushing each sheet with butter and sprinkling each with 2 tablespoons bread crumbs (see pictures and technique on how to butter phyllo, page 129). Spread apple filling over bottom third of pastry, leaving 1½-inch border. Discard any liquid remaining in bowl. Fold narrow ends of phyllo over filling. Using towel as a guide, gently roll up jelly-roll fashion. Place seam-side down on baking sheet. Brush top with butter.

Bake strudel in the 400° oven for 35 to 45 minutes or until golden brown, brushing with butter every 10 minutes. (*) Strudel may be stored wrapped tightly in foil at room temperature overnight, or it may be frozen, if desired. Defrost wrapped strudel at room temperature. Reheat in preheated 400° oven for 10 to 15 minutes before serving.

Sprinkle the top with powdered sugar. Serve warm, cut into 1½-inch diagonal pieces.

Serves 8.

Cherry Goat Cheese Strudel

*This is no ordinary strudel. Its
exciting, innovative taste is created by
combining tangy goat cheese with sweet
sugar, spicy cinnamon and tart cherries.
This distinctive strudel is equally
delicious for brunch or as a snack with
coffee.*

*5 ounces goat cheese (chèvre), such
    as Montrachet, at room
    temperature*
*2 packages (3 ounces each) cream
    cheese, at room temperature*
⅓ cup plus 14 tablespoons sugar
2 large egg yolks
½ teaspoon ground cinnamon
12 sheets phyllo pastry
*¼ pound (1 stick) unsalted butter,
    melted*
*1 can (16 ounces) tart pie cherries,
    well drained*

BAKING PAN
2 rimmed baking sheets

Preheat oven to 375°. Line baking sheets with foil.

Beat goat cheese, cream cheese, ⅓ cup sugar, yolks and cinnamon in
medium-size bowl with electric mixer on low speed or in food
processor fitted with metal blade, until blended. Refrigerate until
chilled.

Stack 6 phyllo leaves, long side facing you, on damp towel, brushing
each sheet with melted butter and sprinkling each with 1 tablespoon
sugar (see pictures and technique on how to butter phyllo, page 129).
Spread half of the cheese filling along one long end, leaving 2-inch
border. Sprinkle half the cherries over the cheese. Fold narrow ends
of phyllo over filling. Using towel as a guide, gently roll up
jelly-roll fashion. Place strudel seam-side down on baking sheet.
Brush top with melted butter and sprinkle with 1 tablespoon sugar.
Repeat to make second strudel. (*) Strudel may be refrigerated on
baking sheet up to 4 hours, if desired.

Bake strudels in the 375° oven for 25 to 30 minutes or until golden
brown. The filling may leak out slightly. Cool for at least 1 hour to
allow the cheese to set up before cutting. Serve lukewarm or at room
temperature.

Makes 2 strudels, about 8 pieces each.

Pineapple Cheese Baklava

In between several layers of flaky phyllo is a tasty filling of ricotta, cream cheese and crushed pineapple. Just before serving this unusual baklava, a lemony-pineapple syrup is spooned generously over the top to intensify its lush flavor.

1 can (1 pound 4 ounces) crushed pineapple in syrup
1 package (8 ounces) cream cheese, at room temperature
1 cup ricotta cheese
½ cup plus ½ cup sugar
2 large egg yolks
1 teaspoon grated lemon peel
1 teaspoon vanilla
12 sheets phyllo pastry
¼ pound (1 stick) unsalted butter, melted
1 teaspoon lemon juice

BAKING PAN
13 x 9-inch baking dish

Drain pineapple well, reserving syrup. Beat cream cheese, ricotta, ½ cup sugar, egg yolks, lemon peel and vanilla in large bowl with electric mixer on medium speed. Scrape down sides of bowl and mix again until well blended. Stir in pineapple.

Preheat oven to 350°. Grease baking dish with some of the melted butter.

Remove 6 sheets of phyllo from the package. Place on damp towel. Using baking dish as a guide, cut phyllo pieces large enough to cover bottom and sides of dish. Brush each sheet with butter. (See pictures on how to butter phyllo, page 129.) Place in baking dish.

Bake in the 350° oven for 15 minutes or until golden. Remove from oven and cool. Spoon in filling. Brush remaining 6 sheets of phyllo with butter. Trim to fit top. Place on top of filling. Mark pastry into approximately 2-inch squares with small, sharp knife, 4 cuts lengthwise and 5 cuts widthwise. Do not cut through all the top sheets of phyllo.

Return to the 350° oven and bake for 40 minutes or until golden. (*) The baklava may be held at room temperature, uncovered, for several hours, if desired. Before serving, reheat in preheated 450° oven for 10 minutes.

As close to serving time as possible, combine ½ cup of reserved pineapple syrup, ½ cup sugar and lemon juice in small saucepan. Bring to a boil, and boil gently for 10 minutes or until syrup thickens slightly. Spoon hot syrup over top of hot baklava. Cut through markings into squares. Serve within 1 hour so phyllo will remain crisp. Serve warm or at room temperature.

Makes 30 squares.

Strawberry Phyllo Napoleon

Traditional napoleons are prepared by layering puff pastry with custard. Irene and Steve Angelo, friends and colleagues from Sacramento, California, suggested that I substitute phyllo for puff pastry. The crunchy phyllo is truly outstanding when combined with an ultra-creamy custard. Once you taste this recipe, you may never crave the classical version again. This is pictured on page 120.

8 sheets phyllo pastry
10 tablespoons (1¼ sticks) unsalted butter, melted
7 teaspoons granulated sugar
1 pint box strawberries, hulled and sliced
Powdered sugar for garnishing
6 to 8 small strawberries for garnishing (optional)

PASTRY CREAM

4 large eggs, at room temperature
2 large egg yolks, at room temperature
2 large egg whites, at room temperature
1 cup plus 1 tablespoon sugar
⅓ cup all-purpose flour
2 cups milk, heated until hot
2 teaspoons vanilla
¼ cup (½ stick) unsalted butter, at room temperature

BAKING PAN
2 rimmed baking sheets

Preheat oven to 350°. Line baking sheets with parchment or foil.

Stack phyllo on damp towel, brushing each sheet with melted butter and sprinkling each with 1 teaspoon sugar. (See pictures on how to butter phyllo, page 129.) Brush top sheet with butter but do not sprinkle with sugar. Cut pastry lengthwise with sharp knife, into 4 rectangles, each about 15 x 3½ inches. Place 2 rectangles on each baking sheet.

Bake in the 350° oven for 12 to 15 minutes or until golden. Remove and cool on rack. Cut each rectangle in half widthwise, making 8 rectangular strips. (*) Rectangles may be stored in airtight container or wrapped tightly in foil at room temperature up to 2 days, or they may be frozen, if desired. Defrost, unwrapped, at room temperature.

PASTRY CREAM
Mix 4 whole eggs, 2 yolks, 1 cup sugar and flour in heavy saucepan until thick and creamy. Place whites in small mixing bowl and set aside. Slowly whisk hot milk into pastry cream. Place over moderate heat and cook, stirring constantly, until mixture comes to a boil. Lower heat to moderately low and continue cooking, stirring constantly, for 3 to 5 minutes, until the custard thickly coats a spoon. The custard may lump as it cooks, but whisking will smooth it out. Remove from heat and stir in vanilla and butter. Cool slightly. Beat the 2 egg whites with electric mixer on low speed until foamy. Add 1 tablespoon sugar and beat on high speed until firm but moist peaks form. Gently fold custard into whites. Press piece of plastic wrap directly on top of custard and refrigerate until chilled and set. (*) Custard may be refrigerated overnight, if desired. Stir before using.

continued

STRAWBERRY PHYLLO NAPOLEON,
CONTINUED

About 2 to 3 hours before serving, assemble dessert. Place 1 phyllo rectangle on serving plate. Spread with ⅓ cup custard cream. Top with layer of sliced strawberries. Repeat with 2 more layers of phyllo, cream and strawberries. Sift powdered sugar over fourth layer. Place on top and garnish with strawberries, if desired. Repeat for second napoleon. Refrigerate for at least 2 hours before serving.

To serve, cut with serrated knife into 1½- to 2-inch slices.

Makes 2 napoleons, each serving 4.

Black Forest Soufflé in Phyllo

Here is a light and original version of Germany's popular Black Forest cake. A bundt pan is lined with layers of phyllo and filled with a dark chocolate-cherry mixture. When unmolded, the phyllo forms a crunchy, golden ring encasing melt-in-your-mouth chocolate soufflé.

6 squares (6 ounces) semisweet chocolate
½ pound (2 sticks) unsalted butter, at room temperature
½ cup sugar
1 tablespoon Kirsch liqueur
5 large egg yolks, at room temperature
4 large egg whites, at room temperature

⅛ teaspoon cream of tartar
2 cans (16 ounces each) pitted bing cherries, drained
8 sheets phyllo pastry
¼ pound (1 stick) unsalted butter, melted
½ cup chocolate or vanilla wafer cookie crumbs (about 10 cookies)

BAKING PAN
12-cup bundt pan

Preheat oven to 350°. Generously butter bundt pan. Melt chocolate in top of double boiler over simmering water. Set aside to cool slightly.

Beat ½ pound butter, sugar and Kirsch in large bowl with electric mixer on medium speed until light and fluffy, about 2 minutes. Add egg yolks one at a time, beating well after each. Mix in cooled, melted chocolate. Beat egg whites in separate medium-size bowl with electric mixer on low speed until foamy. Add cream of tartar and beat on high speed until soft peaks form. Fold egg whites and 1½ cans of the cherries into chocolate mixture. (Reserve remaining half can of cherries for another use.)

Stack phyllo on damp towel, brushing each sheet with melted butter. (See pictures on how to butter phyllo, page 129.) Cut phyllo into thirds. Stack strips in one pile. Lift two strips by ends and set in a "U" in pan, easing it into bottom of pan, with ends extending over edge of pan and covering center hole of bundt pan. Repeat around pan, overlapping strips by a third, until pan is covered by phyllo. Set aside 2 tablespoons cookie crumbs for top. Sprinkle remaining crumbs over phyllo. Spoon in filling. Cut an "X" in middle of pastry over center hole in pan. Fold ends from center over the filling. Fold in pastry ends from outer rim of pan and tuck under as you go so pastry lies flat. Brush top with butter and sprinkle with reserved crumbs. Bake in the 350° oven for 45 to 55 minutes or until golden. Let rest in pan about 30 minutes. Invert onto platter and serve warm.

Serves 10 to 12.

Gorgonzola Pear Dumplings

Gorgonzola cheese is the exciting ingredient in both the filled pears and the pastry they're wrapped in. The tastes and textures of the soft fruit and creamy filling contrasting with the flaky pastry are sensational. Although the Bosc pear is a beautiful shape and has a long, graceful stem, Anjou or Comice pears work equally well. This is pictured on page 120.

BAKING PAN
Baking sheet

GORGONZOLA PASTRY

2 cups all-purpose flour, chilled in freezer
¼ teaspoon salt
½ cup vegetable shortening, chilled in freezer
6 ounces gorgonzola cheese
6 tablespoons ice water

PEARS

4 ripe but firm pears
1 package (3 ounces) cream cheese, at room temperature
3 ounces gorgonzola cheese, at room temperature
1 large egg yolk
1 large egg beaten with 1 tablespoon water for egg wash

PASTRY

Combine flour and salt in food processor fitted with metal blade or in medium-size bowl with a pastry blender. Add shortening and cheese and mix until the mixture is the size of coarse meal. Add ice water and mix until pastry holds together. Do not process into a ball. Remove metal blade if using processor, and invert into plastic bag. Knead dough into 8-inch disc. Refrigerate for at least 1 hour. (*) Dough may be refrigerated up to 2 days, or it may be frozen in heavy plastic bag, if desired. Defrost in refrigerator or at room temperature until just softened enough to roll, but still very cold.

PEARS

Peel pears. Scoop out core from bottom of each with melon baller, leaving stem intact and making a 1-inch diameter cavity, as pictured, see page 209. Mash cream cheese and gorgonzola in small bowl with a fork until well blended. Stir in egg yolk. Divide mixture among the pears, filling the cavities. Cut a small slice off the bottom of each pear so that it will stand upright.

Divide pastry in fourths. Remove one piece, leaving remainder in refrigerator until needed. Roll out pastry on lightly floured board into 8- or 9-inch square, depending on the size of the pears. Trim edges with sharp knife or pastry cutter to make square even. Place pear in center of pastry. Draw corners up over top of pear and pinch together around the stem, like a money bag. Pull down edges of pastry slightly, to make a ruffled border around the stem. Be sure pear is completely covered in pastry. Place on greased baking sheet. Repeat with remaining pears and pastry. Brush pastry with as much egg wash as needed. Refrigerate for at least 1 hour or up to 4 hours.

Preheat oven to 375°. Bake pears for 30 to 40 minutes or until pastry is golden. Serve warm with dessert fork and knife.

Serves 4.

Chocolate Cream Puffs with Chocolate Mocha Mousse

I had never seen a chocolate cream puff until I created this recipe. These are very dark, but not at all sweet. Fill them with any cream—from mousse or ice cream to flavored whipped cream—for a special dessert with a dramatic presentation. See picture on page 120.

CHOCOLATE CREAM PUFFS

1 cup all-purpose flour
2 tablespoons unsweetened cocoa powder
1 cup water
¼ pound (1 stick) unsalted butter, at room temperature, cut into 8 pieces
5 large eggs, at room temperature
1 teaspoon vanilla
1 recipe Chocolate Mocha Mousse (page 147)
Powdered sugar for sprinkling on top

BAKING PAN

Baking sheet

Preheat oven to 425°. Grease baking sheet.

PUFFS

Stir together flour and cocoa in small bowl. Bring water and butter to a full boil in medium-size saucepan over moderate heat. Reduce heat to low. Add flour and cocoa all at once, stirring vigorously with a wooden spoon until thoroughly incorporated and mixture pulls away from sides of pan. Transfer to mixing bowl and beat in eggs one at a time until each is incorporated. Mix in vanilla. Mixture will be thick and glossy.

Place pastry in a pastry bag fitted with a ¾-inch rosette or star tip. Pipe into rosettes or stars about 3 inches across and 2½ inches high, placing them at least 2 inches apart on greased baking sheet. Or, use

1 *Cook, stirring, until mixture leaves the sides of the pan.*

2 *Beat in eggs one at a time. This shows the texture of the pastry after the fifth egg has been added.*

3 *Pipe pastry into rosettes or drop from spoon onto greased baking sheet.*

a soup spoon and drop pastry into 3-inch-wide rounds, placing them at least 2 inches apart. You should have 12 puffs.

Bake in the 425° oven for 35 to 40 minutes or until puffed and firm on the outside. Turn oven off. Split cream puffs in half with serrated knife. Place halves cut-side up on baking sheet. Return to turned-off oven for 5 minutes to dry out insides. Remove from oven and cool on baking sheet. (*) Puffs may be stored well covered overnight, or they may be frozen, tightly wrapped in foil. Defrost, wrapped, at room temperature. Make Chocolate Mocha Mousse.

To serve, fill each puff with scoop of Chocolate Mocha Mousse. Dust tops heavily with powdered sugar. (*) Filled puffs may be refrigerated up to 4 hours.

Serves 12.

VARIATION
1 quart vanilla or chocolate chip ice cream may be substituted for the mousse. Omit powdered sugar and serve with 2 recipes Hot Chocolate Fudge Sauce (page 220) OR Hot Bittersweet Fudge Sauce (page 221).

Almond Cream Puff Ring With Strawberries

Cream puff pastry is baked into a pretty ring. Sprinkled with golden toasted almonds, it's filled with a luscious amaretto cream and fresh strawberry slices.

CREAM PUFF PASTRY
1 cup water
6 tablespoons (¾ stick) unsalted butter, at room temperature and cut into 6 pieces
1 cup all-purpose flour
4 large eggs, at room temperature
1 teaspoon vanilla
1 egg, lightly beaten with 1 teaspoon water for egg wash
¼ cup sliced almonds
2 teaspoons sugar for sprinkling on top

FILLING
1½ cups whipping cream
¼ cup plus 2 tablespoons powdered sugar
3 tablespoons amaretto liqueur
1 pint box strawberries

BAKING PAN
Baking sheet

Preheat oven to 375°. Grease and lightly flour baking sheet. Draw 8-inch circle in center with tip of sharp knife, using a plate or pan lid as a guide.

continued

ALMOND CREAM PUFF RING,
CONTINUED

PASTRY

Bring water and butter to a full boil in medium-size saucepan over moderate heat, stirring until butter melts. Reduce heat to low and add flour all at once, stirring vigorously with wooden spoon until mixture pulls away from sides of pan. Cook, stirring, for 1 to 2 minutes or until mixture is dry. Transfer to mixing bowl and beat in eggs one at a time. Mix in vanilla. Mixture will be thick and glossy.

Spoon dough into pastry bag fitted with plain ½-inch round tip. Pipe dough over circle on baking sheet, joining the ends. Pipe another circle just inside and touching the first one. Put a third ring on top where the two circles join. Or, drop the pastry from a spoon around the circle to make 1 large ring; smooth with a knife. Brush entire surface with as much beaten egg as needed. Sprinkle with sliced almonds and sugar.

Bake in the 375° oven for 35 to 40 minutes or until well puffed and golden brown. Turn oven off. Remove pastry and cut in half horizontally with serrated knife. Place both halves cut-side up on baking sheet and return to turned-off oven for 10 to 15 minutes to dry out inside. Remove from oven and cool on baking sheet completely. (*) The ring may be stored, reassembled and well covered, at room temperature, overnight, or it may be frozen, tightly wrapped in heavy-duty foil. Defrost, wrapped, at room temperature.

FILLING

Beat cream in medium-size bowl with electric mixer on low speed until it begins to thicken. Gradually add ¼ cup powdered sugar and beat on medium speed until soft peaks form. Mix in amaretto. Wash, hull and slice strawberries.

Place bottom of cream puff ring on serving platter. Spread with amaretto cream. Arrange strawberries over cream. Place cream puff top over berries. Cream and berries should show around the sides. Dust top with 2 tablespoons powdered sugar. Refrigerate until ready to serve or up to 6 hours.

Serves 8.

1 *Drop batter by tablespoons at least 3 inches apart onto greased baking sheet.*

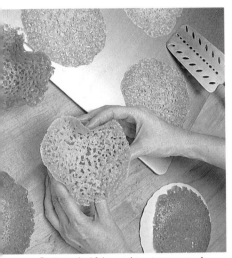

2 *Press half the cookies into custard cups and the other half over the back of a saucer.*

3 *Completed cup and saucer filled with White Coffee Ice Cream.*

Lacy Almond Cookie Cups and Saucers

An almond batter is dropped by spoonfuls onto a cookie sheet. It bakes into delicate lacy cookies which are then shaped into coffee cups and saucers. After they cool they are very crisp and absolutely scrumptious when filled with cold and creamy Incredible White Coffee Ice Cream (see page 166) or Chocolate Mocha Mousse (see page 147).

1⅓ cups whole or slivered blanched almonds (about 6 ounces)
1 cup sugar
⅔ cup all-purpose flour
½ teaspoon salt
½ pound (2 sticks) unsalted butter, at room temperature
⅓ cup whipping cream
Desired mousse or ice cream for filling

BAKING PAN AND MOLD
Baking sheet
4 custard cups (3½ x 1½ inches)
4 coffee cup saucers

Preheat oven to 350°.

Place almonds in food processor fitted with metal blade and process until finely ground. Place on baking sheet. Bake in the 350° oven for 10 minutes or until golden, stirring occasionally.

Place sugar, flour, salt, butter, cream and almonds in heavy large saucepan. Cook over moderately low heat, stirring constantly, until butter is melted and ingredients are incorporated. Remove from heat.

Drop 1 tablespoon batter onto ungreased baking sheet. Leaving at least a 3-inch space between cookies, drop another tablespoon batter, making 4 cookies per sheet.

Bake in the 350° oven for 8 minutes or until cookies are golden and most of bubbling has stopped. Remove baking sheet from oven and let sit 2 to 3 minutes or until cookies are firm enough to remove. Working quickly, ease each cookie off with a spatula and mold 2 of the cookies into custard cups, pushing down gently into cup, as pictured. Mold other 2 on back of inverted saucer. Let set until firm. Continue with remaining batter in same manner, working quickly before batter becomes too thick and cold. If cookies become too firm to remove from the baking sheet, return to oven until warm and softened enough to move. (*) Cookies may be stored airtight at room temperature for several days, or they may be frozen, if desired. Defrost at room temperature.

To serve, fill each cup with a scoop of desired ice cream or mousse and place cup on lacy cookie saucer. Serve on dessert plates.

Makes 8 to 10 cups and saucers, allowing for breakage.

Mousses, Custards and Ice Creams

The egg is probably the simplest yet the most complex ingredient in any recipe. When separated, its two components—the yolk and the white—perform different functions. Egg yolks, for example, are used to give custards or mousses a creamy texture, while the whites add stiffness and firmness and help them set up. This chapter includes a selection of versatile creamy desserts, many of which contain an egg yolk base.

MOUSSES

Mousse is a term commonly used to describe almost any dessert containing whipping cream. Chocolate mousse, perhaps the most popular variety, is the easiest to prepare since chocolate is dense enough to firm up a mousse without the addition of unflavored gelatin. Other mousses usually have a custard or cream base and need gelatin to set it.

When working with unflavored gelatin, timing becomes a critical factor. First, the gelatin must be softened in liquid for about 5 minutes. Then the gelatin must be dissolved in the liquid by heat, either by being stirred into a hot mixture, or by being brought to a simmer. After it is dissolved, it is stirred into the custard or cream base. Before beaten egg whites or whipped cream can be folded together with the base, it must be cooled so the gelatin will thicken. The fastest way to cool the base is to place it in a bowl in a larger bowl of ice water and stir the mixture occasionally until it begins to thicken and set. Then it is ready to be folded into beaten egg whites and/or whipped cream.

- It is very important that the custard-gelatin mixture thicken to the consistency of mayonnaise before it is folded into the whipped cream or beaten egg whites. If the gelatin mixture is too thin, it will sink to the bottom of the dessert; if too thick, it will form lumps. The photos on page 146 will make this technique clear.
- If the custard-gelatin mixture gels before folding in the egg whites or cream, it may be remelted over low heat and then chilled again until the consistency of mayonnaise.
- When whipping egg whites and whipping cream for a mousse, they should hold soft, rounded peaks. If you beat them too stiff, they will be difficult to fold into the mixture and the dessert will not have a soft, fluffy texture.

CUSTARDS

Custards are generally beaten eggs mixed with milk or cream, sugar, and any one of a variety of flavorings. They can be made by two methods: either baked in an oven or cooked on top of a stove. Baked

CLOCKWISE FROM TOP: *Kiwi Mousse with Kiwi Sauce, page 144; Chilled Raspberry-Rimmed Zabaglione, page 156; Southern Praline Maple Mousse, page 148.*

custards are cooked in water baths to keep the cooking temperature constant, to add moisture, and to prevent the custard from boiling or simmering and thus developing unattractive holes. Classic baked custards are done when a knife inserted halfway into the center is removed with only a small amount of custard clinging to it. My Flaming Caramel Flan (page 158), however, which uses evaporated milk rather than fresh, is an exception and should be cooked only until it is a thick cream. It firms up when it cools.

Custards that are made on top of a stove can be cooked either in a double boiler over simmering water or over direct heat in a heavy saucepan. A custard with a high proportion of liquid will take a long time to thicken if cooked in a double boiler. If cooked in a high-quality, heavy saucepan over low heat, the cooking time will be cut in half. Although the latter method is quicker, you must be careful not to burn the custard. I highly recommend that inexperienced or insecure cooks make their custards in a double boiler so there is less chance of scorching or burning.

- If a custard contains a large amount of egg yolks to a small amount of liquid, cook it in a double boiler placed over simmering water. If you cook it over direct heat, you run the risk of scrambling the eggs.
- When making a custard base containing egg yolks that will be set with unflavored gelatin, it is all right to undercook the custard slightly, thus avoiding any chance of scrambling the eggs. The gelatin will set the custard even it it's not as thick as it could have been.
- When cooking a custard in a saucepan on the stove, you may add 1 teaspoon cornstarch as a safeguard against curdling.
- A double boiler can be improvised easily by placing a bowl over a pan of water; make sure the bottom of the bowl does not touch the water when it's gently simmering. The added advantage is that it's sometimes easier to whisk a custard in a wide bowl rather than in a deep double boiler.
- When you unmold a custard from a caramel-lined mold, it is not unusual for part of the caramel to remain hardened in the bottom of the mold.

ICE CREAM

Most ice creams are made with a custard base since it adds richness and creaminess. They can, however, be made more easily by just adding cream and sugar to fruit essence or purée, and then freezing.

- If you make an ice cream that contains alcohol, it will not freeze firm. That's a plus because the end result will be a wonderful, soft-style ice cream.
- When making fruit-flavored ice cream, be sure that the fruit is very ripe. It can even be overripe to the point of *almost* being unusable. The riper the fruit, the more intense the flavor.
- For best results, all ingredients should be cold when put into ice cream machine.

Citus Mousse

Lemon, lime and orange juices blend together to make a delightfully light and creamy dessert. This is pictured on the cover and on page 224.

⅓ *cup lemon juice*
⅓ *cup lime juice*
½ *cup frozen orange juice concentrate, thawed*
2 envelopes unflavored gelatin
6 large eggs, separated and at room temperature
⅔ *cup plus* ½ *cup sugar*
2 tablespoons grated orange peel
1 tablespoon grated lemon peel
1 cup whipping cream

½ *cup whipping cream for garnish (optional)*
Lemon, lime and orange slices for garnish (optional)
Candied citrus peel for garnish (optional; see page 229)

MOLD

6-cup decorative mold

Lightly oil mold. Stir together lemon juice, lime juice, orange juice concentrate and gelatin in small bowl. Set aside for 5 minutes for gelatin to soften.

Beat egg yolks and ⅔ cup sugar in small bowl with electric mixer on medium speed until thick and pale in color, about 3 minutes.

Pour into top of double boiler set over simmering water. Stir in softened gelatin and grated orange and lemon peels. Cook, stirring constantly, until gelatin is dissolved and mixture is very hot to the touch, about 8 to 10 minutes. Remove from heat. Transfer mixture to medium-size bowl. Place bowl in larger bowl of ice water, stirring occasionally until mixture thickens to consistency of mayonnaise and begins to set. Remove from ice water.

Meanwhile, beat egg whites in large bowl with electric mixer on low speed until soft peaks form. Add ½ cup sugar, 2 tablespoons at a time, beating on high speed until stiff but moist peaks form. Pour whites over gelatin mixture, but do not mix in. Beat cream in same bowl, on low speed until thick. Increase speed to high and beat until soft peaks form. Fold gelatin mixture and whites into cream until blended. Pour into mold. Refrigerate, covered with plastic wrap, for several hours or overnight. (*) Mold may be refrigerated up to 2 days.

Before serving, run tip of small knife around edges of mousse. Dip mold briefly in warm water and unmold onto serving plate. If desired, whip ½ cup whipping cream to stiff peaks. Pipe with ½-inch round tip onto top of mousse. Garnish with slices of lemon, lime and oranges, and candied peel if desired.

Serves 6 to 8.

Kiwi Mousse with Kiwi Sauce

The delicate flavor of kiwi really shines in this sensational recipe. A bite of the cream-colored mousse reveals crunchy flecks of the fruit's tiny black seeds. It is served with a lovely, cool, puréed green kiwi sauce. When buying this fruit, look for those which feel firm, but give slightly when pressed. This is pictured on page 140.

4 kiwis, peeled
1¼ cups plus ½ cup sugar
1 tablespoon plus 1 teaspoon unflavored gelatin (about 1½ envelopes)
1¼ cups plain yogurt
1¼ cups sour cream
1½ cups whipping cream
¼ cup water
1 drop green food coloring (optional)
3 drops yellow food coloring (optional)
1 kiwi for garnish (optional)

MOLD

6-cup decorative mold or 9-inch round layer-cake pan

Oil mold or pan. Process kiwis in food processor fitted with metal blade until puréed. You should have 1½ cups purée. Refrigerate ½ cup of the purée for the sauce.

Stir together 1¼ cups sugar and gelatin in medium-size saucepan.

Stir in the 1 cup kiwi purée and let stand 5 minutes for gelatin to soften. Bring to a boil over moderate heat, stirring constantly to dissolve gelatin. Remove from heat and cool to room temperature, about 20 minutes. Whisk in yogurt and sour cream.

Beat cream in large mixing bowl with electric mixer on low speed until thickened. Beat on medium speed until soft peaks form. Fold kiwi mixture into cream. Pour into mold or pan, cover top with plastic wrap and refrigerate for several hours or until set.

To make sauce, bring ½ cup sugar and water to a boil in a small saucepan. Stir until sugar is dissolved. Remove to a bowl and stir in reserved ½ cup kiwi purée. If desired, tint with green and yellow food coloring. Refrigerate until chilled. (*) Mousse and sauce may be refrigerated, covered, overnight, if desired.

Before serving, run small knife around edge and dip mold briefly into warm water. Unmold onto serving platter. Decorate top and sides of mousse with kiwi slices, cut in half, if desired. To serve, slice and top with spoonfuls of kiwi sauce.

Serves 6 to 8.

Lemon Mousse with Crème Fraîche Sauce

Oval, egg-shaped scoops of lemon mousse sit temptingly atop a thin layer of Crème Fraîche Sauce. I first sampled this delectable dessert in Chicago's renowned Ambria Restaurant. I thank them for sharing the recipe with me so I can share it with you. Be sure to begin the Crème Fraîche Sauce a day or more ahead of serving time.

1 recipe Crème Fraîche Sauce
  (see page 219)
1 teaspoon unflavored gelatin
1 tablespoon plus ½ cup fresh
  lemon juice (3 to 4 lemons)
4 large egg yolks
¾ cup sugar
Grated peel of 1½ lemons (about
  1 tablespoon)
2 large egg whites, at room
  temperature

1 cup whipping cream
Candied lemon peel for garnish
  (optional, see page 229)

MOLD
8-inch round or square cake pan

Make Crème Fraîche Sauce as directed. Refrigerate until ready to serve.

Stir together unflavored gelatin and 1 tablespoon lemon juice in small bowl; set aside for gelatin to soften, 5 minutes.

Whisk egg yolks and sugar in top of double boiler off the heat until well blended. Whisk in ½ cup lemon juice and peel.

Place over simmering water and cook, stirring constantly with wooden spoon, until mixture becomes very hot and is thick enough to leave path on wooden spoon when you run finger along it, about 8 to 10 minutes. Do not boil. Stir in softened gelatin until dissolved. Remove from heat and transfer mixture to medium-size bowl. Place bowl in larger bowl of ice water, stirring occasionally until mixture thickens to consistency of mayonnaise and begins to set. Remove from ice water.

Meanwhile, beat egg whites in large bowl with electric mixer on low speed until foamy. Beat on high speed until soft, rounded peaks form; do not beat stiff. Pour whites over lemon mixture; do not mix. In same mixing bowl, beat cream with electric mixer on low speed until thickened. Beat on medium speed until soft peaks form. Gently fold custard and whites into cream until incorporated. Pour into pan, cover with plastic wrap and refrigerate for at least 6 hours or until set. (*) The mousse may be refrigerated overnight, if desired.

As close to serving time as possible, spoon 2 to 3 tablespoons Crème Fraîche Sauce onto each dessert plate, tilting plate to coat it. Using 2 soup spoons dipped in hot water, scoop lemon mousse into egg shape. Place 2 to 3 scoops in center of sauce. Garnish tops with candied lemon peel, if desired.

Serves 4 to 6.

Irish Cream Mousse

Irish Cream Liqueur inside a mousse? There's nothing to it. A day or so before you make this dessert, prepare the simple, homemade liqueur. This subtle blend of chocolate, coffee and whiskey is added to a custard base to make the creamiest mousse ever. The flavor is enhanced by spooning a sauce made with more of this liqueur over the mousse when serving.

1 recipe Irish Cream Liqueur (see page 223)
1 envelope unflavored gelatin
¼ cup cold water
3 large eggs, separated and at room temperature
¼ cup sugar
1 cup plus 6 tablespoons whipping cream

MOLD

5- or 6-cup decorative mold

At least 1 day before making the mousse, make Irish Cream Liqueur as directed.

Lightly oil mold. Stir gelatin into ¼ cup cold water; set aside to soften, 5 minutes.

Whisk egg yolks in top of double boiler off heat until well blended. Whisk in 1 cup Irish Cream Liqueur. Place over simmering water and cook, stirring constantly with a wooden spoon until mixture feels hot to the touch and is thick enough to leave a pattern when your finger runs along the wooden spoon, about 8 to 10 minutes, as pictured. Do not boil. Remove from heat and immediately add softened gelatin, stirring until dissolved. Transfer mixture to medium-size bowl and place in larger bowl of ice water. Stir occasionally until mixture thickens to consistency of mayonnaise and begins to set, as pictured. Remove from ice water.

Meanwhile, beat egg whites in large mixing bowl with electric mixer on low speed until foamy. Gradually beat in sugar, 1 tablespoon at a time, until stiff but moist peaks form. Gently spoon whites over top

1 *Cook the custard thick enough so a path stays on the back of a wooden spoon when you run your finger along it. Stir in gelatin and transfer to a medium-size bowl.*

2 *Stir custard over bowl of ice water until it begins to set.*

3 *Beat egg whites until soft, rounded, moist peaks form.*

4 *Completed mousse garnished with Irish Cream Liqueur Sauce.*

of liqueur mixture; do not mix. Beat 1 cup of the whipping cream in same mixing bowl with electric mixer on low speed until thickened. Beat on medium speed until soft peaks form; do not beat stiff. Fold whites and liqueur mixture into whipped cream until blended. Pour into mold. Cover with plastic wrap and refrigerate until set.

To make sauce, stir together 1 cup Irish Cream Liqueur and 6 tablespoons whipping cream. Refrigerate until ready to serve.
(*) Mousse and sauce may be refrigerated, covered, overnight. Before serving, run knife around edges of mousse and dip mold briefly in warm water. Unmold onto serving plate, slice and top with sauce.

Serves 6 to 8.

Chocolate Mocha Mousse

I can't find another chocolate mousse recipe as rich as this one. Its bold, chocolate flavor lingers on your palate long after you've eaten the last bite. Its smooth, creamy consistency makes it perfect for scooping into balls, if desired.

1 pound semisweet chocolate, chopped
¼ cup (½ stick) unsalted butter
2 teaspoons instant coffee powder or crystals
⅓ cup water
2 large egg yolks
⅓ cup Kahlúa

4 large egg whites, at room temperature
4 tablespoons sugar
1 cup whipping cream

Melt chocolate, butter and coffee with water in top of double boiler over simmering water, stirring occasionally. Mix egg yolks and Kahlúa in small bowl. Remove double boiler from heat. Gradually whisk yolks into chocolate mixture; set aside and cool to room temperature.

Beat egg whites in large bowl with electric mixer on low speed until foamy. Beat on high speed until soft peaks form. Beat in sugar, 1 tablespoon at a time, until firm but still moist peaks form. Spoon over chocolate, but do not mix in. Beat cream in same mixing bowl with electric mixer on low speed until cream thickens. Beat on medium speed until soft peaks form. Fold chocolate and whites into cream.

Pour into medium-size bowl or individual serving dishes. Cover with plastic wrap and refrigerate until firm, at least 4 hours. (*) Mousse may be refrigerated overnight, if desired.

To form balls, dip ice cream scoop into hot water and scoop out mousse. Repeat for each ball.

Serves 8.

Southern Praline Maple Mousse

Homemade Southern-style praline pecan candies are divine, but you can substitute store-bought ones instead of using my recipe. Coarsely chop the candies and generously pile them on top of a maple-scented mousse. The smoothness of the mousse combined with the nutty crunch of pralines make this dessert an unforgettable one. This is pictured on page 140.

SOUTHERN PRALINE PECAN CANDY

1 cup chopped pecans (about 4 ounces)
¾ cup granulated sugar
½ cup firmly packed golden brown sugar
½ cup buttermilk
½ teaspoon baking soda
⅛ teaspoon salt
1½ tablespoons unsalted butter

MOUSSE

2 cups milk
1 tablespoon plus 1½ teaspoons unflavored gelatin (1½ envelopes)
½ cup firmly packed golden brown sugar
¼ teaspoon salt
4 teaspoons maple extract
2 cups whipping cream

BAKING PAN AND MOLD

Baking sheet
2-quart soufflé dish or 7- to 8-cup mold, preferably with a flat bottom surface

CANDY

Preheat oven to 350°. Toast pecans in the 350° oven for 10 to 15 minutes, stirring occasionally, until lightly browned.

Grease baking sheet and set aside.

Combine sugars, buttermilk, baking soda and salt in medium-size saucepan, over moderate heat. Cook, stirring, until sugar dissolves. Increase heat to high, insert a candy thermometer and boil without stirring until mixture reaches 210°. Add pecans and butter and continue cooking, stirring constantly with a wooden spoon, scraping bottom and sides of pan, until thermometer reaches 230°. Remove from heat and cool for 1 minute.

Stir vigorously with wooden spoon until candy begins to form threads as it is stirred. When it feels like it is beginning to thicken, working very quickly, drop by spoonfuls, using another spoon to help remove it from wooden spoon, onto oiled baking sheet. Candy will become opaque and cloudy as it cools and hardens.

When it is completely cool, chop coarsely with a knife. Do not chop in a food processor as it chops it too fine. (*)Candy will keep in an airtight container in the refrigerator for several weeks, or it can be frozen, if desired. Defrost at room temperature.

MOUSSE

Lightly oil soufflé dish or mold. Pour milk into medium-size saucepan. Remove 3 tablespoons and place in small bowl. Stir gelatin into milk in bowl and set aside to soften for 5 minutes. Heat remaining milk to scalding or until bubbles appear around edge. Stir together brown sugar and salt in medium-size bowl. Slowly whisk in hot milk. Add softened gelatin and whisk until completely dissolved. Stir in maple extract. Place bowl in larger bowl of ice water and stir occasionally until mixture thickens slightly and begins to set. Remove from ice water.

Meanwhile, beat cream in large bowl with electric mixer on low speed until cream thickens. Beat on medium speed until soft peaks form; do not beat stiff. Fold maple mixture into cream until blended. Pour mousse into soufflé dish or mold. Cover with plastic wrap and refrigerate for 4 hours or until set. (*) Mousse may be refrigerated overnight, if desired.

Before serving, run small knife around edge of mousse. Dip mold briefly in warm water and invert onto serving platter. Refrigerate until ready to serve. Just before serving, sprinkle praline candy generously over entire top. It can also be pressed into the sides, if desired.

Serves 8.

Chocolate Raspberry Dessert

This elegant recipe is adapted from a recipe in a lovely paperback book entitled The Perfect Chocolate Dessert, *by the editors of* Consumer Guide. *Perched atop each delicate chocolate shell is a scoop of chocolatey mousse that's drizzled with raspberry sauce. These individual desserts take up a lot of room in the refrigerator, so it is best to make them for small dinner parties of about 6 people.*

6 Chocolate Shells (see page 152)
1 recipe Chocolate Mocha Mousse
(see page 147)
1 recipe Ruby-Red Raspberry
Sauce (see page 218)
Fresh raspberries for garnish
(optional)

One or more days before serving, if desired, make chocolate shells, Chocolate Mocha Mousse, and Ruby-Red Raspberry Sauce as directed. Refrigerate all until ready to assemble dessert.

To assemble, place 1 chocolate shell on each dessert plate. Dip ice cream scoop into hot water and then into mousse. Place scoop of mousse in center of each shell. (*) Dessert may be refrigerated up to 4 hours, uncovered, at this point, if desired.

Before serving, spoon raspberry sauce over mousse. Garnish with fresh raspberries, if desired.

Serves 6.

Chocolate Velvet Crown

Crowning a crème de cacao and rum-flavored chocolate cream filling is a majestic ring of ladyfingers. A vanilla custard sauce provides a dramatic taste and color contrast to the intense chocolate flavor of this rich dessert.

2 recipes Vanilla Custard Sauce (see page 216)
1 pound semisweet chocolate, chopped
6 tablespoons (¾ stick) unsalted butter
15 whole ladyfingers (approximately 4 ounces)
¼ cup white crème de cacao
½ cup powdered sugar, sifted
3 large eggs, separated and at room temperature

2 tablespoons light rum
1 teaspoon instant coffee powder or crystals dissolved in 2 teaspoons warm water
2 cups whipping cream

MOLD
8 x 3-inch or 8½ x 2-inch springform pan

Make Vanilla Custard Sauce as directed. Refrigerate until ready to use.

Melt chocolate and butter in top of double boiler over simmering water, set aside and cool to room temperature.

Cut ladyfingers in half lengthwise. Place on baking sheet cut-side up. Sprinkle with 2 tablespoons of the crème de cacao. Stand ladyfingers around sides of springform, cut-side facing inward. Cover bottom with remaining ladyfingers. It is not necessary to cover the bottom completely.

Beat powdered sugar, egg yolks, rum, remaining 2 tablespoons crème de cacao and coffee in large bowl with electric mixer on medium speed until well blended. Mix in chocolate-butter mixture. Beat egg whites in large bowl with electric mixer on low speed until foamy. Beat on high speed until soft, rounded peaks form. Pour whites over chocolate mixture; do not mix. Beat whipping cream in same mixing bowl on low speed until thickened. Beat on medium speed until soft peaks form. Fold chocolate mixture and whites into cream until no streaks of white remain. Turn mixture into prepared pan, smoothing top evenly with a spatula. Cover the top with plastic wrap and refrigerate several hours or until set. (*) Dessert may be refrigerated up to 2 days, or it may be frozen tightly wrapped with foil, if desired. Defrost in refrigerator overnight.

Several hours before serving, run sharp knife around sides of pan. Remove sides of springform pan and place dessert on serving platter. Spoon enough Vanilla Custard Sauce on each dessert plate to coat plate. Place a slice of dessert in center of each plate. Pass remaining sauce.

Serves 8 to 10.

Frozen Crunchy Strawberry Cloud

Egg whites and strawberries are whipped together to make a voluminous pink and creamy cloud. Layered with buttery, toasted brown sugar-pecan crumbs, it is a light and luscious dessert which keeps beautifully in the freezer.

CRUMB MIXTURE
¼ *pound (1 stick) unsalted butter*
1 *cup all-purpose flour*
¼ *cup firmly packed golden brown sugar*
1 *teaspoon vanilla*
½ *cup chopped pecans (about 2 ounces)*

STRAWBERRY FILLING
1 *package (10 ounces) frozen strawberries with syrup, defrosted*
2 *large egg whites, at room temperature*
½ *cup sugar*
3 *tablespoons lemon juice*
1 *cup whipping cream*
1 *teaspoon vanilla*

SERVING DISH
2-quart decorative bowl, preferably glass, which can be put in freezer

CRUMB MIXTURE
Preheat oven to 350°.

Place butter, flour, brown sugar, vanilla and pecans in food processor fitted with metal blade. Pulse on and off until mixture is crumbly. Place crumbs on cookie sheet. Bake in the 350° oven for 15 to 20 minutes, stirring occasionally with a fork to break mixture up, until crumbs are lightly toasted; watch carefully toward end of baking time so they don't burn. Set aside to cool completely.

FILLING
Meanwhile, beat strawberries, egg whites, sugar and lemon juice in large bowl with electric mixer, on medium speed until mixture begins to thicken. Increase speed to high and continue beating until mixture forms very stiff peaks, about 15 minutes; do not underbeat. Whip cream and vanilla in separate bowl with electric mixer on low speed until thickened. Beat on medium speed until soft peaks form; do not beat stiff. Fold into strawberry mixture.

Sprinkle a third of the crumbs in bottom of dish. Spoon half the strawberry mixture over crumbs. Sprinkle with another third of crumbs and spread with remaining strawberry mixture, smoothing top with spatula. Sprinkle remaining crumbs over top. Cover tightly with foil and freeze overnight. (*) Dessert may be frozen up to 1 month, if desired.

Remove from freezer 30 to 45 minutes before serving so it becomes soft enough to spoon. Serve in shallow bowls or on dessert plates.

Serves 10.

Chocolate Shells for Mousse or Ice Cream

These shells make beautiful, edible holders for any type of ice cream or mousse. Topped with a complementary sauce, they are sure to evoke raves from your guests.

8 ounces semisweet chocolate, chopped
Desired filling, such as ice cream or mousse

EQUIPMENT
Scallop shells and regular-strength aluminum foil

Stir chocolate in top of double boiler over simmering water until melted. Set aside to cool slightly.

Line outside of scallop shells with foil, tucking about ½ inch of foil underneath. With hands, smooth out as many wrinkles as possible. Spread a thin layer of chocolate with a small spatula or knife over outside of each shell, going to within ¼ inch of edge. Be careful not to let chocolate run underneath the shell. Refrigerate for 5 minutes. Repeat with a second layer of chocolate. Refrigerate for at least 8 hours. (*) Shells may be refrigerated, covered, up to 1 week, if desired.

To remove chocolate from shell, work with one shell at a time, leaving remaining in refrigerator. Gently lift foil from the shell. Pull back on foil, tearing it in pieces away from the chocolate. It is important not to touch the chocolate more than necessary, as the heat of your hand will cause it to melt. Refrigerate until ready to use. (*) Shells may be refrigerated for several days in airtight container, or they may be frozen in airtight container, if desired. Defrost in refrigerator. Serve chilled, filled with desired filling.

Makes 6 to 8 shells.

1 *Smooth the foil with your fingers to heighten the shell motif, then spread with melted chocolate. Refrigerate until hard and then spread with a second layer.*

2 *Carefully pull away the foil.*

3 *Chocolate shells filled with Chocolate Mocha Mousse, topped with Ruby-Red Raspberry Sauce, page 149.*

Chocolate Cups for Mousse or Ice Cream

4 ounces semisweet chocolate,
  chopped
Desired filling

EQUIPMENT

16 to 20 fluted paper or foil
  baking cups

Stir chocolate in top of double boiler over simmering water until melted. Set aside to cool slightly. Double up baking cups.

Brush or spread chocolate with brush or small knife about ⅛ inch thick on bottom and up sides of double thickness of cups. Place in muffin pan cups and refrigerate until firm, at least 8 hours. Gently pull back on paper, handling chocolate as little as possible. (*) Cups may be refrigerated for several days in an airtight container, or they may be frozen, if desired. Defrost in refrigerator. Serve chilled filled with desired filling.

Makes 8 to 10 cups.

Chocolate Peppermint Angel Dessert

Indulge in lofty layers of angel food cake that are crowned with creamy, mint-flavored chocolate mousse. It tastes just like an exquisite chocolate after-dinner mint.

1½ cups chocolate chips (about 9
  ounces)
2 tablespoons sugar
2 tablespoons milk
¼ teaspoon peppermint or mint
  extract
3 large eggs, separated and at room
  temperature
2 cups whipping cream
1 large angel food cake (about 18
  ounces), homemade or
  store-bought
1 cup whipping cream for garnish
  (optional)

MOLD

8 x 3-inch or 8½ x 2-inch
  springform pan

Stir chocolate chips, sugar, milk and mint extract in top of double boiler over simmering water until chocolate is melted. Remove from heat. Whisk egg yolks in small bowl until blended; whisk into chocolate. Beat egg whites in medium-size bowl with electric mixer on low speed until foamy. Beat on high speed until soft, rounded peaks form. Spoon over chocolate without mixing. Beat cream in same mixing bowl on low speed until thickened. Beat on medium speed until soft peaks form. Fold chocolate mixture and whites into cream until no streaks of white remain.

Cut angel food cake into 1-inch pieces. Place layer of cake pieces on bottom of springform, using half the cake. Top with half the mousse. Repeat second layer of cake and remaining mousse in same manner. Smooth top evenly with a spatula. Cover with plastic wrap and refrigerate overnight. (*) Dessert may be refrigerated up to 2 days, or it may be frozen, covered with plastic wrap and foil, if desired. Defrost wrapped, in refrigerator overnight.

Several hours before serving, remove sides of springform. Beat remaining whipping cream until stiff. Spoon into pastry bag fitted with 1-inch rosette or star tip and pipe rows of whipped cream going up the sides and 1 rosette in the center. Or, spread whipped cream over top and sides, if desired.

Serves 8 to 10.

Warm Champagne Zabaglione

Zabaglione, or Sabayon, is an Italian custard quickly whisked up into a frothy, creamy dessert and served warm from the stove. This version substitutes champagne for the traditional Marsala, which makes a more delicate and subtle custard.

4 large egg yolks, at room temperature
¼ cup sugar
½ cup champagne

Place yolks and sugar in top of double boiler or in a bowl which can be placed over a saucepan. Beat with an electric mixer or whisk until mixture is pale yellow and very creamy. Place over, not touching, simmering water and stir in champagne. Continue beating or whisking until mixture foams and then thickens into soft mounds, about 10 minutes. Spoon into champagne glasses or large wine goblets and serve immediately.

Serves 6.

Chilled Raspberry-Rimmed Zabaglione

Zabaglione is a golden custard delicately flavored with Marsala wine. In this version, a portion is blended with a purée of frozen raspberries. Spoonfuls of the raspberry zabaglione are placed in a champagne glass and topped with the golden custard. The raspberry custard borders the sides of the glass, making a glamorous and delicious rim. This is pictured on page 140.

**6 large egg yolks, at room
   temperature**
¾ cup sugar
⅓ cup all-purpose flour
2 cups milk
⅓ cup Marsala wine
1 cup whipping cream
**1 package (10 ounces) frozen
   raspberries in syrup, thawed**

Whisk egg yolks, sugar, flour, milk and Marsala in a medium-size heavy saucepan until well blended. Cook over moderate heat, stirring with whisk until mixture comes to a boil and thickens, about 15 minutes. Lower heat and cook, stirring constantly, for 2 minutes. Do not be concerned if it lumps slightly as it comes to a boil; whisking will smooth it out. Remove from heat and immediately pour into a bowl. Place in larger bowl of ice water and stir occasionally until cooled to room temperature. Beat whipping cream in mixing bowl with electric mixer on low speed until thickened. Beat on medium speed until soft peaks form. Fold into cooled custard.

Drain raspberries, reserving syrup. Place raspberries in food processor fitted with metal blade and add ¼ cup of the syrup. Process until puréed. Pour into bowl and stir in 1 cup of the custard. (*) Golden and raspberry custards may be refrigerated, well covered, for several hours, if desired.

Up to 2 hours before serving, put 3 heaping tablespoons of raspberry custard into each of 8 champagne glasses. Carefully ladel golden custard into center of raspberry mixture until glass is nearly full. Refrigerate until serving time.

Serves 8.

Duke of Nottingham's Fruit Trifle

It's so easy to make a sophisticated trifle if you begin with packaged pound cake and frozen mixed fruit. After it's marinated overnight in a delicate amaretto custard, the frozen fruit actually tastes as flavorful as fresh. This is a terrific dessert to transport to friends as your contribution to a holiday dinner.

2 packages (16 ounces each) frozen mixed fruit, thawed
4 large eggs, at room temperature
4 large egg yolks, at room temperature
1 cup sugar
2 tablespoons cornstarch
3 cups half and half
2 tablespoons plus ¼ cup amaretto liqueur
2 teaspoons vanilla
1 loaf pound cake (12 ounces), fresh or frozen, thawed
¼ cup dark rum

WHIPPED CREAM TOPPING
  (Optional)
¼ cup sliced almonds
1 cup whipping cream
2 tablespoons sugar
½ teaspoon vanilla
1 tablespoon dark rum

SERVING DISH
Attractive 2- or 2½-quart glass bowl

Pour thawed fruit into strainer set over bowl and let drain for 2 hours or longer. Pat fruit dry on paper towels.

To make custard, beat eggs and yolks together in medium-size bowl with electric mixer on medium speed or whisk until light and creamy. Beat in sugar, cornstarch and half and half until blended. Transfer mixture to heavy saucepan. Cook over moderate heat, stirring and whisking constantly, until mixture comes to a boil, about 5 minutes. Lower heat slightly and cook, stirring, for 2 minutes. The custard may lump slightly as it comes to a boil, but whisking will smooth it out. Remove from heat and whisk in 2 tablespoons amaretto and vanilla. Place pan in larger bowl of ice water and stir occasionally until cold.

Slice cake into ½-inch-thick slices. Cut each slice into quarters and place them on work surface. Stir together rum and ¼ cup amaretto in a small bowl. Sprinkle evenly over cake slices.

Line bottom of glass bowl with a third of the cake slices. Spoon a third of the fruit over cake. Spoon a third of the custard over fruit. Repeat with 2 more layers of cake, fruit and custard. Cover with plastic wrap and refrigerate overnight.

TOPPING
Before serving, if desired, make topping. Toast almonds in preheated 350° oven for 10 to 15 minutes or until lightly browned. Beat cream in medium-size bowl with electric mixer on low speed until thick. Add sugar, vanilla, and rum and beat on medium speed until soft peaks form. Spoon into pastry bag fitted with a ¾- to 1-inch rosette or star tip and pipe rosettes of cream around top. Or, spoon dollops of cream over top. Sprinkle center with toasted almonds.

Serves 10.

Flaming Caramel Flan

This is my favorite custard. The use of evaporated milk creates a density that intensifies the creaminess and flavor. Flaming Grand Marnier poured over when serving adds a new dimension to its goodness and creates a dramatic presentation, as well.

1 cup plus ¾ cup sugar
¼ cup water
3 large eggs
5 large egg yolks
2 cans (13 ounces each) evaporated milk
2 teaspoons vanilla
1 orange, sliced for garnish (optional)
¼ cup Grand Marnier

BAKING PAN
9-inch round layer-cake pan

Preheat oven to 300°.

Melt 1 cup sugar with the water in small saucepan or skillet over moderate heat, stirring once to dissolve sugar completely; after about 30 seconds it will become a clear syrup. Bring to a boil, swirling and rotating the pan, not stirring, until sugar turns mahogany, about 5 minutes. Watch carefully, as it goes from mahogany to burnt very quickly. Hold cake pan with pot holder in one hand. Carefully pour hot caramel into pan, tilting and turning to completely cover sides and bottom, as pictured. Set aside until cool and caramel hardens.

Mix eggs, yolks and ¾ cup sugar in large bowl with wire whisk until blended. Whisk in milk and vanilla until incorporated. Do not whisk until bubbly, as this will incorporate airholes in the finished custard. Place caramel-lined mold in shallow baking pan or skillet with an ovenproof handle. Pour custard through fine strainer into mold. Place on oven rack and pour enough hot tap water into pan to come halfway up sides of mold, being careful not to let water splash into custard.

Bake in the 300° oven for 70 to 75 minutes or until outer 3 inches are set, but center is still very loose and looks like creamy soup. It will appear underbaked, but will set up as it cools. Remove mold from water and cool to room temperature. Cover with plastic wrap and refrigerate overnight. (*) Custard may be refrigerated, well covered, up to 2 days, if desired.

Before serving, run small knife around edge of custard. Invert onto rimmed serving platter which is at least 2 to 3 inches larger than custard. The caramel will have become a sauce. Decorate platter with orange slices, if desired. Heat Grand Marnier in ladle or small pan until very hot, but not boiling. Bring to the table, if desired. Ignite and pour flaming over custard, spooning caramel over custard until flames die out. Spoon caramel over custard when serving.

Serves 8.

1 *Pour in caramelized sugar, rotating the pan until it is coated with the caramel.*

2 *Strain custard into the caramel-lined pan.*

3 *Completed flan decorated with orange slices and flambéed with warm Grand Marnier.*

Classic Caramel Custard

This is a lush, shiny, satiny custard drenched with a silky topping of mahogany caramel.

1 cup plus ½ cup sugar
¼ cup water
2¼ cups milk
1½ cups half and half
6 large eggs
3 large egg yolks
⅛ teaspoon salt
2 teaspoons vanilla

BAKING PAN
6-cup ring mold

Preheat oven to 325°.

Melt 1 cup sugar and water together in small saucepan or skillet over moderate heat, stirring once to dissolve sugar completely. After about 30 seconds it will become·a clear syrup. Bring to a boil, swirling and rotating the pan without stirring, until sugar turns mahogany, about 5 minutes. Watch carefully as it can go from mahogany to burnt very quickly. Pick up mold with pot holder in one hand. Carefully pour hot caramel into to it, tilting and turning mold to completely cover sides and bottom. Set aside until cool and caramel hardens.

Bring milk and half and half to a simmer in medium-size saucepan, stirring frequently. Whisk together eggs, yolks, ½ cup sugar and salt in medium-size bowl until blended. Very slowly whisk in hot milk and vanilla. Do not whisk until bubbly, as this will incorporate air holes into the finished custard.

Place mold in shallow baking pan or skillet with ovenproof handle. Pour custard through fine strainer into a pitcher. Pour into mold. Place on oven rack. Fill pan half full of hot tap water, being careful not to let water splash into custard.

Bake in the 325° oven for 45 to 55 minutes or until small knife or cake tester inserted into center of custard comes out almost clean. A little custard adhering to knife will ensure it is creamy and not overbaked. Be careful not to cut through to bottom of custard when testing. Remove mold from water and cool to room temperature. Cover with plastic wrap and refrigerate for several hours or until chilled. (*)Custard may be refrigerated, well covered, overnight, if desired.

Before serving, run small knife around edge of custard. Invert onto rimmed serving platter which is slightly larger than mold. Spoon melted caramel over custard when serving.

Serves 10.

Crème Brûlée

Cold, smooth, creamy vanilla custard creates a dramatic contrast to a crunchy, hot, bubbly brown-sugar topping.

2 cups half and half
½ cup granulated sugar
2 teaspoons vanilla
7 large egg yolks
6 to 9 tablespoons golden brown sugar

BAKING DISHES

Six ½-cup soufflé dishes or ramekins

Preheat oven to 325°.

Bring half and half and sugar to a boil in medium-size saucepan, stirring until sugar is dissolved. Remove from heat and stir in vanilla.

Whisk egg yolks in medium-size bowl, just until broken up. Slowly whisk in half and half. Pour through fine strainer into pitcher or bowl. Place baking dishes in shallow baking pan. Fill dishes with the custard. Place on oven rack and pour about 1 inch of hot tap water into pan.

Bake in the 325° oven for 35 to 40 minutes or until center of custards jiggle slightly and a cake tester comes out almost clean. Remove dishes from water and cool to room temperature. Cover with plastic wrap and refrigerate until chilled. (*) Custards may be refrigerated, well covered, up to 2 days.

Before serving, rub brown sugar between your fingers to soften it and make sure it is free of lumps. If the sugar is hard, it may be necessary to put it through a strainer. Sprinkle 1 to 1½ tablespoons sugar over top of each custard to cover by about ⅛ inch.

Broil under medium heat or about 3 inches from flame for 2 to 3 minutes or until part of the sugar is golden brown, melted and bubbling. Some of it will not look melted. Watch very carefully as it burns quickly. Remove from heat and set aside 5 minutes for sugar to harden. Serve immediately or refrigerate up to 1 hour.

Serves 6.

Vanilla Pots de Crème

Tiny dishes filled with light, ivory-colored custard make a perfect dessert for any occasion.

2 cups half and half
¾ cup sugar
2 teaspoons vanilla
7 large egg yolks

BAKING DISHES

Six ½-cup pots de crème, ramekins or soufflé dishes

Preheat oven to 325°.

Stir half and half and sugar together in medium-size saucepan. Bring just to a boil. Remove from heat and stir in vanilla.

Whisk egg yolks in medium-size bowl just until broken up. Slowly whisk in cream mixture. Pour through fine strainer into pitcher. Place baking dishes in shallow baking pan. Pour custard into dishes. Place on oven rack and pour about 1 inch of hot tap water into pan.

Bake in the 325° oven for 35 to 40 minutes or until centers jiggle slightly and a cake tester inserted near center come out almost clean. Remove dishes from pan to wire rack and cool to room temperature. Cover with plastic wrap and refrigerate until chilled. (*) The pots de crème may be refrigerated, well covered, up to 2 days, if desired.

Serves 6.

Coffee Pots de Crème

Now you can drink your coffee and eat it, too. These individual desserts contain three great "C's"—coffee, cream and Cognac.

2 cups half and half
1 cup sugar
3 tablespoons instant coffee powder or crystals
2 teaspoons vanilla
2 tablespoons Cognac or brandy
7 large egg yolks

BAKING DISHES

Six ½-cup pots de crème, ramekins or soufflé dishes

Preheat oven to 325°.

Stir half and half, sugar and coffee together in medium-size saucepan. Bring just to a boil, stirring until coffee is dissolved. Remove from heat and stir in vanilla and Cognac or brandy.

Whisk yolks in medium-size bowl, just until broken up. Slowly whisk in hot cream mixture. Pour through fine strainer into pitcher. Place baking dishes in shallow baking pan. Pour custard into dishes. Place on oven rack and pour about 1 inch of hot tap water into pan.

Bake in the 325° oven for 30 to 35 minutes or until centers jiggle slightly and cake tester inserted near center comes out almost clean. Remove dishes from pan to rack and cool to room temperature. Cover with plastic wrap and refrigerate until cold. (*) The pots de crème may be refrigerated, well covered, up to 4 days, if desired.

Serves 6.

Chocolate Pots de Crème

These pots de crème are richer and creamier than any mousse you've ever eaten. It's almost sinful that such a decadent dessert could be so simple to make.

2 cups milk
8 ounces semisweet chocolate, chopped
1 cup sugar
2 teaspoons vanilla
2 tablespoons brandy
7 large egg yolks
Whipped cream for garnishing (optional)

BAKING DISHES
Eight ½-cup pots de crème, ramekins or soufflé dishes

Preheat oven to 325°.

Heat milk in medium-size heavy saucepan until hot. Add chocolate and sugar. Whisk constantly over low heat until chocolate is completely melted and smooth. Remove from heat and stir in vanilla and brandy. Set aside to cool slightly.

Whisk egg yolks in medium-size bowl until blended. Slowly whisk in chocolate mixture. Place dishes in shallow baking pan. Pour custard through a strainer into pitcher. Fill dishes with the custard. Place on oven rack and pour about 1 inch of hot tap water into pan.

Bake in the 325° oven for 30 to 35 minutes or until centers jiggle slightly when pan is shaken. Remove dishes from water and cool completely. Cover with plastic wrap and refrigerate until chilled. (*) Pots de crème may be refrigerated, well covered, up to 4 days.

If desired, top each with a rosette or dollop of whipped cream before serving.

Serves 8.

Irish Whiskey Ice Cream

A homemade version of Irish Cream Liqueur is the flavor base for this extraordinary ice cream. As it contains some alcohol, it never freezes firm, but remains soft and creamy.

1 recipe Irish Cream Liqueur (see page 223)
3 cups whipping cream
1 cup milk
¾ cup sugar
4 large egg yolks

EQUIPMENT
Ice cream machine

At least 1 day before making the ice cream, make Irish Cream Liqueur as directed. Refrigerate until ready to use.

Stir cream, milk and sugar in large heavy saucepan over moderate heat until mixture is hot and sugar is dissolved. Whisk egg yolks in medium-size bowl until blended. Slowly stir 1 cup hot cream mixture into yolks. Return to saucepan with the cream. Cook over moderate heat, stirring constantly with wooden spoon, until mixture is thick enough to leave path on back of wooden spoon when you run a finger along it. Do not boil. Remove from heat and pour through fine strainer into bowl. Cool to room temperature. Stir in 1¼ cups Irish Cream Liqueur. Cover and refrigerate several hours or until well chilled. (*) Custard may be refrigerated, well covered, up to 4 days, if desired. The custard will thicken in the refrigerator.

Pour cold custard into ice cream machine and freeze according to manufacturer's directions. (*) The ice cream may be stored in the freezer for several weeks as it never freezes solid, but stays soft and creamy.

Serve topped with spoonfuls of Irish Cream Liqueur.

Makes 1 quart.

VARIATION
To make Crème de Grand Marnier Ice Cream, substitute 1 recipe Crème de Grand Marnier (see page 223) for the Irish Cream Liqueur.

Oreo Espresso Ice Cream

Coffee and chocolate are a popular pair. Chunks of Oreo cookies in an intensely coffee-flavored ice cream add a new dimension to this dynamic duo.

1 quart half and half
¾ cup sugar
⅓ cup instant coffee powder or crystals
4 large egg yolks
10 Oreo creme sandwich cookies

EQUIPMENT
Ice cream machine

Heat half and half, sugar and coffee in heavy medium-size saucepan, stirring until sugar and coffee are dissolved.

Whisk egg yolks in medium-size bowl until blended. Slowly pour in 1 cup of the hot liquid, whisking constantly. Return to saucepan and cook over moderate heat, stirring constantly with wooden spoon, until mixture is thick enough to leave a path on wooden spoon when you run a finger along it. Remove from heat and cool to room temperature. Cover and refrigerate for several hours or until well chilled. (*) Custard may be refrigerated, well covered, up to 2 days, if desired.

Pour into ice cream machine and freeze according to manufacturer's directions. Just before ice cream is frozen to desired consistency, break Oreo cookies with hands into coarse pieces and add to ice cream. Continue processing until frozen. Serve immediately or freeze up to 1 week.

Makes 1 quart.

Marvelous Mango Ice Cream

As there's no need to make a custard base, no cooking is required when preparing this simple recipe. On a sweltering summer day, it's a perfect, most refreshing cold dessert. It boasts a lovely, delicate orange color and a fresh tropical taste.

*2 very ripe mangos, about
    14 ounces each
1½ cups half and half, chilled
1½ cups milk, chilled
1½ cups sugar
¼ cup lemon juice, chilled
⅔ cup orange juice, chilled*

EQUIPMENT

Ice cream machine

Peel mangos. Cut pulp into 1-inch chunks and place in food processor fitted with metal blade. Process until puréed. Mangos are extremely fibrous and must be puréed very well. You should have about 1½ cups purée. Spoon into large pitcher or bowl and stir in half and half, milk, sugar, lemon and orange juice. Pour into ice cream maker and freeze according to manufacturer's directions. Serve immediately or freeze up to 1 week.

Makes 1 quart.

Fresh Peach Ice Cream

A spoonful of this soothing ice cream will conjure up images of fresh-from-the-tree peaches blended with whipping cream in grandmother's hand-cranked freezer. Use the ripest peaches possible to get the utmost flavor.

2 cups whipping cream
2 cups half and half
¾ cup sugar
4 large egg yolks
1 teaspoon vanilla
¼ teaspoon almond extract
5 to 7 ripe peaches (about 2 pounds)

EQUIPMENT

Ice cream machine

Heat cream, half and half, and sugar in heavy medium-size saucepan, until hot and sugar is dissolved. Whisk yolks in medium-size bowl until blended. Whisking constantly, slowly pour in about 1 cup of the hot cream. Return to saucepan and cook over moderate heat, stirring constantly with a wooden spoon, until mixture is thick enough to leave a path on wooden spoon when you run a finger along it. Do not boil. Remove from heat and pour through fine strainer into bowl. Stir in vanilla and almond extracts. Cool to room temperature and refrigerate until cold. (*)Custard may be refrigerated, covered, up to 2 days, if desired.

Peel peaches by dropping them into a pan of boiling water to cover for 20 seconds. Remove with slotted spoon and run under cold water. When cool enough to handle, slip off peel. Cut up peaches and pit them. Purée peaches in food processor fitted with metal blade. You should have about 3½ cups purée. Stir peach purée into cold custard base. Pour into ice cream machine and freeze according to manufacturer's directions. It is best served the same day.

Makes 1½ quarts.

Incredible White Coffee Ice Cream

Your eyes may tell you that this is just vanilla, but your taste buds will flip for the distinct, rich-brewed coffee flavor. Whole coffee beans steep in cream, releasing their fresh roasted essence and giving this ice cream a pure coffee flavor unlike any you've ever tasted. It's wonderful served in Lacy Almond Cookie Cups and Saucers (see page 139).

1 quart half and half
1 cup sugar
4 ounces whole aromatic coffee beans, such as French Roast
4 large egg yolks

EQUIPMENT

Ice cream machine

Bring half and half and sugar to a boil in large saucepan, stirring to dissolve sugar. Remove from heat. Add coffee beans, cover and set aside for 3 hours. Strain cream into large, heavy saucepan. Discard coffee beans.

Whisk egg yolks in small bowl until blended. Whisk into coffee-cream mixture. Cook over moderate heat, stirring occasionally with wooden spoon, until mixture is thick enough to leave a path on the spoon when you run a finger along it. Do not boil. Remove from heat and cool to room temperature. Cover and refrigerate until well chilled. (*) Custard may be refrigerated, well covered, up to 2 days, if desired.

Place cold coffee mixture in ice cream maker and freeze according to manufacturer's directions. Serve immediately or freeze up to 1 week.

Makes 1 quart.

White Chocolate Ice Cream

White chocolate transforms this ice cream into an ethereal treat.

6 ounces white chocolate, chopped (see notes on chocolate, pages 7–8)
½ cup plus 1½ cups milk
3 large egg yolks, at room temperature
⅓ cup sugar
1 cup half and half
1 teaspoon vanilla

EQUIPMENT
Ice cream machine

Melt chocolate with ½ cup milk in top of double boiler over simmering water. Remove from heat and cool slightly.

Whisk egg yolks and sugar in medium-size heavy saucepan until blended. Gradually whisk in 1½ cups milk and half and half. Cook over medium heat, stirring constantly with wooden spoon, until mixture is thick enough to leave a path on wooden spoon when you run a finger along it. Remove from heat. Stir in white chocolate and vanilla. Cool to room temperature. Cover and refrigerate until cold. (*)The custard may be refrigerated, well covered, up to 2 days, if desired.

Place cold custard in ice cream maker and freeze according to manufacturer's directions. Serve immediately or freeze up to 1 week.

Makes 1 quart.

Soufflés and Meringues

The recipes in this chapter have an important ingredient in common—egg whites. The whites, however, are employed in two different, distinctive ways. Egg whites beaten with sugar until stiff and glossy and then baked form dry and crispy meringues. Whites whipped only to soft, moist peaks and then folded into a custard base create a light and airy soufflé.

COLD SOUFFLÉS

A cold soufflé is actually a mousse presented in a soufflé dish, frequently with the mousse rising above the rim of the dish. To achieve this effect, the dish is fitted with a "collar" before the mousse mixture is poured in. To make a collar, tear a piece of regular strength, 12-inch-wide aluminum foil, long enough to wrap around the soufflé dish. Fold in half and place around the dish, making a collar extending at least 3 inches over the top of the dish. Tie with a string or clip in place with paper clip.

HOT SOUFFLÉS

Most dessert soufflés contain a custard base. The thicker the custard, the more substantial and pudding-like the soufflé will be. I'm particularly partial to these types. My Amaretto and Raspberry Soufflés are both very thick and creamy, and although the outside will be set, the inside will remain soft and saucy.

It is important to beat egg whites to the correct consistency so the soufflé will have the proper texture. The whites should hold a soft peak when the beater is lifted from them, and you should be able to see beads of moisture in them.

To incorporate the base and the whites together, first stir a dollop of whites into the custard base to lighten it. Then pour that mixture over the whites, folding from the bottom of the bowl over the top, until only a small amount of whites can be seen.

TIPS

- If in doubt, slightly overbeat whites rather than underbeat. The soufflé may not rise as high, but it will still achieve some volume. If egg whites are underbeaten, they won't possess enough substance and firmness to lift the soufflé and make it rise.
- Do not let egg whites stand after they are beaten or they will lose their air and deflate. Fold them into the soufflé base as soon as they are whipped.
- When folding beaten egg whites into other ingredients, be careful not to overmix them. It's customary that streaks of white appear, even in a chocolate soufflé batter. The streaks generally disappear during the baking process.

CLOCKWISE FROM TOP: *Raspberry Floating Islands, page 180; Hazelnut Meringue Torte with Apricot Cream, page 184; Frosty Daiquiri Soufflé, page 173.*

- A tablespoon or two of sugar from the recipe added to the egg whites when they are beaten gives the whites greater holding power and makes them easier to fold into the soufflé base.
- For the prettiest and highest soufflé, make sure the batter in the soufflé dish comes up almost to the rim.
- To test a soufflé for doneness, insert a knife near the center; it should come out almost clean. Soufflés are not meant to be cooked through until firm; they should be puffed and golden brown, but their centers should almost always remain soft.

MERINGUES

Hard baked meringues, either shells or layers, can stand alone. They contain a lot of sugar, usually about ¼ cup for each white, which stabilizes the whites and keeps them from breaking down.

When beating egg whites for hard, crisp meringues, begin mixing at low speed until the whites become foamy. Increase the mixer to high speed and continue mixing until soft peaks form. Then add the sugar a tablespoon at a time, beating constantly until about half has been added and stiff peaks have formed. You may then add the remaining sugar a little faster until all is incorporated and the mixture is the consistency of marshmallow cream. The amount of time it takes to incorporate all the sugar varies with different models of mixers. It usually takes about 10 minutes. Meringues should be baked in a very slow oven, 200° to 250° degrees, so they remain white, but become absolutely dry. They should then be left in the turned off oven with the oven door closed to continue drying.

TIPS

- When beating egg whites for meringues, be sure to add the sugar slowly. If you add the sugar too quickly, it will cause the whites to soften.
- It's so important not to make meringues on a humid day. The meringue will absorb the moisture in the air and become sticky.

Iced Lemon Soufflé

A maximum amount of lemon juice and a minimum amount of gelatin make this soufflé amazingly tangy and light. As an added plus, it can be served straight from the mold, for easy entertaining.

¾ cup fresh lemon juice (4 to 5 lemons)
1 tablespoon plus 1½ teaspoons unflavored gelatin (1½ envelopes)
6 large eggs, separated and at room temperature
1 cup plus ½ cup sugar
3 tablespoons grated lemon peel (from about 3 lemons)
1½ cups whipping cream

GARNISH (optional)
1 cup whipping cream, whipped to stiff peaks
Candied Lemon Peel or Notched Lemon Slices (page 229)

SOUFFLÉ DISH
5- to 6-cup soufflé dish

Tear piece of regular strength aluminum foil 12 inches wide and long enough to wrap around soufflé dish. Fold in half lengthwise and place around dish, making a collar extending at least 3 inches above top of dish. Tie or clip it in place.

Measure lemon juice into glass measuring cup. Stir in unflavored gelatin and set aside to soften, about 5 minutes. Mix egg yolks and 1 cup sugar in small mixing bowl with electric mixer on medium speed or whisk until thick and pale yellow, about 3 minutes. Stir in lemon peel. Pour into the top of a double boiler placed over simmering water and cook, stirring constantly with wooden spoon, until the mixture thickens slightly and feels very hot to the touch, about 10 minutes. Do not boil. Remove from heat and immediately add gelatin mixture, stirring until dissolved. Pour mixture into medium-size bowl and set in large bowl of ice water. Stir occasionally until mixture thickens to consistency of mayonnaise and begins to set. Remove from ice water.

Meanwhile, beat egg whites in large bowl with electric mixer on low speed until foamy. Beat on high speed until soft, rounded peaks form. Slowly add ½ cup sugar, 1 tablespoon at a time, beating until whites form stiff, but not dry, peaks. Pour over lemon mixture; do not mix. Beat whipping cream in same mixing bowl on low speed until thickened. Beat on medium speed until soft peaks form; do not beat stiff. Gently fold lemon mixture and whites into cream. Spoon mixture into soufflé dish, smoothing top with a spatula. Refrigerate until firm and then cover with plastic wrap. (*) Soufflé may be refrigerated overnight, or it may be frozen, if desired. Defrost in refrigerator overnight.

Before serving, gently remove collar from soufflé. If desired, place whipping cream in pastry bag fitted with a ¾- to 1-inch rosette or star tip. Pipe rosettes of whipped cream around top of soufflé and garnish with candied lemon peel or lemon slices, if desired.

Serves 8.

Chilled Mandarin Orange Soufflé

What a fabulous finale for Oriental dinners! These creamy, orange, individual soufflés beautifully complement the flavors of Eastern entrées. When topped with tiny paper parasols, they add the perfect accent to help carry out your party's theme.

12 almond or coconut macaroon cookies (1½ cups crumbs)
1 can (6 ounces) frozen orange juice concentrate, thawed
⅓ cup water
1 envelope unflavored gelatin
3 large eggs, separated and at room temperature

2 large eggs, at room temperature
⅓ cup sugar
2 tablespoons Grand Marnier
½ cup whipping cream
1 can (11 ounces) mandarin oranges, well drained
1 cup whipping cream, whipped for garnish (optional)

SOUFFLÉ DISH

Six ½-cup individual soufflé dishes

Preheat oven to 350°. Tear pieces of regular strength aluminum foil long enough to go around soufflé dishes. Fold in half and wrap around outside of soufflé dishes, extending 1½ inches above rims. Tie in place.

Crumble cookies with your hands and place on baking sheet. Bake in the 350° oven until lightly browned, stirring once, about 10 minutes. Place in food processor fitted with metal blade and process into crumbs. Sprinkle 1 tablespoon of the crumbs into bottom of each soufflé dish. Reserve remaining crumbs for garnishing.

Stir together orange juice concentrate and ⅓ cup water in small bowl. Sprinkle gelatin over liquid and set aside to soften, about 5 minutes. Whisk egg yolks, 2 whole eggs and sugar in top of double boiler, until well blended. Set over simmering water and cook, stirring constantly, until mixture feels very hot to the touch and thickens slightly, about 10 minutes. Do not bring to a boil. Stir softened gelatin mixture into hot custard until dissolved. Remove from heat and immediately pour custard into medium-size bowl. Place bowl into bowl of ice water and stir occasionally until mixture thickens and begins to set. Remove from ice water and stir in Grand Marnier.

Meanwhile, beat egg whites in large bowl with electric mixer on low speed until foamy. Beat on high speed until soft, rounded peaks form. Pour over orange mixture; do not mix. Beat cream in same mixing bowl on low speed until thickened. Beat on medium speed until soft, not stiff, peaks form. Fold orange mixture and whites into cream until no streaks of white remain.

Reserve 6 mandarin slices for garnish and fold remainder into orange mixture. Spoon into prepared soufflé dishes. Refrigerate for several hours or until set. (*) Soufflés may be refrigerated, covered with plastic wrap, overnight, or they may be frozen, if desired. Defrost in refrigerator overnight. Before serving, gently remove collars by carefully pulling back the foil. Press reserved macaroon crumbs around outside edges of soufflés. Decorate top with rosettes of whipped cream, if desired, and reserved mandarin orange segments.

Serves 6.

Frosty Daiquiri Soufflé

This soufflé of tropical flavors—lemon, lime and rum—is unmolded and teamed up with the pretty spring colors of green pistachios and crystallized violets for a dreamy daiquiri dessert. This is pictured on page 168.

1 tablespoon plus 1½ teaspoons unflavored gelatin (1½ envelopes)
⅓ cup light rum
7 large eggs, separated and at room temperature
1½ cups sugar
⅓ cup lemon juice
⅓ cup lime juice
Grated peel of 1 lemon
Pinch salt

1½ cups plus 1 cup whipping cream
½ cup shelled pistachio nuts, very finely chopped
Crystallized violets and mint leaves for garnish (optional)

SOUFFLÉ DISH
1½-quart (6 cup) soufflé dish

Tear piece of regular strength aluminum foil 12 inches wide and long enough to wrap around soufflé dish. Fold in half lengthwise and place around dish, making a collar at least 3 inches above top of dish. Tie or clip it in place.

Sprinkle unflavored gelatin over rum in small bowl and set aside to soften, about 5 minutes. Beat egg yolks in small mixing bowl with electric mixer on medium speed until light and fluffy. Add sugar and beat until thick and pale yellow. Add lemon and lime juices, grated peel, and pinch of salt. Mix until well blended. Pour into top of double boiler and stir over simmering water until mixture thickens and feels very hot to the touch. Do not boil. Remove from heat and immediately stir gelatin mixture into hot custard until gelatin is dissolved. Pour custard into medium-size bowl. Place bowl in larger bowl of ice water and stir occasionally until mixture thickens to consistency of mayonnaise and begins to set. Remove from water.

Meanwhile, beat egg whites in large bowl with electric mixer on low speed until foamy. Beat on high speed until they form soft, rounded peaks. Pour on top of custard mixture; do not mix. Beat 1½ cups of the whipping cream in same bowl with mixer on low speed until thickened. Beat on medium speed until soft peaks form. Fold whites and custard into cream. Pour into soufflé dish. Smooth top with spatula. Refrigerate until firm and then cover with plastic wrap. (*) Soufflé may be refrigerated up to 2 days, or it may be frozen, if desired. Defrost in refrigerator overnight.

Before serving, carefully remove collar. Press pistachio nuts onto sides of soufflé. Whip remaining 1 cup cream in medium-size bowl until stiff peaks form. Spoon into pastry bag fitted with ¾- to 1-inch rosette or star tip. Pipe rosettes around top of soufflé. Decorate with crystallized violets and mint leaves, if desired.

Serves 8.

Fudgy Brownie Soufflé

If a hot chocolate brownie was so incredibly moist and fudgy that it could sensuously melt in your mouth, it would taste like a spoonful of this sinful soufflé.

1 recipe Creamy Vanilla Sauce for serving (see page 217)
1 tablespoon instant coffee powder or crystals
1 tablespoon Grand Marnier
¼ pound (1 stick) unsalted butter, at room temperature
2 squares (2 ounces) semisweet chocolate, chopped
2 squares (2 ounces) unsweetened chocolate, chopped
½ cup plus ½ cup sugar

4 large egg yolks, at room temperature
1 teaspoon vanilla
¼ cup all-purpose flour
5 large egg whites, at room temperature
⅛ teaspoon cream of tartar

SOUFFLÉ DISH

1½-quart (6 cup) soufflé dish

Make Creamy Vanilla Sauce as directed. Refrigerate, covered, until ready to use. Butter the soufflé dish.

Dissolve coffee in Grand Marnier in small cup. Melt butter and chocolates in heavy medium saucepan, over very low heat, stirring constantly until melted and smooth. Remove from heat. Stir coffee, ½ cup sugar, egg yolks and vanilla into chocolate mixture. Stir in flour. The mixture will look grainy and will not be smooth. (*)Chocolate mixture may be covered and held at room temperature at this point, up to 4 hours, if desired. Reheat slightly before using.

Preheat oven to 400°.

Beat egg whites in large bowl with electric mixer on low speed until foamy. Add cream of tartar and beat on high speed until soft, rounded peaks form. Gradually add remaining ½ cup sugar, a tablespoon at a time, beating until stiff but moist peaks form. Fold a quarter of the whites into the chocolate mixture to lighten it. Pour chocolate over whites. Carefully fold together until only a few streaks of white remain; do not overfold. Carefully pour into soufflé dish. (*) Soufflé may be held covered at room temperature up to 3 hours.

Place soufflé dish on baking sheet. Bake at 400° for 25 to 30 minutes or until soufflé is well puffed, but center is still moist. Serve immediately with Creamy Vanilla Sauce.

Serves 6.

Amaretto Soufflé

This recipe is everything a soufflé should be—light, puffed, and golden brown. It tastes like a warm, creamy amaretto custard.

2 tablespoons plus ⅓ cup sugar
1½ cups milk
3 large egg yolks, at room
    temperature
½ teaspoon almond extract
2 tablespoons cornstarch
¼ cup amaretto
2 tablespoons dark rum
8 large egg whites, at room
    temperature
⅛ teaspoon cream of tartar

SOUFFLÉ DISH
1½-quart (6 cup) soufflé dish

Butter soufflé dish. Sprinkle inside with 2 tablespoons sugar, tilting to coat the dish and shaking out excess.

Bring milk to a simmer in heavy medium-size saucepan. Beat egg yolks, ⅓ cup sugar and almond extract in small bowl with electric mixer on medium speed until thick and lemon colored, about 3 minutes. Mix in cornstarch on low speed. Add hot milk in a stream, mixing constantly. Pour custard into saucepan in which milk was heated. Bring to a boil over moderate heat, stirring and whisking constantly until mixture is very thick and smooth. The custard may lump slightly as it comes to a boil, but whisking will smooth it out. Immediately transfer custard to a bowl and whisk in amaretto and rum. Place a piece of plastic wrap directly on surface to keep skin from forming. Cool to room temperature. (*) Custard may be prepared up to 4 hours ahead and held at room temperature, if desired.

Preheat oven to 375°.

Beat egg whites in large bowl with electric mixer on low speed until frothy. Add cream of tartar and beat on high speed until whites form soft, rounded peaks. Stir custard until smooth. Stir quarter of whites into custard to lighten it. Then gently fold custard into remaining whites until a few streaks of white remain; do not overfold. Carefully pour mixture into prepared soufflé dish.

Place soufflé dish on baking sheet. Bake in the 375° oven for 35 minutes or until puffed and browned. The center will be soft. Remove from oven and serve immediately.

Serves 6.

Hot Raspberry Soufflé

High and glorious, this soufflé is smooth, creamy and bursting with pure raspberry flavor.

SOUFFLÉ DISH
1½-quart (6 cup) soufflé dish

2 packages (10 ounces each) frozen raspberries in syrup, thawed
1 tablespoon lemon juice
1 cup milk
3 large egg yolks, at room temperature
¼ cup granulated sugar

½ teaspoon vanilla
2 tablespoons cornstarch
8 large egg whites, at room temperature
⅛ teaspoon cream of tartar
Powdered sugar for sprinkling on top

Butter soufflé dish.

Place strainer over medium-size saucepan. Press raspberries through strainer, scraping the bottom often with wooden spoon; discard seeds. Bring to a boil over high heat. Cook until syrup is reduced by about half to measure 1 cup, about 8 minutes. Set aside and cool to room temperature. Stir in lemon juice.

Bring milk to a simmer in heavy medium-size saucepan. Beat egg yolks, ¼ cup sugar and vanilla in small mixing bowl with electric mixer on medium speed, until thick and light colored, about 3 minutes. Mix in cornstarch on low speed. Add hot milk in a stream, mixing constantly. Pour custard into saucepan in which milk was heated. Bring to a boil over moderate heat, stirring and whisking constantly, until very thick and smooth. Do not be concerned if it lumps slightly, as whisking will smooth it out. Transfer custard to a bowl and stir in raspberry purée. Place piece of plastic wrap directly on surface to keep skin from forming. Cool to room temperature. (*) Custard may be prepared several hours ahead to this point.

Preheat oven to 375°. Beat egg whites in large bowl with electric mixer on low speed until frothy. Add cream of tartar and beat on high speed until whites form soft, rounded peaks. Stir quarter of the whites into the custard to lighten it. Then gently fold custard into

1 *Push raspberries through a medium-size (not fine) strainer using a wooden spoon. Scrape bottom of the strainer often.*

2 *Cook custard until very thick, then stir in raspberry purée.*

3 *Gently fold a small amount of whites into custard to lighten it, and then gently fold custard into whites.*

4 *Completed soufflé dusted with powdered sugar.*

whites just until slight streaks of white remain. Do not overfold. Carefully pour mixture into prepared soufflé dish.

Place soufflé dish on baking sheet. Bake in the 375° oven for 30 minutes or until center jiggles slightly and soufflé is well puffed and brown. Sprinkle top with powdered sugar and serve immediately.

Serves 6.

Candlelight Chocolate Soufflés for Two

This recipe is for lovers. It makes two exquisite soufflés that should be savored by candlelight after a romantic dinner à deux.

2 tablespoons milk
1 teaspoon cornstarch
1 square (1 ounce) semisweet chocolate, chopped
2 teaspoons instant coffee dissolved in 1 tablespoon boiling water
1 teaspoon Grand Marnier
1 tablespoon plus 1 teaspoon sugar
1 teaspoon unsalted butter

1 large egg yolk, at room temperature
2 large egg whites, at room temperature
Dash cream of tartar
½ cup whipping cream, lightly whipped for serving

SOUFFLÉ DISH
Two ¾-cup soufflé dishes

Preheat oven to 400°. Butter soufflé dishes. Sprinkle with sugar, tilting to coat and shaking out any excess.

Mix milk and cornstarch in heavy, very small saucepan. Place over moderate heat and cook, stirring constantly, until mixture comes to a boil and thickens. Remove from heat and stir in chocolate until melted. Whisk in coffee and Grand Marnier until blended. Whisk in 1 tablespoon sugar, butter and egg yolk until smooth. (*) Chocolate mixture may be covered and held several hours at room temperature, if desired. Reheat slightly before using.

Beat egg whites in small bowl on low speed until foamy. Add cream of tartar and beat on high speed until soft peaks form. Add 1 teaspoon sugar and continue beating until whites form firm but still very moist peaks. Pour chocolate mixture over whites and fold together quickly and lightly until only a few streaks of white remain. Do not overmix. Spoon into prepared soufflé dishes to about ¼ inch from the top.

Place on baking sheet and bake in the 400° oven for 10 minutes or until soufflés have risen well above rim of dishes and shake slightly when jiggled. Serve immediately with softly whipped cream.

Serves 2.

NOTE
The recipe may be doubled, if desired.

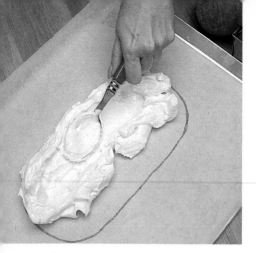

1 *Spread meringue over pattern, pushing up sides of meringue with the back of a spoon to make a nest.*

2 *Pipe rosettes around sides.*

3 *Completed fruit-filled meringue.*

Heavenly Fruit-Filled Meringue

Fill a crunchy meringue shell with layers of sliced bananas, strawberries, peaches, kiwis and mounds of whipped cream. This beautiful combination is my interpretation of a Pavlova, a meringue dessert named for the Russian ballerina. It probably receives as many rave reviews and "bravos" as she once did. Since the meringue is baked free-form on a baking sheet, you can shape it to fit any of your platters. It is best to make this type of meringue on a humidity-free day, as it tends to absorb moisture from the air. (This is pictured on page 224.)

BAKING PAN
Baking sheet

MERINGUE

MERINGUE

6 large egg whites, at room
   temperature
1/8 teaspoon salt
1/2 teaspoon cream of tartar
1 1/2 cups superfine sugar

FILLING

3 to 4 ripe peaches (about 1 1/2
   pounds)
2 cups whipping cream
2 bananas, peeled and sliced
2 to 3 kiwis, peeled and sliced
1 pint box strawberries, hulled and
   sliced
1 pint box strawberries, whole and
   hulled

MERINGUE

Preheat oven to 225°. Place a dab of shortening in each of the corners of the baking sheet. Line with parchment or brown paper bag cut to fit. Draw 10-inch circle or oval on paper. Grease the circle.

Beat egg whites until foamy in large bowl with electric mixer on low speed. Add salt and cream of tartar. Beat on high speed until soft peaks form. Slowly add sugar, 2 tablespoons at a time, beating continuously for about 10 minutes or until meringue forms very stiff peaks and is shiny and glossy like marshmallow cream.

Spread meringue evenly over the pattern, building up sides with a spoon to make a nest. If desired, spoon about one quarter of the meringue into a pastry bag fitted with a 1/2-inch rosette or star tip. Pipe rosettes around sides of meringue nest, as pictured. Bake in the 225° oven for 2 hours or until very dry and crisp, but not brown. Turn off oven and let meringue dry out in oven with door closed for several hours or overnight. (*) Meringue may be kept at room temperature, uncovered, overnight, if desired.

FILLING

To assemble the dessert: plunge the peaches into a pot full of boiling water to cover for 20 seconds. Run under cold water. When cool enough to handle, peel, pit and slice. Whip cream in medium-size bowl with electric mixer on low speed until thickened. Beat on medium speed until soft peaks form. Place meringue on serving platter. Spread a thin layer of whipped cream over meringue. Arrange banana slices overlapping on cream. Alternate layers of cream and fruit, making each layer smaller in diameter than the previous one, as pictured. Decorate the top with rosettes or dollops of whipped cream. Refrigerate for at least 2 hours before serving.

Serves 10.

Toffee-Crunch Meringue Torte

Three layers of crunchy meringue make a luscious dessert when sandwiched with whipped cream studded with pieces of store-bought chocolate and nut-coated toffee candy.

6 large egg whites, at room temperature
1 teaspoon vanilla
½ teaspoon cream of tartar
⅛ teaspoon salt

2 cups sugar
8 ounces English Toffee, Almond Roca or Heath bars
2 cups whipping cream

BAKING PAN
2 baking sheets

Preheat oven to 250°. If possible, use 2 ovens and bake in the center of each. If not, place oven racks in upper and lower third of oven. Place dab of shortening in each of the corners of baking sheets. Cover with parchment paper or brown paper bag, cut to fit. Draw two 8-inch circles on each. Grease the circles.

Beat egg whites in large mixing bowl with electric mixer at low speed until frothy. Add vanilla, cream of tartar and salt and beat on high speed until whites form soft, rounded peaks. Increase speed to high and gradually add sugar, 1 tablespoon at a time, beating until meringue forms very stiff peaks and is shiny and glossy like marshmallow cream.

Divide meringue among the 4 circles; spread evenly to inside edge of circle. Bake in the 250° oven for 1 hour or until meringues feel firm. If baking both sheets in one oven, reverse their positions after 30 minutes. Turn off heat and let meringues dry out in oven with door closed for at least 2 hours. (*) Meringues may be stored at room temperature, covered with plastic wrap, overnight, if desired.

Place half the candy in food processor fitted with metal blade and process until chopped into small pieces. Repeat with remaining candy. Reserve ¼ cup chopped candy for garnish. Whip cream in medium-size bowl with electric mixer on low speed until thickened. Beat on medium speed until soft peaks form. Fold candy into whipped cream. Place one meringue disc on serving plate. Spread a layer of cream on top and continue with remaining meringues and cream, ending with a meringue disc on top. Frost top and sides with cream, covering torte completely. Refrigerate uncovered for at least 10 to 12 hours before serving so the meringues soften. (*) Torte may be refrigerated overnight, if desired.

Before serving, sprinkle top of torte with reserved candy. Cut into wedges with serrated knife to serve.

Serves 10 to 12.

Raspberry Floating Islands

Floating islands are actually egg-shaped meringues sailing on a sea of vanilla custard. A much prettier version is created by adding raspberry purée to the meringues. Their texture remains light and airy and they turn a delicate blushing pink. This is pictured on page 168.

1 recipe Vanilla Custard Sauce (see page 216)
2 packages (10 ounces) frozen raspberries in syrup, thawed
5 large egg whites, at room temperature
⅛ teaspoon cream of tartar
½ cup sugar

SERVING DISH
8-cup shallow rimmed dish or bowl, preferably glass

Make Vanilla Custard Sauce as directed. Refrigerate, covered, until ready to use.

Place raspberries and their syrup in strainer placed over bowl. Press raspberries through strainer, discarding the seeds, as pictured on page 176. Measure 1 cup of the purée and place in medium-size saucepan. Reserve remaining purée in refrigerator for garnishing. Bring purée to a boil over high heat, stirring occasionally, until reduced to ⅔ cup, about 5 minutes. Cool to room temperature. (*) Purée may be refrigerated, covered, for several days, if desired.

Beat egg whites in large bowl with electric mixer on low speed, until foamy. Add cream of tartar and beat on high speed until soft, rounded peaks form. Add sugar, 1 tablespoon at a time, beating continuously until meringue forms very stiff peaks and is shiny and glossy like marshmallow cream. Fold in raspberry purée.

As close to serving time as possible, fill a large skillet with about 1 inch of water. Bring to a simmer over moderate heat. Using an oval or round ice cream scoop or 2 soup spoons, form scoops of meringue and drop them into gently bubbling water. Poach for about 1 minute or until top looks set. Remove with slotted spoon to paper towels to drain. Repeat until all the meringue is used. You will have about 12 to 14 scoops.

To assemble, pour custard sauce into shallow rimmed dish. Gently set raspberry eggs on top. Drizzle ribbons of reserved raspberry purée over all.

Serves 6.

Crunchy Meringue Ice Cream Sandwich with Hot Fudge Sauce

Chopped semisweet chocolate, pecans and vanilla cookies flavor meringue rounds that are sandwiched with your favorite ice cream. Serve in wedges with heaping spoonfuls of thick hot fudge sauce. The sandwich keeps beautifully in the freezer for last-minute guests.

1 quart chocolate or vanilla ice cream, softened slightly
2 squares (2 ounces) semisweet chocolate
20 shortbread or vanilla wafer cookies
¾ cup shelled pecans (about 3 ounces)
4 large egg whites, at room temperature
⅛ teaspoon cream of tartar

1½ cups powdered sugar
½ teaspoon vanilla
1 recipe Hot Chocolate Fudge Sauce (see page 220) or Hot Bittersweet Fudge Sauce (see page 221)

MOLD AND BAKING PAN

9-inch round cake pan
2 baking sheets

Line cake pan with foil. Spread softened ice cream in pan and smooth top with a spatula. Cover with foil and freeze until firm, preferably overnight or for several days, if desired.

Preheat oven to 350°. If possible, use 2 ovens and bake 1 meringue in center of each. If not, place oven racks in upper and lower third of oven. Place a dab of shortening in each of the corners of each of the baking sheets. Line them with parchment or foil. Trace 9-inch circle in the center of each, using cake pan as a guide. Grease circles. Chop chocolate in food processor fitted with metal blade into coarse chunks. Add cookies and pecans and process until finely chopped; set aside.

Beat egg whites in large bowl with electric mixer on low speed until foamy. Add cream of tartar and beat on high speed until soft peaks form. Gradually add powdered sugar, a tablespoon at a time, beating until meringue forms very stiff peaks and is shiny and glossy like marshmallow cream. Beat in vanilla. Fold in chocolate-nut mixture. Divide meringue in half and spread half on each circle, being careful to stay within the edges. Smooth tops with a spatula. Bake in the 350° oven for 15 to 20 minutes or until lightly browned. If baking in one oven, reverse positions after 8 minutes. Remove from oven and cool 10 minutes. While still slightly warm, loosen edges with spatula, leaving meringues on baking sheets until completely cool.

To assemble, remove 1 meringue layer from paper and place top-side up on cutting board. Remove foil and ice cream from pan, and remove foil from ice cream. Place ice cream on meringue. Top with second meringue top-side up. Wrap in heavy foil and freeze. (*) The sandwich may be frozen up to 1 month, if desired.

Make sauce as directed. Remove ice cream sandwich from freezer 10 to 15 minutes before serving to soften slightly. Cut into wedges and serve with sauce.

Serves 8 to 10.

Chocolate Meringue Butterflies

These whimsical works of art literally look too pretty to eat. A crunchy chocolate meringue is piped into sculptured butterflies. Chocolate mousse becomes an edible pedestal.

BAKING PAN
2 baking sheets

3 large egg whites, at room temperature
⅛ teaspoon salt
⅛ teaspoon cream of tartar
¾ cup sugar
6 tablespoons unsweetened cocoa powder

1 recipe Chocolate Mocha Mousse (see page 147)
½ cup whipping cream, whipped to stiff peaks

Preheat oven to 250°. Using the photos as guides, draw a pair of wings 4½ inches high and 2 inches wide on a piece of cardboard. Cut them out and trace them on parchment or wax paper cut to fit two baking sheets. Place dab of shortening in each of the corners of the baking sheets. Line baking sheets with the paper writing-side down. Grease paper and set aside.

Beat egg whites in large mixing bowl with electric mixer on low speed until foamy. Add salt and cream of tartar and beat on high speed until soft peaks form. Gradually add sugar, 1 tablespoon at a time, beating until meringue forms very stiff peaks, shiny and glossy like marshmallow cream. Reduce speed to low and add cocoa, a tablespoon at a time, mixing until blended.

Fit pastry bag with a ¼-inch writing tip. Fill bag with chocolate meringue and pipe out wings following the pattern, about ¼ inch wide. Pipe out bodies about 3 inches long and ⅜ inch thick, as pictured.

Bake in the 250° oven for 30 to 40 minutes, or until the top of the meringue feels firm but the inside feels soft. Remove from the oven and cool completely on baking sheet. When cool and firm, remove by gently pulling back on paper. (*) Butterflies may be stored at room temperature in an airtight container for several days, or they may be frozen, if desired. Defrost, uncovered, at room temperature.

As close to serving time as possible, place a scoop of mousse in center of each dessert plate. Prop butterfly body in center of mousse. Slant wings into each side of mousse, as pictured. Place whipping cream in pastry bag fitted with small star tip. Pipe 3 stars of cream on each side of body. Refrigerate until serving time, but not more than 2 hours.

Makes about 8 servings.

1 *Trace pairs of wings onto paper. Turn paper over, grease it, then pipe chocolate meringue around outline of wings about ¼ inch thick.*

2 *Pipe bodies about 3 inches long and about ⅜ inch thick.*

3 *Completed butterflies on a scoop of Chocolate Mocha Mousse.*

Hazelnut Meringue Torte with Apricot Cream

A slightly sweet, dried apricot cream filling is separated by two layers of delicate hazelnut meringue. This is a lovely dessert when you want something not too rich, but very impressive. This is pictured on page 168 with an optional garnish of whipped cream rosettes and candied dried apricot halves.

FILLING
4 ounces dried apricots
¼ cup granulated sugar
1 tablespoon lemon juice
1 cup whipping cream
2 tablespoons powdered sugar

MERINGUES
2 cups hazelnuts or filberts (about 8 ounces)
6 large egg whites, at room temperature
1½ cups sugar
½ teaspoon white vinegar
1½ teaspoons vanilla

BAKING PANS
Two 9-inch round cake pans

FILLING

Cover the apricots with water in small saucepan. Bring to a boil. Cover and remove from heat. Let stand several hours or overnight to soften.

Pour off all but 3 to 4 tablespoons of the water in which the apricots were soaking. Add the sugar and lemon juice. Simmer, covered, about 30 minutes or until very soft. Mash with fork or potato masher until mixture is fairly smooth. Set aside and cool completely. Beat cream with powdered sugar in medium-size bowl with electric mixer on low speed until thickened. Beat on medium speed until stiff. Fold apricot mixture into cream until blended.
(*) Filling may be refrigerated up to 4 days, or it may be frozen, if desired. Defrost at room temperature.

MERINGUES

Preheat oven to 375°. Grease and flour cake pans, shaking out excess.

Grind nuts in food processor fitted with metal blade until finely ground. Spread on baking sheet. Bake in the 375° oven for 8 to 10 minutes or until lightly browned, stirring once or twice. Watch carefully so they do not burn. Let the nuts cool while you prepare the meringue. Leave oven on 375°.

To make meringues, beat egg whites in a large bowl with electric mixer on low speed until foamy. Increase speed to high and beat until soft peaks form. Gradually add sugar, a tablespoon at a time, beating until meringue forms very stiff peaks and is shiny and glossy like marshmallow cream. Beat in vinegar and vanilla. Gently fold in ground hazelnuts until thoroughly combined. Divide meringue evenly between prepared pans, smoothing tops with a spatula.

Bake in 375° oven for 25 to 30 minutes or until lightly browned and tops are firm; do not overbake. Cool for 10 minutes. Turn meringues out of pans onto wire racks to cool. (*) Meringues may be held at room temperature overnight, if desired. Store on plates, loosely covered with plastic wrap.

Up to 8 hours before serving, assemble torte. Place 1 meringue layer on serving plate. Spread with about one fourth of the apricot cream. Top with second meringue layer. Spread top and sides with remaining cream. Refrigerate until serving time, but not more than 8 hours.

Serves 8 to 10.

VARIATION
Two cups shelled pecans (8 ounces) can be substituted for the hazelnuts, if desired.

Coffee Meringues with Hazelnut Cream

Reminiscent of tortes found in the finest European patisseries, this one combines coffee-flavored meringues with a thick filling of toasted hazelnut cream.

MERINGUES

3 large egg whites, at room
   temperature
2 teaspoons instant coffee powder
   or crystals
⅛ teaspoon cream of tartar
¾ cup granulated sugar

FILLING

1 cup hazelnuts or filberts (about 4
   ounces)
1½ cups whipping cream
3 tablespoons powdered sugar

BAKING PAN

2 baking sheets

Preheat oven to 225°. Place dab of shortening in each corner of baking sheets. Line with parchment or brown paper bag cut to fit. Using an 8-inch cake pan as a guide, draw one 8-inch circle on each sheet and grease circles.

Place egg whites and coffee in large bowl. Let stand 5 minutes for coffee to soften. Beat whites with electric mixer on low speed, until foamy. Add cream of tartar and beat on high speed until soft peaks form. Gradually add granulated sugar 1 tablespoon at a time, beating continuously until meringue forms very stiff peaks and is glossy and shiny like marshmallow cream. Divide meringue between the 2 circles, spreading them evenly with a spatula. Bake at 225° for 2 hours or until meringues are firm and dry. They will have puffed up. Reverse pan positions after 1 hour. Turn off heat and let meringues dry out in oven with door closed for at least 1 hour. When thoroughly cooled, carefully remove from paper. (*) Meringues may be stored, loosely covered with plastic wrap, overnight.

FILLING

Preheat oven to 350°. Chop nuts in food processor with metal blade until finely ground. Place on baking sheet and bake for 7 to 10 minutes, stirring occasionally, until lightly browned. Cool to room temperature. Beat cream with electric mixer at low speed until thickened. Add powdered sugar, increase speed to high and beat until stiff peaks form. Fold in nuts.

Assemble torte 6 to 8 hours before serving. Place 1 meringue disc on serving plate, top-side up. Spread with one third hazelnut cream. Place second meringue layer on top. Press down gently. Do not be concerned if meringue breaks. Cover top and sides with remaining cream. Refrigerate, uncovered, 6 to 8 hours before serving to allow meringues to soften.

Serves 8.

Chocolate Meringue Shells

Light colored and crisp on the outside, these meringues are cocoa-brown and fudgy within. Although designed to be containers for ice cream or mousse, they are absolutely delicious eaten alone.

¼ cup powdered sugar
¼ cup unsweetened cocoa powder
3 large egg whites, at room temperature
⅛ teaspoon cream of tartar
¾ cup granulated sugar
Desired mousse or ice cream for filling

BAKING PAN
Baking sheet

Preheat oven to 225°. Place a dab of shortening in each corner of the baking sheet. Line it with parchment paper or brown paper bag cut to fit. Grease the paper. Sift powdered sugar and cocoa into bowl; set aside.

Beat egg whites in large bowl with electric mixer on low speed, until frothy. Add cream of tartar and beat on high speed until soft peaks form. Add granulated sugar 1 tablespoon at a time, beating continuously until meringue forms stiff peaks and is glossy and shiny like marshmallow cream. Reduce mixer to low speed and gradually beat in cocoa mixture, scraping down sides of bowl and mixing until incorporated.

Drop meringue by large spoonfuls into six 3-inch mounds on prepared baking sheet. Make well with back of spoon in the center of each mound, pushing up sides to form a nest. Bake in the 225° oven for 1 hour and 30 minutes. They will still feel soft, but will firm up as they cool. Turn oven off and let meringues cool in oven with door closed for 2 hours. (*) Shells may be kept at room temperature, uncovered, overnight, or they may be frozen in an airtight container. Defrost at room temperature.

Before serving, fill with mousse or ice cream.

Makes 6 shells.

Meringue Swans

If you really want to make a splash at your next dinner party, make these elegant swans for dessert. They are much easier to prepare than they look.

6 large egg whites, at room
   temperature
½ teaspoon cream of tartar
1½ cups superfine sugar
1 recipe Satin Strawberry Sauce
   (see page 218)
1 quart strawberry ice cream

BAKING PAN
2 or 3 baking sheets

Place a dab of shortening in each corner of the baking sheets. Line the sheets with parchment or a brown paper bag cut to fit. Using the photos as guides, draw a swan's neck about 4 inches high and a pair of wings about 2½ inches long on cardboard. Cut them out. Trace 8 necks and 7 pairs of wings on the paper (the extras allow for breakage), leaving room in between for expansion. Grease the paper. On separate baking sheet, draw 6 ovals 3½ inches long and 2 inches wide for the bodies. Grease paper.

Preheat oven to 225°. Beat egg whites in large bowl with electric mixer on low speed until foamy. Add cream of tartar and beat until soft peaks form. Increase speed to high and gradually add sugar 1 tablespoon at a time, beating continuously until whites hold stiff, glossy peaks and are shiny like marshmallow cream.

Fit pastry bag with a ⅝-inch rose tip. Fill with about half the meringue. Pipe out necks and right and left wings, as pictured. If the meringue becomes too soft to pipe, it may be returned to the mixing bowl and beaten until stiff.

Bake in the 225° oven for 30 minutes or until dry on top. If you have used 2 baking sheets, rotate their position in the oven halfway through the baking time. Remove from oven and cool completely.

Meanwhile, spoon mounds of meringue onto each oval. Make a well in the center using a large spoon. Swirl one end slightly upward for the tail, as pictured. Bake in center of oven for 60 minutes or until crisp and dry. Turn oven off and cool in oven for 1 hour. Remove from oven and cool to room temperature.

Make Satin Strawberry Sauce as directed. Refrigerate until serving time. (*) Swan bodies, necks and wings may be kept, uncovered, at room temperature overnight, or they may be frozen in an airtight container. Defrost at room temperature.

Up to 8 hours before serving, place a scoop of strawberry ice cream in each swan's body. Insert neck and wings, as pictured. Freeze, uncovered, until ready to serve.

To serve, spoon enough strawberry sauce on each dessert plate to thickly cover bottom of plate. Place swan in center of plate. Pass remaining sauce.

Makes 6 swans.

1 *Draw neck and wings on paper-lined baking sheet. Turn over paper and grease it. Using a ⅝-inch rose tip, pipe out necks and right and left wings.*

2 *Draw 6 bodies on second baking sheet. Turn over paper and grease it. Spoon a mound of meringue onto each oval, making a nest with the back of a spoon. Swirl up one end for the tail.*

3 *Meringue Swan filled with strawberry ice cream on Satin Strawberry Sauce.*

Fruits

POACHING FRUIT	• Although it's often thought that underripe fruit works best for poaching, I do not agree. It may soften properly, but the flavor will not be intense enough. Ideally, the fruit you select for poaching should be ripe, but firm. • It's important that poaching liquid maintain a constant simmer. If it boils, the fruit may fall apart. If the temperature is too low, the juices may escape from the fruit before it's tender.
FRUIT AS A CONTAINER	• When scooping out the pulp from a fruit with a thick skin or rind, always consider the possibility of using the rind as a serving dish. For example, a scooped out orange or lemon makes a lovely container for sorbet. A melon half can be scalloped and filled with fresh fruit.
FRUIT ICES	• To make an intensely flavored ice, use the ripest fruit possible. The fruit should be almost mushy. • Before leftover fruits begin to spoil, try combining them to make mixed fruit ices. First, purée the fruit. Then make a sugar syrup by boiling equal parts sugar and water until the sugar is dissovled. Add syrup to taste to the fruit purée and freeze in your ice cream machine.
TIPS	• An easy way to core pears and apples when they do not need to remain whole is to cut the fruit in half and then remove the seeds with a melon baller. • It is easier to cut firm fruit and melon with a serrated cutter, the type that is often sold for cutting French fries. It's quick, simple to do and the fruit will look attractive. Often, when you use a melon baller you are left with much wasted fruit.

CLOCKWISE FROM TOP: *Honeydew Melon Sherbet, page 213; Peach Melba, page 205; Strawberries in Crème de Grand Marnier, page 196.*

Tropical Fruit in Pineapple Rickshaw

Put your creativity to work on a fresh fruit dessert that is always the star of any buffet. Although it looks as if you spent hours making it, it's actually very easy to prepare. If there are more than 8 guests expected, slice extra fruit and arrange it around the base of the rickshaws. Garnish with fresh flowers.

2 large pineapples
1 papaya
1 large orange
2 bananas
1 kiwi
¼ cup chopped pitted dates
¼ cup shredded coconut
1 cup seedless red grapes
Flowers for garnish (optional)

Cut 1 pineapple in half lengthwise, cutting through the frond. With grapefruit knife, remove pineapple flesh from both halves. Reserve both shells as base for rickshaw. Remove core and cut pineapple into 1-inch cubes and place in large bowl.

Peel papaya, remove seeds and cut into cubes. Peel orange and cut segments into thirds. Remove seeds. Peel and slice bananas. Peel and chop kiwi. Place all fruit in bowl with pineapple. Stir in dates and coconut. Reserve 4 grapes for garnish and add rest to fruit mixture. Refrigerate, covered with plastic wrap, for several hours or until well chilled.

Place the second pineapple on its side on cutting board. Cut off frond and reserve. Slice crosswise right through the peel of the pineapple, making four ½-inch-thick round slices. These 4 slices are the wheels. They should be as close to the same size as possible. Place a wheel on each side of pineapple half, placing them about 2 inches from end where frond joins the pineapple, as pictured. Secure in place with half a wooden pick. Place a red grape over the exposed end of the wooden pick. Repeat with second pineapple half.

As close to serving time as possible, place rickshaws on large platter. Tilt rickshaws forward slightly by propping the backs with a piece of pineapple. Fill each rickshaw with fruit. Cut second pineapple frond in half lengthwise. Place frond leaf-side up over cut-side of frond on rickshaw, as pictured. Garnish with fresh flowers, if desired.

Serves 8.

1 *Scoop out fruit with a grapefruit knife.*

2 *Attach a slice of pineapple to each side for wheels.*

3 *Tropical Fruit in Pineapple Rickshaw.*

Cantaloupe Alaska

Here's an innovative update of baked Alaska that's wonderful for a light dinner or brunch. Soft ripe cantaloupes filled with scoops of vanilla ice cream are topped with swirls of golden-brown meringue.

2 pints vanilla ice cream
3 small ripe cantaloupes, chilled
4 large egg whites, at room
  temperature
¼ teaspoon cream of tartar
Dash salt
½ cup sugar

BAKING DISH

Oven-to-table platter

Scoop vanilla ice cream into 6 balls, each large enough to fit into cavity of half a melon. Place scoops on baking sheet covered with foil and freeze solid.

When ready to serve, preheat oven to 500°. Cut cantaloupes in half and scoop out seeds. Cut small slice off bottom so halves sit flat.

Beat egg whites in large bowl with electric mixer on low speed until foamy. Add cream of tartar and salt and beat on high speed until soft peaks form. Beat in sugar, 1 tablespoon at a time, until whites form stiff peaks, glossy and shiny like marshmallow cream. Place cantaloupes on ovenproof platter or board. Fill each half with scoop of ice cream. Spread meringue over cut side of melon and ice cream to completely cover the melon and ice cream, but leave rind uncovered. Make swirls and peaks in the meringue with back of a teaspoon.

Bake in the 500° oven for 3 to 5 minutes or until golden brown. Serve immediately.

Serves 6.

Minted-Melon Mélange

A colorful compote of mixed melon balls is delicately sweetened with just a little honey, orange liqueur and a hint of fresh mint.

About ⅛ watermelon
½ honeydew melon
½ large cantaloupe or crenshaw
  melon
1 cup fresh blueberries
⅓ cup Cointreau or other
  orange-flavored liqueur

3 tablespoons honey
1 tablespoon chopped fresh mint

SERVING DISH

1½- to 2-quart glass bowl or
  compote

Remove seeds from melons. Scoop each melon with melon baller into balls. You should have about 2 cups of each. Place in glass bowl or compote dish. Add blueberries. Stir together orange liqueur and honey in small bowl. Pour over fruits and toss well. Refrigerate for 2 to 3 hours. Before serving, sprinkle with mint and toss lightly.

Serves 4 to 6.

Macaroon-Filled Apricots

Fresh golden apricot halves are topped with mounds of crumbled macaroons, toasted pecans, sweet butter and cinnamon. It tastes exactly like eating a rich cookie with ripe fruit and makes a beautiful addition to a fresh fruit platter.

⅔ **cup chopped pecans (about 3 ounces)**
6 **ounces soft coconut macaroon cookies (about 1 cup crumbs)**
3 **tablespoons unsalted butter, melted**
⅛ **teaspoon ground cinnamon**
⅛ **teaspoon ground nutmeg**
12 **whole fresh apricots, halved and pits removed**

BAKING PAN
Baking sheet

Preheat oven to 350°. Toast pecans on baking sheet, stirring occasionally, until lightly browned, about 10 minutes. Cool.

Chop macaroons into fine crumbs in food processor fitted with metal blade. Add toasted nuts, butter, cinnamon and nutmeg. Process with pulses until well combined.

Place apricots cut-side up on platter. Spoon cookie mixture with a teaspoon into hollows, mounding slightly. Cover and refrigerate until chilled. (*) Filled apricots may be refrigerated overnight, tightly covered.

Makes 24 halves.

Hawaiian Fruit in Honey-Nut Yogurt

Every premium tropical flavor is used to create this ultra-refreshing honey-yogurt fruit salad.

1 *orange*
½ *pineapple, cut into cubes (about 2 cups)*
1 *large papaya, peeled, seeded and cut into cubes (about 2 cups)*
1 *large mango, peeled, pitted and sliced*

1 *tablespoon honey*
¾ *cup plain yogurt*
1 *tablespoon chopped fresh mint*
2 *bananas*
¼ *cup chopped macadamia nuts*
¼ *cup shredded coconut*

Peel orange and divide into segments; seed and cut each in half. Place in large bowl with pineapple, papaya and mango. Cover and refrigerate until well chilled. Stir together the honey, yogurt and mint in small bowl. Cover and chill.

Before serving, peel and slice bananas. Stir into mixed fruit. Toss gently with yogurt dressing. Spoon into dessert dishes and top with nuts and coconut.

Serves 6.

Strawberries in Crème de Grand Marnier

Crème de Grand Marnier, an easily prepared homemade liqueur, keeps in the refrigerator for more than a month. When spooned over fresh fruit, it tastes as if you spent hours in the kitchen making an elegant Grand Marnier custard sauce. This is pictured on page 190.

*1 recipe Crème de Grand Marnier
  (see page 223)
2 pint boxes strawberries*

At least 1 day before serving, make Crème de Grand Marnier as directed.

Hull strawberries and cut in half if large. Before serving, divide berries among 4 to 6 shallow dessert dishes, wine goblets or champagne glasses. Spoon 2 tablespoons Crème de Grand Marnier over each serving.

Serves 4 to 6.

VARIATION
One pint raspberries may be substituted for the strawberries.

Chocolate-Nougat Fondue with Fresh Fruit

I use Toblerone chocolate when making fondue because it doesn't burn as easily as many other chocolates. When this special candy bar melts, ribbons of white nougat swirl throughout the chocolate. The real surprise when tasting this fantastic fondue is the honey-almond crunch rippling through ultra-smooth chocolate.

*6 ounces Toblerone Swiss milk
  chocolate with almond and
  honey nougat, chopped
6 ounces Toblerone bittersweet
  chocolate with almond and
  honey nougat, chopped
½ to 1 cup whipping cream
2 tablespoons light rum, kirsch or
  Grand Marnier
Assorted fruit for dipping such as
  strawberries, pineapple chunks,
  banana slices, apple slices, pear
  slices, dried apricots, dried figs*

EQUIPMENT
Fondue pot or small chafing dish

Chop chocolate. Place in top of double boiler with ½ cup of the cream. Stir over low heat until chocolate is melted. Stir in liqueur.

Transfer mixture to fondue pot or small chafing dish. Keep warm. The chocolate should coat the fruit when it is dipped into it. If too thick, stir in additional cream as needed. (*) Leftover fondue may be refrigerated, covered, and reheated.

Serves 6.

Fresh Fruit Medley with Orange-Kirsch Marinade

The fresh flavors of ripe fruit are spirited with a splash of imported kirsch.

2 oranges
1 pineapple, cut into chunks
2 bananas, peeled and sliced
2 apples, peeled, cored and cut into pieces
1 medium-size melon such as cantaloupe, honeydew or crenshaw

3 tablespoons sugar
3 tablespoons orange juice
3 to 4 tablespoons kirsch, imported preferred

Grate peel of oranges into small bowl; set aside. Peel oranges and divide into segments. Seed and cut each segment into 2 or 3 pieces and place in large serving bowl. Add pineapple chunks, banana slices and apple. Cut melon in half and remove seeds. Scoop melon into balls or cut into pieces using serrated cutter. Add to fruit.

Stir sugar, orange juice and kirsch into grated orange peel. Pour over fruit and toss gently but thoroughly. Cover with plastic wrap and refrigerate until ready to serve or up to 6 hours.

Serves 8 to 10.

Fluffy Orange Dip

Mayonnaise is the secret ingredient which creates the cloud-like, marshmallow-cream texture in this orange-scented dip.

½ cup sugar
⅓ cup light corn syrup
2 large egg whites, at room temperature
⅓ cup mayonnaise
1 tablespoon vanilla
2 tablespoons orange juice
Grated peel of 2 oranges
Strawberries, peach slices, orange segments, apple slices or other desired fruits for dipping

Beat egg whites in medium-size bowl with electric mixer on low speed until foamy. Beat on hight speed until stiff peaks form. Combine sugar and corn syrup in small saucepan. Bring to a boil, stirring constantly. Add sugar syrup in a steady stream, beating on high speed. Fold in mayonnaise, vanilla, orange juice and peel until thoroughly combined. Refrigerate several hours before serving. Serve with desired fruits. (*) Dip may be refrigerated, well covered, up to 2 days. Or, it may be frozen and served directly from the freezer since it does not freeze solid.

Yields 1½ cups.

Fresh Raspberry Alaska

Raspberry sherbet is generously topped with fresh raspberries and drizzled with kirsch or framboise. Cloaked with clouds of airy meringue, it's baked until golden brown and served immediately. It's cold, hot, smooth and crunchy—a dazzling bouquet of taste sensations.

2 pints raspberry sherbet, softened slightly
3 large egg whites, at room temperature
Dash cream of tartar
½ cup granulated sugar
2 tablespoons kirsch or framboise
1½ pints fresh raspberries
Powdered sugar

BAKING DISH
9 x 1½-inch gratin dish or oven-to-table baking dish

Spread softened sherbet in baking dish, smoothing top with a spatula. Cover with foil and freeze until solid.

Preheat oven to 500°. Beat egg whites in large bowl with electric mixer on low speed until foamy. Add cream of tartar and beat on high speed until soft peaks form. Beat in sugar, 1 tablespoon at a time, until meringue forms smooth, glossy, stiff peaks. Beat in 1 tablespoon liqueur.

Remove sherbet from freezer. Top with layer of raspberries. Sprinkle with 1 tablespoon liqueur. Spread layer of meringue over top, sealing to edges. Using a pastry bag fitted with a rosette or star tip, pipe meringue into decorative rosettes or swirl into peaks with the back of a spoon. Sprinkle top with powdered sugar. Bake in the 500° oven for 3 to 5 minutes or until top is golden brown. Serve immediately.

Serves 6.

Orange-Glazed Oranges

Great for brunch or a light dessert, these peeled, pre-sliced oranges are served reassembled as whole ones. To heighten their natural flavor, they are drizzled with a soft orange-scented syrup flecked with glazed orange peel.

8 navel oranges
4 cups plus ½ cup water
2 cups sugar
¼ cup Grand Marnier or other orange-flavored liqueur
Fresh mint for garnish (optional)

EQUIPMENT
Candy thermometer

Remove orange part from skins of oranges (no white pith) with a vegetable peeler. Cut into very thin julienne strips. Place in small saucepan with 4 cups of water. Bring to a boil. Lower heat and simmer for 10 to 15 minutes or until peel is tender when bitten into. Drain, discarding the water. Rinse peel under cold water and dry on paper towels. Peel may be refrigerated overnight, if desired.

Cut away all the white membrane from the oranges with sharp paring knife. Slice each orange into 3 to 4 horizontal slices. Reshape each orange into its original shape. Place in serving dish or on a rimmed platter. Cover and refrigerate until chilled.

Combine sugar, ½ cup water and Grand Marnier in heavy medium-size saucepan. Bring to a boil over moderate heat, stirring once to help dissolve sugar. Increase heat to moderately high, insert candy thermometer and boil until syrup reaches 244°, or forms a firm ball. Immediately drop in the blanched orange peel and boil for 1 to 2 minutes or until syrup has thickened again. Orange peel should be glazed with the syrup. Remove from heat and transfer to heatproof bowl. (*) Syrup may be kept covered at room temperature for several hours, if desired.

Before serving, spoon syrup and glazed orange peel over oranges. Decorate with small sprigs of mint, if desired.

Serves 8.

Baby Papaya Birds

Your guests are sure to smile when they're served fruit or salad in these cute little birds.

½ papaya per serving plus 1 extra whole papaya for cutting
Currants
Sliced almonds
Leaves from pineapple top
Hawaiian Fruit in Honey-Nut Yogurt (see page 195) or desired fruit or salad

Remove seeds from papaya half. Cut a small slice off the bottom so the papaya will sit flat. Cut 2 slits in wide end for the tail, as pictured. Cut extra papaya in half and remove seeds. Cut out 1 ball with melon baller. Break wooden pick in half and place part of it into papaya ball. Attach ball with wooden pick to wide end of papaya for bird's head. Insert 1 currant on each side for eyes and 1 sliced almond for the beak. Make wings by attaching 2 to 3 pineapple leaves to each side, securing in place with half a wooden pick. (*) Bird may be refrigerated, covered with plastic wrap, up to 8 hours. Before serving, fill with Hawaiian Fruit in Honey-Nut Yogurt or desired fruit or salad.

Makes 1 bird.

1 *Cut 2 slits in the wide end for a tail. From the other half, scoop out a head with a melon baller.*

2 *Attach head, currant eyes, sliced almond beak and pineapple leaves on each side for wings.*

3 *Baby Papaya Birds filled with Hawaiian Fruit in Honey-Nut Yogurt.*

Cinnamon-Scented Winter Fruit

Winter fruits taste especially fresh when enlivened with a marinade of orange and apple juice, a cinnamon stick and a hint of cloves.

1 cup apple juice
1 cinnamon stick
4 whole cloves
½ cup fresh orange juice
2 tart green apples, peeled, cored and cut into ½-inch pieces
1 cup seedless red or green grapes, halved
3 navel oranges, peeled, sectioned and each section cut into 3 pieces
3 kiwis, peeled and cut into ½-inch slices

Combine apple juice, cinnamon stick and cloves in medium-size saucepan. Bring to a boil. Lower heat and simmer for 10 minutes. Remove from heat and cool. Stir in orange juice and strain into bowl. Stir in apples, grapes, oranges, and kiwis. (*) Fruit mixture may be refrigerated overnight.

Serves 4.

Fresh Figs in Vanilla-Lemon Syrup

Fresh figs, although scarce, can now be found more frequently in our supermarkets. They are truly a delicacy, especially when served in a sugar syrup fragrant with vanilla and lemon.

¾ cup water
¾ cup sugar
1 teaspoon vanilla
2 tablespoons lemon juice
1 teaspoon grated lemon peel
8 fresh figs

Combine water and sugar in medium-size saucepan. Bring to a boil, stirring to dissolve sugar. Lower heat and simmer for 3 minutes. Remove from heat and cool to room temperature. Stir in vanilla, lemon juice and peel.

Cut figs in half lengthwise and place in large bowl. Pour syrup over figs. Cover and refrigerate for 4 hours, but no more than 8 hours.

To serve, place 4 fig halves in each dessert bowl. Spoon a generous amount of syrup over top.

Serves 4.

Pears in Praline Cream

Softly poached pears are covered with fleecy meringue, whipped cream and crunchy candy-coated almonds.

1 cup plus ½ cup plus 1 tablespoon sugar
4 cups water
1 teaspoon vanilla
6 ripe but firm pears
Juice of 1 lemon
½ cup whole blanched almonds
1 large egg white, at room temperature
⅛ teaspoon cream of tartar
1 cup whipping cream

BAKING PAN
Baking sheet

In saucepan large enough for pears to stand upright, combine 1 cup of sugar and water. Bring to a boil, stirring occasionally. Lower heat and add vanilla. Cover and simmer 5 minutes.

Meanwhile, peel pears. Drop them into bowl of water to which juice of 1 lemon has been added to keep them from discoloring. Cut core out from bottom of pears with melon baller or small knife, leaving top and stem intact, as pictured on page 209. If necessary, cut small slice off bottom of each pear so it stands up straight. Stand pears in the sugar-water. Cover and simmer slowly until pears are tender when pierced with tip of small knife, about 15 to 30 minutes. Cooking time will depend on type, size and ripeness of pear. As pears test done, remove from syrup and cool.

(*) Pears may be returned to cool syrup and refrigerated several hours or overnight, if desired.

Grease baking sheet. To make praline, melt ½ cup sugar in medium-size saucepan over low heat, stirring once to help dissolve the sugar. Increase to moderate heat and cook without stirring until sugar turns a mahogany color. Remove from heat and immediately stir in almonds. Pour mixture onto baking sheet and set aside to cool and harden. When hard, place in food processor fitted with metal blade. Pulse on and off until chopped into very small pieces.
(*) Praline may be refrigerated in airtight container for several weeks, or it may be frozen. Defrost at room temperature.

Three to 4 hours before serving, beat egg white in small bowl with electric mixer on low speed until foamy. Add cream of tartar and beat on high speed until soft peaks form. Add 1 tablespoon sugar and beat at high speed until very stiff peaks form. Beat whipping cream in separate mixing bowl with electric mixer on low until thickened. Beat on medium speed until soft peaks form. Fold whites and 4 tablespoons of the praline into cream. Remove pears from syrup and blot dry. Spread cream onto outside of pears, covering all but the stem. Place on serving plate or individual dessert plates. Sprinkle remaining praline on cream. Refrigerate until serving time, up to 4 hours.

Serves 6.

Prunes in Port

These prunes are baked and marinated in a spiced mixture of cinnamon sticks, cloves, brown sugar, port and citrus slices. Keep some in the refrigerator for a family snack or serve them with crème fraîche to unexpected guests.

1½ pounds dried pitted prunes
1 cinnamon stick, broken into pieces
2 whole cloves
1 cup firmly packed dark brown sugar
½ vanilla bean, split and seeds scraped out
1 cup tawny port wine
½ lemon, thinly sliced
½ orange, thinly sliced
Crème Fraîche (see page 219) or sour cream for serving (optional)

BAKING DISH
13 x 9-inch glass baking dish

Place prunes in large heatproof bowl. Cover with boiling water and soak for several hours. If prunes float to top of bowl, place plate over them to keep them immersed in the water.

Preheat oven to 325°.

Drain prunes. Combine prunes in large bowl with cinnamon, cloves, brown sugar, vanilla, wine, lemon and orange slices. Pour mixture into baking dish.

Bake in the 325° oven, uncovered, for 40 minutes. (*) Prunes may be refrigerated up to 1 month, well covered.

Serve warm or chilled, topped with crème fraîche or sour cream, if desired.

Serves 6 to 8.

Lemon-Cream Peaches with Blueberry Sauce

Sweet, lightly poached peaches are topped with a creamy scoop of lemon-flavored cream cheese and spoonfuls of blueberry sauce.

4 ripe but firm peaches
1½ cups water
¼ cup plus ⅓ cup sugar
1 recipe Blueberry Sauce
  (see page 218)
6 ounces cream cheese, at room
  temperature
1½ teaspoons grated lemon peel
1 teaspoon lemon juice

Cut peaches in half and remove pits. In large skillet in which peaches fit in one layer, combine water and ¼ cup sugar. Bring to a boil, stirring once to help dissolve the sugar. Lower heat and simmer, covered, for 10 minutes. Place peaches cut side down in sugar syrup. Poach, uncovered, very gently for 5 to 8 minutes, turning over once with slotted spoon. Cooking time will depend upon ripeness of peaches. They should feel slightly soft when pierced with tip of small knife, but still remain firm. Do not overcook. Remove peaches from syrup with slotted spoon and place in shallow dish. When cool enough to handle, slip off peel. Cool syrup to room temperature and pour over peaches. Refrigerate, covered, for several hours or overnight.

Make Blueberry Sauce as directed. Refrigerate until ready to serve.

Beat cream cheese and ⅓ cup sugar in large bowl with electric mixer on medium speed or in food processor fitted with metal blade until blended. Mix in lemon peel and juice.

Before serving, remove peaches from syrup and blot lightly with paper towels. Spoon dollop of cream cheese mixture into each peach half. Place 2 halves in shallow dessert dish and top with spoonfuls of sauce.

Serves 4.

VARIATION
Nectarines may be substituted for the peaches.

Peach Melba

There's something wonderful about combining deep ruby-red, tart raspberries with sunshiny gold, sweet peaches. In this version of peach melba, the peaches are poached very lightly and peach ice cream is substituted for the more traditional vanilla. This is pictured on page 190.

6 ripe but firm peaches
2 cups water
½ cup sugar
Juice of ½ lemon
1 cup raspberry pancake syrup or
   ½ cup syrup from frozen
   raspberries
1 recipe Ruby-Red Raspberry Sauce
   (see page 218)
1 recipe Fresh Peach Ice Cream
   (see page 166) or 1 quart
   commercial peach ice cream
½ pint box fresh raspberries

Cut peaches in half and remove pits. In large saucepan or skillet in which peaches fit in one layer, combine water, sugar, lemon juice and syrup. Bring to a boil, stirring to dissolve the sugar. Lower heat and simmer, covered, for 10 minutes. Place peaches cut-side down in syrup and poach, uncovered, very gently for 5 to 8 minutes, turning over once with a slotted spoon. Cooking time will depend upon ripeness of peaches. They should feel slightly soft when pierced with tip of a knife, but still remain firm. Do not overcook. Remove peaches from syrup with slotted spoon. When cool enough to handle, slip off peel and place peaches in a bowl. Cool syrup to room temperature and pour over peaches. Refrigerate peaches, covered, for several hours or overnight.

Make Raspberry Sauce as directed. Refrigerate until ready to use.

To assemble dessert, place 1 or 2 peach halves in dessert goblet or wine glass. Place scoop of ice cream in center of each. Top with spoonfuls of raspberry sauce and garnish with fresh raspberries.

Serves 6.

Pineapple and Bananas Flambé

Fresh pineapple and bananas drenched in a warm caramel sauce are served over vanilla ice cream for a tasty impromptu dessert.

1 pineapple
4 bananas
4 tablespoons (½ stick) unsalted butter
1 cup firmly packed golden brown sugar

¼ cup Cointreau or other orange-flavored liqueur
¼ cup dark rum
1 quart vanilla ice cream

EQUIPMENT
Chafing dish or large skillet

Cut slice off each end of pineapple. Cut pineapple in half lengthwise. Remove fruit by cutting between rind and fruit with a grapefruit knife. Remove center core and discard. Cut pineapple into 1-inch pieces. Peel bananas. Slice in half lengthwise and crosswise, cutting each into 4 pieces.

Melt butter in large skillet or chafing dish. Add brown sugar and cook, stirring, until melted. Stir in pineapple and cook until heated through. Stir in Cointreau. Add bananas to pan and move them around gently until heated through. Heat rum in ladle or small pan until very hot; do not let boil. Ignite and pour over fruit. Shake pan until flames die out. Scoop vanilla ice cream into serving dishes. Spoon fruit and sauce over top.

Serves 8.

Baked Grapefruit Streusel

A sweet, buttery topping bakes like a cookie over grapefruit halves. It's super for breakfast or dessert.

2 whole firm grapefruit
⅓ cup all-purpose flour
¼ cup sugar
4 tablespoons (½ stick) unsalted butter, cold and cut into 4 pieces

BAKING PAN
Baking sheet

Preheat oven to 400°.

Cut grapefruit in half. Loosen sections by cutting around them with grapefruit knife. Place halves on baking sheet.

Mix flour, sugar and butter in medium-size bowl with pastry blender or 2 knives until mixture resembles coarse meal. Sprinkle each grapefruit half with ¼ cup streusel.

Bake in the 400° oven for 25 minutes or until streusel is lightly browned. Cool 15 to 20 minutes before serving.

Serves 4.

Spiced Fruit Compote

Mixed dried fruit is gently poached to soften before it's immersed in a lively orange-honey sauce splashed with brandy.

½ cup pine nuts
2 tablespoons plus 2 tablespoons sugar
3 packages (8 ounces each) mixed dried fruit
2 oranges
¼ cup honey
⅛ teaspoon ground allspice
⅛ teaspoon ground ginger
3 tablespoons brandy

BAKING EQUIPMENT
Baking sheet

Preheat oven to 300°. Place pine nuts on baking sheet. Sprinkle 2 tablespoons sugar over nuts. Bake until nuts are lightly browned, about 15 minutes. Set aside to cool. Reserve for garnish.

Remove pits from prunes, if desired. Place fruit in medium-size saucepan and add enough water to barely cover fruit. Simmer over moderate heat for 15 minutes or until fruit is soft but still holds its shape. Remove fruit with slotted spoon to a bowl. Reserve cooking liquid in saucepan.

Remove the outer orange peel (no white pith) with a vegetable peeler from the oranges. Cut into thin matchstick strips. Squeeze juice from oranges into reserved liquid in saucepan. Add orange strips, honey, allspice, ginger, brandy and 2 tablespoons sugar. Bring to a boil and cook until mixture thickens slightly and orange peel is tender, about 20 minutes. Cool to room temperature and pour over fruit. Cover and refrigerate. (*) Compote may be refrigerated, covered, up to 4 days.

Serve chilled or at room temperature. Before serving, sprinkle with toasted pine nuts.

Serves 6 to 8.

Truffle-Filled Chocolate-Glazed Pears

The glossy, dark chocolate glaze which coats these pears is spectacular, but the real delight comes when you cut into them. Hidden inside the juicy poached pear is a rich, creamy, chocolate truffle filling.

EQUIPMENT
Baking sheet

PEARS

1 cup sugar
4 cups water
3 tablespoons lemon juice plus juice of 1 lemon
2 cinnamon sticks
4 whole cloves
6 firm but ripe pears
Sprigs of mint for garnish (optional)

FILLING AND GLAZE

4 ounces German sweet chocolate, chopped
7 squares (7 ounces) semisweet chocolate, chopped
¼ pound (1 stick) unsalted butter
⅓ cup whipping cream, at room temperature

PEARS

In saucepan large enough for pears to stand upright, combine sugar, water, 3 tablespoons lemon juice, cinnamon sticks and cloves. Bring to a boil. Lower heat and simmer, covered, for 15 minutes. Stir to make sure sugar is dissolved.

Meanwhile, peel pears. Drop them into bowl of water to which juice of 1 lemon has been added to keep pears from discoloring. Scoop out core with a melon baller, from bottom of each pear, leaving stems intact and making 1-inch diameter cavity, as shown. If necessary, cut small slice off bottoms so they stand upright. Stand pears in simmering liquid and poach, covered, until pears are tender when pierced with tip of small knife, about 15 to 30 minutes. Cooking time will depend on the type, size and ripeness of pears. As each pear is done, remove with slotted spoon to baking sheet or wire rack to cool. Pears may be returned to cool poaching liquid and refrigerated several hours or overnight, if desired.

FILLING AND GLAZE

Several hours before serving, melt both chocolates and butter in top of double boiler over simmering water, stirring occasionally. When smooth, remove from heat. Measure ⅓ cup, remove to small bowl and stir in whipping cream. Cool this truffle mixture in refrigerator or over a bowl of ice water, stirring often, until mixture is thick enough to hold its shape. Leave the remaining chocolate mixture in double boiler over warm water.

Blot pears dry with paper towels. Line a baking sheet with waxed paper. Using a small spatula, fill cavities of pears with truffle mixture. Reheat chocolate mixture in top of double boiler over water until hot, if necessary. Holding pear carefully by its stem, dip each into glaze mixture, tilting pear and spooning glaze to cover pear completely. Place on wax paper lined baking sheet and refrigerate for several hours. Before serving, remove with spatula to serving plate. Garnish each pear with a sprig of mint, if desired.

Serves 6.

1 *Scoop out seeds of pear with a melon baller, leaving stem intact.*

2 *Fill poached pears with chocolate truffle filling.*

3 *Dip pears into glaze, tilting them and spooning glaze over until pears are completely coated.*

4 *Truffle-Filled Chocolate-Glazed Pears garnished with sprigs of mint.*

Sugar-and-Spice Baked Apples

Sugar and spice and literally everything nice is spooned inside these warm baked apples. When the brandy-scented cream cheese filling meets the hot fruit, it delectably begins to melt.

6 baking apples
6 teaspoons granulated sugar
1 package (8 ounces) cream cheese, at room temperature
5 tablespoons firmly packed golden brown sugar
1½ teaspoons brandy
¼ teaspoon ground cinnamon
Dash ground cloves
⅛ teaspoon ground nutmeg

BAKING DISH

11 x 7-inch baking dish

Preheat oven to 325°. Grease baking dish.

Core apples. Place in baking dish and sprinkle each with 1 teaspoon granulated sugar.

Bake in the 325° oven, basting occasionally, for 40 to 45 minutes or until tender. Remove from oven and cool 15 minutes.

Meanwhile, beat cream cheese, brown sugar, brandy, cinnamon, cloves and nutmeg in small bowl with electric mixer on medium speed until smooth. Spoon mixture into cavities of the warm apples. Serve immediately.

Serves 6.

Tangerine Slush

This simple-to-prepare ice is best served right from your ice cream maker so it stays soft and creamy. It possesses a very pure, tart, tangerine taste.

2 cans (6 ounces each) frozen tangerine juice concentrate, thawed
4 juice cans water
1 cup light corn syrup

EQUIPMENT

Ice cream machine

Stir all ingredients together in large pitcher or bowl. Refrigerate until well chilled. Pour into ice cream machine and freeze according to manufacturer's directions. Serve immediately.

Makes 1½ quarts.

Papaya-Yogurt Freeze

Wow! This tastes so creamy, you'll think you're eating rich ice cream. Actually, it's a lower calorie treat without one drop of cream. Papaya, egg white and yogurt whip up to a delectable dessert easily made in the food processor.

1 very ripe papaya
1 large egg white, at room temperature
⅓ cup sugar
2 teaspoons lemon juice
1 cup vanilla yogurt

Peel, seed and dice papaya into ½-inch cubes. You should have about 2 cups. Beat egg white, papaya, sugar and lemon juice in large bowl with electric mixer on medium speed until blended. Scrape down sides of bowl and beat on high speed for 5 minutes. Add yogurt and mix on low speed until blended. Pour into ice cube trays or bowl. Freeze, tightly covered, overnight.

Before serving, remove cubes from tray or cut frozen mixture into 2-inch chunks. Place in food processor fitted with metal blade and pulse on and off until mixture is broken up. Continue processing, stirring with a spatula once or twice, until mixture is smooth and consistency of sherbet. Serve immediately.

Makes ¾ pint. Serves 4.

Lemon Chardonnay Snow

The unique ingredient in this intermezzo is white wine. Although you can experiment with any white wine, Chardonnay adds a depth of flavor to this cool palate refresher. The texture is somewhere between cream and snow.

1 cup white wine
1 cup water
1 cup sugar
1 cup lemon juice (about 6 lemons)
2 large egg whites

EQUIPMENT
Ice cream machine

Mix wine, water and sugar in medium-size saucepan. Bring to a boil over moderate heat, stirring to dissolve sugar. Lower heat and simmer for 3 to 5 minutes or until sugar is dissolved. Cool to room temperature. Stir in lemon juice. Refrigerate until chilled. (*) Syrup may be refrigerated indefinitely.

Place syrup in ice cream machine and freeze 25 to 30 minutes or until slushy. Meanwhile, beat egg whites in medium-size bowl with electric mixer on low speed until frothy. Beat on high speed until stiff but glossy peaks form. With ice cream machine running, pour whites into wine mixture. Continue freezing according to manufacturer's directions until desired consistency. Serve immediately.

Makes 1 quart.

Piña Colada Sherbet

The delightfully creamy texture of this pineapple-rum flavored sherbet comes from adding a can of cream of coconut. This sherbet is a spoonable version of the drink.

1½ cups sugar
3 cups water
1 medium-size fresh ripe pineapple
1 can (6 ounces) frozen pineapple
    concentrate, thawed but cold
1 can (8½ ounces) cream of coconut
¼ cup light rum

EQUIPMENT

Ice cream machine

Combine sugar and water in medium-size saucepan. Bring to a boil, stirring to dissolve sugar. Lower heat and simmer for 5 minutes or until sugar is dissolved. Cool to room temperature and refrigerate until cold. (*)Syrup may be refrigerated indefinitely.

Cut pineapple in half. Remove fruit by cutting between rind and fruit with a grapefruit knife. Remove center core and discard. Cut pineapple into chunks and place in food processor fitted with metal blade. Pulse on and off 5 to 10 times or until mixture is puréed and resembles slush. You should have about 1½ cups. Transfer to a large bowl or pitcher and stir in chilled sugar syrup, pineapple juice concentrate, cream of coconut and light rum. Pour into ice cream machine and freeze according to manufacturer's directions. Serve immediately or freeze up to 1 week.

Makes 1½ quarts.

Fresh Strawberry Ice

This strawberry-red, thirst-quenching ice blends fresh berries with a simple sugar syrup and tangy lemon juice.

⅔ cup sugar
⅔ cup water
2 pints fresh strawberries, hulled
¼ cup lemon juice

EQUIPMENT

Ice cream machine

Combine sugar and water in medium-size saucepan. Bring to a boil, stirring to help dissolve the sugar. Lower heat and simmer for 3 to 5 minutes or until sugar is dissolved. Cool to room temperature and refrigerate until cold. (*) Syrup may be refrigerated indefinitely.

Process strawberries in food processor fitted with metal blade until puréed. You should have about 3 cups. Stir in sugar syrup and lemon juice. Pour into ice cream maker and freeze according to manufacturer's directions. Serve immediately or freeze up to 1 week.

Makes about 1 quart.

Honeydew Melon Sherbet

The outstanding features of this sorbet are the pure, natural taste and the pastel shade of honeydew. Midori melon liqueur heightens the sweetness and adds deep green color. To obtain the utmost flavor, use an overripe, almost mushy melon. This is pictured on page 190.

1 cup sugar
1 cup water
1 very ripe honeydew melon
1 tablespoon lime juice (1 lime)
1 tablespoon grated lime peel (3 limes)
½ cup Midori melon liqueur
2 egg whites

EQUIPMENT

Ice cream machine

Combine sugar and water in medium-size saucepan. Bring to a boil, stirring to dissolve sugar. Lower heat and simmer for 3 to 5 minutes. Cool to room temperature. Refrigerate until chilled. (*) Syrup may be refrigerated indefinitely.

Cut melon in half. Remove seeds and cut melon into 1-inch cubes. You should have about 4 cups.

Stir together chilled syrup, melon, lime juice and peel and liqueur in large bowl. Pour a third of the mixture into food processor fitted with metal blade. Process until mixture is puréed and smooth. Remove to bowl and repeat 2 more times.

Pour melon mixture into ice cream machine. Freeze 25 to 30 minutes or until slushy. Meanwhile, beat egg whites in medium-size bowl with electric mixer on low speed until frothy. Beat on high speed until stiff but glossy peaks form. With machine running, pour whites into melon mixture. Freeze until desired consistency is obtained. Serve immediately.

Makes 1 quart.

Sauces and Toppings

What would a hot fudge sundae be without the fudge sauce? Sauces, when spooned over desserts, transform the simple into the sublime. They add complementary tastes, contrasting colors and varying flavors. Many of the dessert recipes in this book call for sauces from this chapter, but don't limit yourself to the suggestion given. After you have sampled a number of sauces, you may find personal favorites with which you can mix and match.

There are two varieties of vanilla sauce included in the following pages—Creamy Vanilla and Vanilla Custard. The Creamy Vanilla Sauce is thicker and sweeter than the Vanilla Custard and is exceptionally good spooned over desserts that call for a whipped-cream-type topping. Vanilla Custard is a light, pourable sauce that's great served over denser desserts. I have also included two recipes for hot fudge sauce: One I call Hot Bittersweet Fudge Sauce and the other Hot Chocolate Fudge Sauce. Although both sauces are incredibly rich and creamy, the Hot Chocolate Fudge Sauce is lighter in color and flavor than the more traditional Hot Bittersweet Fudge Sauce. These two sauces are interchangeable.

Dessert sauces are easy to prepare and keep well in covered containers in the refrigerator.

Vanilla Custard Sauce

This very light custard, in French called Crème Anglaise, *is so versatile that it's excellent for topping fruit, plain cakes, mousses and steamed puddings. It is a fragile, delicate sauce so please follow my directions carefully.*

**6 large egg yolks, at room
     temperature**
⅓ cup sugar
1½ teaspoons cornstarch
2¼ cups milk, heated until very hot
1 teaspoon vanilla

Place fine strainer over medium-size bowl. Place bowl in larger bowl of ice water and set aside.

Beat egg yolks and sugar in large bowl with electric mixer on medium speed until thick and light colored, about 3 minutes. Beat in cornstarch. Slowly pour in the hot milk beating continuously. Pour mixture into top of double boiler over simmering water. Place candy thermometer in pan. Cook, stirring occasionally, until mixture thickens slightly and reaches 170°. It is done when you can run your finger down the back of the spoon and a path remains in the custard for several seconds. Immediately strain into the bowl over ice water and cool, stirring occasionally. Stir in vanilla. When cooled to room temperature, cover and refrigerate. (*) Sauce may be refrigerated up to 2 days.

Serve chilled.

Makes 2¼ cups.

Creamy Vanilla Sauce

This sauce takes the place of whipped cream when you want a thicker, sweeter topping.

1 cup powdered sugar
3 tablespoons unsalted butter, melted
1 large egg yolk, at room temperature
¼ teaspoon vanilla
⅛ teaspoon salt
1 cup whipping cream

Whisk together powdered sugar, melted butter, egg yolk, vanilla and salt in medium-size bowl until well blended and fluffy. Whip cream in separate bowl, with electric mixer on low speed until thickened. Beat on medium speed until soft peaks form. Fold whipped cream into sugar mixture. (*) Sauce may be refrigerated, covered, overnight.

Serve chilled.

Makes 1¾ cups.

Hard Sauce

A traditional sauce which can be served with any type of steamed pudding.

1¼ cups powdered sugar
¼ pound (1 stick) unsalted butter, at room temperature
2 to 3 tablespoons dark rum or brandy

Sift powdered sugar onto sheet of waxed paper. In small bowl, beat butter until fluffy with electric mixer at medium speed. Reduce speed to low and gradually beat in powdered sugar. Beat until mixture is light and fluffy. Add liquor to taste, mixing well. (*) May be kept covered at room temperature overnight.

Makes about 1¼ cups.

Ruby-Red Raspberry Sauce

2 packages (10 ounces each) frozen
*   raspberries in syrup, thawed*
¼ cup seedless raspberry jam
1 tablespoon arrowroot or corn-
*   starch*
1 tablespoon kirsch or framboise

Place strainer over small saucepan (do not use a fine strainer). Push raspberries through strainer with a wooden spoon to extract as much juice as possible; discard seeds. (See pictures for Hot Raspberry Soufflé, page 176.) Add jam to juice in saucepan and bring to a boil. Remove from heat. Dissolve arrowroot or cornstarch in liqueur in small cup. Whisk into sauce. Cook over moderate heat, whisking or stirring constantly, until sauce comes to a boil and thickens. Refrigerate until ready to use. (*) Sauce may be refrigerated, covered, up to 1 week. Serve chilled.

Makes 1½ cups.

Satin Strawberry Sauce

2 packages (10 ounces each) frozen
*   strawberries in syrup, thawed*
1 tablespoon lemon juice

Place strainer over bowl. Press strawberries through strainer with a wooden spoon to extract as much juice as possible. Scrape bottom of strainer often. Stir in lemon juice. (*) Sauce may be refrigerated, covered, up to 2 weeks.

Serve chilled.

Makes 1½ cups.

Blueberry Sauce

1 pint fresh or frozen blueberries
*   (2 cups)*
½ cup sugar
1 teaspoon grated lemon peel
½ teaspoon ground cinnamon
¼ teaspoon ground nutmeg
¼ cup water

Mix all ingredients in medium-size saucepan. Bring to a boil over moderate heat and cook, stirring often, for 8 to 10 minutes or until sauce thickens slightly and sugar is dissolved. The sauce will continue to thicken as it cools. (*) Sauce may be refrigerated, covered, up to 2 weeks.

Serve at room temperature.

Makes about 2½ cups.

Berries and Cherries Jubilee

A pretty deep red and blue ice cream topping, great for impromptu summer desserts.

¼ cup water
¼ cup sugar
1 cup blueberries
1½ cup fresh cherries, pitted and halved

2 tablespoons unsalted butter, at room temperature
1 cup strawberries, hulled and sliced
2 tablespoons kirsch
1 quart vanilla ice cream for serving

Combine water and sugar in medium-size skillet or chafing dish. Cook over moderate heat, stirring until sugar is dissolved. Stir in blueberries and cherries and cook over moderate heat for 2 to 3 minutes, stirring until fruits are coated. Add butter and strawberries and stir gently until butter is melted. Heat kirsch in ladle or small saucepan until hot, but not boiling. Ignite and pour over fruit. Spoon flames over fruit. Serve immediately over vanilla ice cream.

Serves 6.

Crème Fraîche Sauce

At least 24 hours before making the sauce, stir together buttermilk and cream to make crème fraîche—a thickened, soured cream, perfect for topping fresh fruits. In this version, sugar and lemon juice are added for a thinner consistency and greater flavor.

CRÈME FRAÎCHE

1 cup whipping cream
2 tablespoons buttermilk

SAUCE

4 teaspoons sugar
Dash salt
1 tablespoon lemon juice
1 to 2 tablespoons milk (optional)

CRÈME FRAÎCHE
Stir cream and buttermilk together in 2-cup glass jar or measuring cup. Cover top loosely with plastic wrap and let stand at room temperature for 24 hours or until thickened. (*) Crème Fraîche may be refrigerated, covered, up to 2 weeks.

To make sauce, whisk together crème fraîche, sugar, salt and lemon juice in small bowl. Thin with milk, if desired.

Serve chilled.

Makes 1 cup sauce.

Lemon Sauce

½ cup sugar
1 tablespoon cornstarch
1 cup boiling water
2 tablespoons unsalted butter
Pinch salt
2½ tablespoons lemon juice
1 teaspoon grated lemon peel

Stir together sugar and cornstarch in heavy small saucepan. Add the boiling water, whisking constantly. Bring to a boil over moderate heat and boil 5 minutes, stirring constantly. Remove from heat and stir in butter, salt, lemon juice and peel until butter is melted. Cool to room temperature. (*) Sauce may be refrigerated, covered, for several weeks. Gently reheat, if desired.

Serve warm or at room temperature.

Makes about 1 cup.

Hot Chocolate Fudge Sauce

Substituting sweetened condensed milk for sugar makes for a richer taste and a creamier texture. This sauce is heavenly —thick, rich and fudgy.

6 squares (6 ounces) semisweet chocolate, chopped
1 can (14 ounces) sweetened condensed milk
⅔ cup water
1 teaspoon vanilla
Pinch salt

Melt chocolate with milk, water, vanilla and salt in heavy medium-size saucepan over low heat, stirring until chocolate melts. Continue cooking, over moderate heat, stirring constantly until mixture comes to a full boil. Whisk over moderate heat until thickened, about 3 to 5 minutes. (*) Serve immediately or refrigerate in wide-mouth container up to 1 month. Reheat by placing container in pan of simmering water, or sauce in top of a double boiler over simmering water.

Serve warm.

Makes 2¾ cups.

Hot Bittersweet Fudge Sauce

Although any unsweetened cocoa powder will give you excellent results when making this sauce, a Dutch-process cocoa powder such as Droste will give you a wonderfully dark, rich, bittersweet sauce.

6 tablespoons unsalted butter, in small pieces
⅔ cup granulated sugar
⅔ cup firmly packed dark brown sugar
1 cup unsweetened cocoa powder
⅔ cup whipping cream
⅛ teaspoon salt

Combine butter, granulated sugar, brown sugar, cocoa powder, cream and salt in heavy medium-size saucepan. Cook over moderate heat until butter is melted, stirring occasionally. Reduce heat to low and continue to stir, scraping bottom and sides of the pan until the sugar is melted and the sauce is smooth. (*) Serve immediately or store in wide-mouth container in refrigerator up to 1 month. Reheat by placing container in pan of simmering water, or sauce in top of double boiler over simmering water.

Serve warm.

Makes 2 cups.

Sabayon Sauce

The flavor of this light custard sauce is determined by the type of wine you choose. It's fabulous over fresh fruit or any dessert with a non-assertive flavor.

3 large egg yolks, at room temperature
½ cup sugar
⅔ cup white wine, preferably Chablis or Riesling
½ teaspoon grated lemon peel

Whisk egg yolks and sugar in top of double boiler until well blended. Place over simmering water and stir in wine and lemon peel. Cook, stirring with wooden spoon, until very hot to the touch and thick enough to leave path on wooden spoon when you run finger along it. Remove from heat and immediately pour into bowl. Place in larger bowl of ice water and stir occasionally until cool. (*) Sauce may be refrigerated, covered, up to 2 days. Reheat in top of double boiler over simmering water, if desired.

Serve warm or at room temperature.

Makes 1 cup.

Rum Sauce

A thin, caramel-colored sauce that is very heady with rum.

1½ cups sugar
½ cup water
2 teaspoons light corn syrup
1 cup dark rum

Stir together sugar, water and corn syrup in medium-size heavy saucepan over moderately high heat until sugar has dissolved and mixture comes to a boil. Continue cooking, twirling and rotating the pan, without stirring, until syrup turns a caramel color.

Immediately remove pan from heat and, standing back, carefully pour in about 1 tablespoon of the rum. It is important to do this cautiously; the hot syrup will splatter when the rum is added. Continue to add the rum, about a tablespoon at a time, until it no longer splatters. Then stir well, and gradually stir in remaining rum. Cool to room temperature. (*) Sauce may be kept covered at room temperature up to 2 weeks. Do not refrigerate.

Serve at room temperature.

Makes about 2 cups.

Brandy Cream Sauce

This sauce is so good I've had guests who have eaten it straight from the sauceboat!

3 large egg yolks
1½ tablespoons cornstarch
¼ cup water
½ cup sugar
1 cup milk
4 to 6 tablespoons brandy
1 teaspoon vanilla

Lightly whisk egg yolks in heavy medium-size saucepan. Dissolve cornstarch in the water in small bowl; whisk into yolks. Whisk in sugar and milk. Cook over moderate heat, whisking constantly, until sauce comes to a boil and thickens. Remove from heat and stir in brandy to taste and vanilla. Place a piece of plastic wrap directly on top of sauce and let cool to room temperature. Serve immediately or cover and refrigerate. (*) Sauce may be refrigerated, covered, up to 2 months. Stir well before using.

Serve chilled or at room temperature.

Makes about 2 cups.

Crème de Grand Marnier

Grand Marnier, when mixed with condensed milk and eggs, becomes rich and creamy. Drink it after dinner, pour it over fruit, or use it as the base for Crème de Grand Marnier ice cream (see page 164).

¾ cup Grand Marnier liqueur
1 can (14 ounces) sweetened condensed milk
3 large eggs, at room temperature

Place Grand Marnier, milk and eggs in blender and mix until smooth. Refrigerate overnight. Stir well before using. (*) Cream may be refrigerated, covered, up to 1 month.

Serve chilled.

Makes about 2½ cups.

Irish Cream Liqueur

Bailey's Irish Cream liqueur is a commercial, cream-based after-dinner drink that takes the place of dessert. Here is my rendition of the liqueur which is not only delicious to drink, but is the base for Irish Cream Mousse (see page 146) and Irish Whiskey Ice Cream (see page 164).

¾ cup Irish or Scotch whiskey
1 can (14 ounces) sweetened condensed milk
2 tablespoons chocolate syrup
2 tablespoons instant coffee dissolved in 1 tablespoon boiling water
3 large eggs, at room temperature

Place whiskey, milk, syrup, coffee and eggs in blender and mix until smooth. Refrigerate overnight. Stir well before using. (*) Liqueur may be refrigerated, covered, up to 1 month. Stir well before using.

Serve chilled.

Makes about 3 cups.

Garnishes and Flourishes

To garnish or not to garnish, that is the question. Many people prefer the simple beauty and coarse texture of an unfrosted cake and the creamy fluffiness of an unadorned mousse. Others, however, find a dessert without decoration too plain or too unfinished. Just as we should season food to our own taste, so should we decorate for our own pleasure. I have only one steadfast rule when it comes to garnishing: It should be fun or it shouldn't be done. As for me, I think of my cakes and pies as a canvas on which I am free to create a design as simple or ornate as I wish, depending on my mood, the occasion and my schedule. Here are a few helpful hints to make decorating easier.

TIPS

- It is best to garnish a dessert using one or more of the ingredients from the recipe. Chocolate desserts should be garnished with chocolate, nut desserts with nuts, etc.
- Pastry bags are available in different materials. If possible, buy disposable ones made from plasticized paper. They are easy to use and they can be simply thrown away.
- When using a pastry bag, put desired tip in the bag and place bag tip-side down in a drinking glass. This leaves both your hands free to fill the bag.
- It is easiest to work with a pastry bag when it is filled only ⅔ full.
- Dip whole or part of dried fruit, nuts or fresh fruit, such as strawberries, orange segments, lemon slices and pineapple, into melted chocolate for a lovely garnish (see page 25).
- When decorating a plain dessert with powdered sugar, place a lacy doily on top of the dessert. Sprinkle it heavily with sugar, and then carefully lift up the doily.

CLOCKWISE FROM TOP: *Citrus Mousse, page 143; Heavenly Fruit-Filled Meringue, page 178; White Chocolate Cake, page 21.*

Chocolate Dough

This marvelous, easily prepared dough is pliable enough to roll, cut or bend into any shape imaginable. It doesn't melt like plain chocolate, which makes its uses limitless. It is so much fun to work with, I call it adult play-dough. And it tastes good, too. The recipe can be doubled, if desired. Use this dough to make chocolate triangles, bands and curls.

6 ounces semisweet chocolate chips or 6 squares semisweet chocolate, chopped
¼ cup (2 ounces) light corn syrup

In top of double boiler over simmering water, melt chocolate and syrup, stirring with rubber spatula, until mixture is smooth. Pour into a small bowl and cool to room temperature. Cover with plastic wrap directly on the dough. Let stand in a cool place for 4 to 6 hours, or until the mixture forms a soft, shiny, pliable dough.

(*) Dough may be held, covered, at room temperature until ready to use, or for several months. It will harden. Place the bowl in a pan of simmering water until the dough begins to melt and becomes soft enough to remove from bowl. Do not refrigerate it.

Work with all or half the dough at a time. With your hands, remove dough from bowl and place on a sheet of wax paper. It should be soft. If too firm, put in a warm place to soften. Shape into a flat disc. Roll dough between 2 sheets of wax paper, as pictured. Remove top sheet of paper by carefully pulling back on the paper. If the dough is too sticky to pull off the paper, let it stand until it becomes firm. Turn dough over and pull off second sheet of paper. Cut into desired shapes or roll into curls, as pictured. Repeat with remaining dough. Dough may be remelted and reused as desired.

Chocolate decorations

Roll Chocolate Dough between 2 sheets of wax paper to desired thickness.

Chocolate triangles

Roll dough ⅛ inch thick. Draw pattern of a triangle measuring 3 inches on each side. Cut around pattern as shown.

Chocolate bands

1 *Roll dough ¼ inch thick. Measure height and circumference of your cake. Make 2 bands each the height of the cake and ½ the circumference.*

2 *Wrap each band around half the cake, fitting the two ends together. Pictured here is the White Chocolate Cake. See page 21 for the recipe.*

Chocolate curls

Roll dough as thin as possible. Cut edges even. Cut into rectangles about 3½ inches long and 1½ inches wide. Roll until edges overlap slightly. Place seam side down.

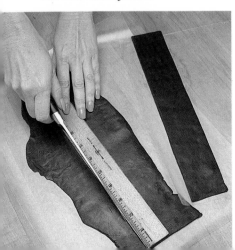

Chocolate Shavings

Dark and white chocolate are equally lovely for shavings. Sprinkle them on top of desserts or onto the sides of cakes.

Use as large a block of chocolate as possible. It should be a little warmer than room temperature. If the shavings break, then the chocolate is too cold and should be placed on top of a stove or in a warm place. Draw a knife at an angle along the face of the chocolate, letting shavings fall.

Chocolate Leaves

Heavy-veined leaves make the prettiest chocolate ones. You may use dark chocolate, white chocolate, or any of the colored chocolates available from candymaking stores.

1 *Spread melted chocolate on underside of clean leaf. Refrigerate until firm.*

2 *Gently pull back on leaf, separating it from the chocolate, touching the chocolate as little as possible. Refrigerate chocolate leaves until ready to use.*

3 *White Chocolate Cake wrapped in chocolate band and decorated with chocolate leaves. See page 21 for cake recipe.*

Notched Lemon or Orange Slices

Half slices of lemons or oranges make a lovely border around the top of a dessert or on a platter. They are also nice tucked into rosettes of whipped cream.

Pull lemon stripper down length of lemon at ¼-inch intervals. Slice and use as desired.

Candied Citrus Peel

An elegant garnish which adds flavor and texture as well as eye appeal.

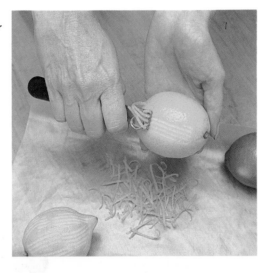

1 *Using a 5-holed zester or a lemon grater, make slivers of peel from 1 to 2 lemons, oranges or limes.*

2 *In a medium-size saucepan, bring ¾ cup water and ¾ cup sugar to a boil, stirring occasionally. Simmer 5 minutes or until sugar is dissolved. Add the peel and simmer for 2 minutes. Remove from heat. Leave peel in syrup until cool and ready to use. May be refrigerated up to 2 days in covered container. Before using, remove peel from syrup and blot dry with paper towels.*

Index

Absolutely Divine Devil's Food Cake, 14–15
air-cushioned baking sheets, 6
Alaska, cantaloupe, 194
Alaska, fresh raspberry, 198
Alaska roll, sherbet filled, 31–32
alcohol, in ice cream, 142
all-purpose flour, 3–4
all-purpose pastry, 85–86
almond cookie cups and saucers, 139
Almond Cream Puff Ring with Strawberries, 137–138
almond date cake, glazed, 38
almond lemon tart, 109
Almond Paste Chocolate Chip Strudel, 128–129
almond praline, for Pears in Praline Cream, 202
Amaretti Fruit Tartlets, 117
amaretto cream filling for cream puff ring, 137–138
Amaretto Soufflé, 175
Ambria Restaurant, 145
Angelo, Irene and Steve, 133
Anjou pears, 9
appetizer, Triple Cheese Flan, 47
apple cake, hot, with caramel pecan sauce, 34–35
apple cinnamon bread pudding, 71
Apple Lemon Tart, 91
apple pie with custard, double-crust, 92–93
apples, 7
    coring of, 191
    for strudel, 130
    sugar-and-spice baked, 21
Apple Streusel Tart, 94–95
apple strudel, Viennese, 130
apple tart, open-face, 124–125
Apricot Cheesecake, 61
Apricot Cobbler, 77
apricot cream, hazelnut meringue torte with, 184–185
apricot glaze, for New York Cheesecake, 49
apricot–Grand Marnier glaze for bread pudding, 72
apricot-orange bundt cake, 42
apricots, macaroon-filled, 195
Apricot Strudel, 127

Apricot Upside-Down Ginger Cake, 36
arrowroot, 4

Baby Papaya Birds, 200
Bailey's Irish Cream, 223
baked apples:
    sugar-and-spice, 210
    varieties for, 7
baked crusts, freezing of, 84
baked custards, 141–142
Baked Grapefruit Streusel, 206
Baker's semisweet chocolate, 8
Baker's unsweetened chocolate, 7
baking equipment, 6–7
    baking pan, size of, 11
    baking sheets, 6
baking of cheesecakes, 5, 45
baking questions, 1–5
baking rules, for cakes, 11
baklava, pineapple cheese, 132
banana cake, with banana frosting, 18–19
Banana Fritters, 79
banana frosting, for banana cake, 18–19
Banana Fudge Cheesecake, 57–58
banana pineapple pie, 96
bananas and pineapple flambée, 206
Bartlett pears, 9
beating of cake batter, 11
beets, in devil's food cake, 14–15
Berries and Cherries Jubilee, 219
Berries and Cream Tart, 97
biscuit, chocolate, for strawberry shortcake, 80–81
biscuit topping:
    for Mixed Fruit Cobbler, 75
    for rhubarb peach cobbler, 78
bitter chocolate, 7
bittersweet chocolate, 8
Bittersweet Fudge Sauce, 215
    hot, 220
Bittersweet Fudge Torte, 23
Blackberry Cobbler, 77
Black Forest Soufflé in Phyllo, 134
blind baking, 84
Blueberry Fritters, 79
blueberry glaze, for New York Cheesecake, 49
blueberry pudding, steamed, with lemon sauce, 66
blueberry puff, warm, 79

Blueberry Sauce, 218
    lemon-cream peaches with, 203
Blueberry Turnovers, 126
boiled custards, 142
Bosc pears, 9
bottled lemon juice, 5
Bourbon Street Fudge Cake, 39
Boysenberry Cobbler, 77
Brandy and Ginger Peach Tart, 99
Brandy Cream Sauce, 222
    light and dark steamed pudding with,
        64–65
bread flour, 3
bread puddings, 63
    bread for, 63
    Cinnamon Apple Bread Pudding, 71
    Mexican Bread and Cheese Pudding, 73
    Olde English Bread Pudding, 72
brownie soufflé, 174
brown sugar, 9
bundt cakes:
    Grand Marnier Nut Cake, 43
    Orange-Apricot Bundt Cake, 42
    Bourbon Street Fudge Cake, 39
    Holiday Egg Nog Cake, 41
    Persimmon Spice Cake, 40
bundt pans, 6
butter, 7
    beating of, for cakes, 11
    margarine substituted for, 4
    unsalted, 3
butter cream:
    coffee, 13
    white chocolate, 22
butterflies, chocolate meringue, 182–183
butter pastry, 83

cake batter, beating of, 11
cake flour, 3
    all-purpose substituted for, 4
cake pans, 6
cake rolls:
    Espresso Chocolate Soufflé Roll, 32–33
    Lemon Meringue Spiral, 27–28
    Sherbet Alaska Roll, 31–32
    Strawberry Shortcake Roll, 29–31
cakes:
    Absolutely Divine Devil's Food Cake,
        14–15
    Apricot Upside-Down Ginger Cake, 36
    to bake, 11
    doneness test, 11
    Fresh Banana Cake with Banana
        Frosting, 18–19
    Glazed Almond Date Cake, 38
    Hot Apple Cake with Caramel Pecan
        Sauce, 34–35
    Orange Sponge Cake, 16–18

cakes (cont'd)
    Strawberry Cream Sponge Tart, 37–38
    White Chocolate Cake, 21–22
    see also Bundt cakes; Cake rolls
Candied Lemon or Orange Peel, 229
Candlelight Chocolate Soufflés for Two,
    177
candy, Southern Praline Pecan, 148
Cantaloupe Alaska, 194
caramel custard, 160
Caramel Custard Fruit Tart, 106–107
caramel flan, flaming, 158–159
caramel-lined molds, custard in, 142
caramel pecan sauce, hot apple cake with,
    34–35
Caramel Pumpkin Pudding, 69
champagne zabaglione, warm, 155
Chardonnay lemon snow, 211
cheddar and pear tart, 102
cheese, cream, for cheesecakes, 45
cheese and bread pudding, Mexican, 73
cheesecakes, 45
    Apricot Cheesecake, 61
    baking of, 5
    Banana Fudge Cheesecake, 57–58
    Chocolate Truffle Cheesecake, 52
    Classic New York Cheesecake with
        Choice of Toppings, 48–49
    Hazelnut Praline Cheesecake, 60
    Lemonade Chiffon Cheesecake, 53
    Miniature Fruit-Glazed Cheesecakes, 54
    My Favorite Cheesecake, 58–59
    Oreo Cheesecake, 50–51
    Peanut Butter Chocolate Chip
        Cheesecake, 56
    Piña Colada Cheesecake with Pineapple
        Glaze, 55
    Triple Cheese Flan, 47
    White Chocolate Cheesecake, 46–47
cheese pineapple baklava, 132
cherries and berries jubilee, 219
Cherry Goat Cheese Strudel, 131
Cherry Quiche, 100
Chicago, Ambria Restaurant, 145
chiffon pies:
    gelatin in, 3
    lightness of, 2
    Pumpkin Praline Chiffon Pie, 103
    White Chocolate Mousse Pie, 104–105
Child, Julia, 14
Chilled Mandarin Orange Soufflé, 172
Chilled Raspberry-Rimmed Zabaglione,
    156
chocolate:
    Absolutely Divine Devil's Food Cake,
        14–15
    bittersweet fudge sauce, 220
    Bourbon Street Fudge Cake, 39

chocolate (cont'd)
    Fudgy Brownie Soufflé, 174
    melting of, 4–5
    Mocha Fudge Torte, 26–27
    types of, 7–8
    white:
        cake of, 21–22
        ice cream, 167
        mousse pie, 104–105
chocolate chip almond paste strudel,
    128–129
chocolate chip peanut butter cheesecake,
    56
chocolate chips, semisweet, 8
Chocolate Cream Puffs with Chocolate
    Mocha Mousse, 136–137
Chocolate Cups, 154
Chocolate Curls, for garnish, 21
    Chocolate-Kahlúa Cream Torte, 20–21
    Espresso Chocolate Soufflé Roll, 32–33
Chocolate Dough, 226–227
chocolate espresso soufflé roll, 32–33
chocolate fudge banana cheesecake, 57–58
chocolate fudge sauce, hot, 220
chocolate glaze, for nut torte, 24–25
chocolate-glazed pears, truffle-filled,
    208–209
Chocolate-Kahlúa Cream Torte, 20–21
Chocolate Leaves, 228
Chocolate Meringue Butterflies, 182–183
Chocolate Meringue Shells, 187
Chocolate Mocha Mousse, 147
    chocolate cream puffs with, 136–137
    Chocolate Meringue Butterflies, 182
    Chocolate Raspberry Dessert, 149
chocolate mousse, 141
Chocolate-Nougat Fondue with Fresh
    Fruit, 196
Chocolate Nut Torte, 24–25
Chocolate Pastry, 89
    Banana Fudge Cheesecake, 57
    Chocolate Truffle Cheesecake, 52
Chocolate Peppermint Angel Dessert,
    154–155
Chocolate Pots de Crème, 163
chocolate pudding, steamed, with creamy
    vanilla sauce, 67
Chocolate Raspberry Dessert, 149
Chocolate Shavings, 228
Chocolate Shells, 152–153
    Chocolate Raspberry Dessert, 149
chocolate soufflé, fudgy brownie, 174
chocolate soufflés for two, 177
Chocolate Strawberry Shortcake, 80–81
Chocolate Truffle Cheesecake, 52
Chocolate Truffle Tartlets, 118
Chocolate Velvet Crown, 150
Christmas Cranberry Pudding, 70–71

Cinnamon Apple Bread Pudding, 71
Cinnamon-Scented Winter Fruit, 201
cinnamon streusel crust, for plum tart, 98
Citrus Mousse, 143
Classic Caramel Custard, 160
Classic New York Cheesecake with
    Choice of Toppings, 48–49
cobblers, 63
    Fresh Blackberry Cobbler, 77
    Fresh Peach Cobbler, 76–77
    Mixed Fruit Cobbler, 74–75
cocoa powder, unsweetened, 8
coconut cream tartlets, 119
coconut frosting for sponge cake, 17
Coffee Butter Cream, 13
Coffee Fudge Ice Cream Torte, 115
coffee ice cream, white, 166–167
Coffee Macadamia Torte, 12–13
Coffee Meringues with Hazelnut Cream,
    186
Coffee Pots de Crème, 162–163
cold soufflés, 169
    Chilled Mandarin Orange Soufflé,
        172
    Frosty Daiquiri Soufflé, 173
    gelatin in, 3
    Iced Lemon Soufflé, 171
Comice pears, 9
compote, dried fruit, spiced, 207
confectioners' sugar, 9
containers:
    Baby Papaya Birds, 200
    Chocolate Meringue Shells, 187
    fruit as, 191
    Lacy Almond Cookie Cups and
        Saucers, 139
    Meringue Swans, 188–189
cookie cups and saucers, almond, 139
cookie pastry, 83, 88
    chocolate, for Peanut Butter Chocolate
        Chip Cheesecake, 56
    for Classic New York Cheesecake, 48
    graham cracker crumb, 53, 59
    Oreo, for Oreo Cheesecake, 50
cooking equipment, 6–7
coring of fruits, 191
cornstarch, 4
    added to boiled custard, 142
Cortland apples, 7
cracking of cheesecakes, to prevent, 5
Cranberry Pear Pie, 101
cranberry pudding, 70–71
cream, to whip, 2, 9
cream and berries tart, 97
cream cheese, for cheesecakes, 45
Cream Cheese Pastry for Tartlets, 90
cream of tartar, 8
cream puff pastry, 121

cream puff ring, almond, with
    strawberries, 137–138
cream puffs, chocolate, with chocolate
    mocha mousse, 136–137
Creamy Vanilla Sauce, 215, 217
    Bittersweet Fudge Torte, 23
    Fudgy Brownie Soufflé, 174
    steamed chocolate pudding with, 67
Crème Anglaise, 216
Crème Brûlée, 161
Crème de Grand Marnier, 223
    strawberries in, 196
Crème de Grand Marnier Ice Cream, 164
Crème Fraîche, 219
Crème Fraîche Sauce, 219
    lemon mousse with, 145
crumb crusts, 83
Crunchy Meringue Ice Cream Sandwich
    with Hot Fudge Sauce, 181
crunchy strawberry cloud, frozen, 151
crusts:
    amaretti cookie, for cheesecake, 58
    amaretti–graham cracker crumb, 117
    cheddar cheese, 102
    for cheesecake, 48
    chocolate cookie, 114–115
    chocolate cookie, for peanut butter
        cheesecake, 56
    cinnamon streusel, 98
    graham cracker, for cheesecake, 59
    graham cracker and nut, 97
    ice cream cone crust, 116
    macadamia nut, 96
    Oreo cookie, for cheesecake, 50
    vanilla wafer almond, 105
    see also Pastry
cups, chocolate, 154
cups and saucers, almond, 139
custard-gelatin mixtures, to thicken, 3
custard pies:
    Caramel Custard Fruit Tart, 106–107
    Lemon Almond Tart, 109
    Zesty Lemon Custard Pie, 108
custards, 141–142
    Caramel Pumpkin Pudding, 69
    Chocolate Pots de Crème, 163
    Christmas Cranberry Pudding, 70–71
    Classic Caramel Custard, 160
    Coffee Pots de Crème, 162–163
    Crème Brûlée, 161
    double-crust apple pie with, 92–93
    Flaming Caramel Flan, 158–159
    Vanilla Pots de Crème, 162
cutting of fruits, 191

daiquiri soufflé, frosty, 173
dark brown sugar, 9
date almond cake, glazed, 38

Devil's Food Cake, 14–15
dip, fluffy orange, 197
doneness of cake, test of, 11
doneness of soufflé, test for, 170
double boiler, custard cooked in, 142
Double-Crust Apple Pie with Custard,
    92–93
double-crust pies, pastry for, 85, 87
Droste cocoa, 8
dry ingredients, combining of, 11
Duke of Nottingham's Fruit Trifle, 157
dumplings, gorgonzola pear, 135
dusting with powdered sugar, 9

Easy Puff Pastry, 122–123
egg nog cake, 41
egg whites, 141, 169–170
    folding in, 2
    frozen, uses of, 2
    leftover, frozen, 2
    to whip, 1, 8
egg yolks, 141
    frozen, uses of, 2
    leftover, frozen, 2
eggs, 8
    beating of, for cakes, 11
    to separate, 1
electric mixer method, cookie pastry, 88
equipment, 6–7
Espresso Chocolate Soufflé Roll, 32–33
Espresso Oreo ice cream, 164–165

figs, fresh, in vanilla-lemon syrup, 201
fillings:
    apricot cream, for hazelnut meringue
        torte, 184–185
    chocolate-Kahlúa cream, for torte, 20
    coffee butter cream, for macadamia
        torte, 12–13
    cream, Kirsch-scented, for sponge tart,
        37–38
    hazelnut cream, for coffee meringues,
        186
    lemon, for Lemon Meringue Spiral,
        27–28
    orange custard, for sponge cake, 17
    strawberry, for orange sponge cake, 18
    strawberry, for shortcake roll, 29–31
    white chocolate butter cream, 22
flambéed pineapple and bananas, 206
Flaming Caramel Flan, 158–159
flan rings, 7
floating islands, raspberry, 180
flour, 8
    sifting of, 4, 11
    thickening with, 4
    types of, 3–4
flouring of pans, for cakes, 11

flourless cakes:
    Bittersweet Fudge Torte, 23
    Chocolate Nut Torte, 24–25
    see also Tortes
Fluffy Orange Dip, 197
folding in of beaten egg whites, 2, 169
fondue, chocolate-nougat, with fresh fruit,
        196
food processor method:
    chocolate pastry, 89
    cookie pastry, 88
    grinding of nuts, 8
    pastry, 85–86
    shortening pastry, 87
Fournous' Ovens, 113
freezing methods:
    egg whites and yolks, 2
    flour, 8
    nuts, 8
    pastry, 84
Fresh Banana Cake with Banana Frosting,
        18–19
Fresh Blackberry Cobbler, 77
Fresh Blueberry Turnovers, 126
Fresh Figs in Vanilla-Lemon Syrup, 201
Fresh Fruit Medley with Orange-Kirsch
        Marinade, 197
Fresh Peach Cobbler, 76–77
Fresh Peach Ice Cream, 166
    Peach Melba, 205
Fresh Raspberry Alaska, 198
Fresh Strawberry Ice, 212
fritters, blueberry, 79
frostings:
    banana, for banana cake, 18–19
    chocolate, for chocolate-Kahlúa cream
        torte, 21
    coconut, for sponge cake, 17
    fudge, for devil's food cake, 14–15
    strawberry, for shortcake roll, 29–31
    whipped cream, for orange sponge
        cake, 18
Frosty Daiquiri Soufflé, 173
frozen cream puffs, 121
frozen desserts:
    Fresh Strawberry Ice, 212
    Frozen Crunchy Strawberry Cloud, 151
    Honeydew Melon Sherbet, 213
    Lemon Chardonnay Snow, 211
    Papaya-Yogurt Freeze, 211
    Piña Colada Sherbet, 212
    in springform pans, 6
    Tangerine Slush, 210
    see also ice creams; ices; sherbet
frozen lemon juice, 5
frozen phyllo, 121
frozen puff pastry, 121
frozen whipping cream, 9

fruit, 191
    for cobblers, 63
    glazed, for garnish, 225
fruit Amaretti tartlets, 117
fruitcakes, Orange-Apricot Bundt Cake,
        42
fruit compote, spiced, 207
fruit desserts:
    Baked Grapefruit Streusel, 206
    Blueberry Fritters, 79
    cakes:
        Apricot Upside-Down Ginger Cake,
            36
        Glazed Almond Date Cake, 38
        Hot Apple Cake with Caramel
            Pecan Sauce, 34–35
        Persimmon Spice Cake, 40
        Strawberry Cream Sponge Tart,
            37–38
    Cantaloupe Alaska, 194
    Chocolate-Nougat Fondue with Fresh
        Fruit, 196
    Chocolate Strawberry Shortcake, 80–81
    Cinnamon-Scented Winter Fruit, 201
    Duke of Nottingham's Fruit Trifle, 157
    Fluffy Orange Dip, 197
    Fresh Blackberry Cobbler, 77
    Fresh Figs in Vanilla-Lemon Syrup, 201
    Fresh Fruit Medley with Orange-Kirsch
        Marinade, 197
    Fresh Peach Cobbler, 76–77
    Fresh Raspberry Alaska, 198
    Fresh Strawberry Ice, 212
    Hawaiian Fruit in Honey-Nut Yogurt,
        195
    Honeydew Melon Sherbet, 213
    Lemon Chardonnay Snow, 211
    Lemon-Cream Peaches with Blueberry
        Sauce, 203
    Macaroon-Filled Apricots, 195
    Minted Melon Melange, 194
    Mixed Fruit Cobbler, 74–75
    Orange-Glazed Oranges, 199
    Papaya-Yogurt Freeze, 211
    Peach Melba, 205
    Pears in Praline Cream, 202–203
    Piña Colada Sherbet, 212
    Pineapple and Bananas Flambée, 206
    Prunes in Port, 203
    Rhubarb Peach Cobbler with Lattice
        Biscuit, 78
    Spiced Fruit Compote, 207
    Strawberries in Crème de Grand
        Marnier, 196
    Sugar-and-Spice Baked Apples, 210
    Tangerine Slush, 210
    Tropical Fruit in Pineapple Rickshaw,
        192–193

fruit desserts (cont'd)
    Truffle-Filled Chocolate-Glazed Pears,
        208–209
    Warm Blueberry Puff, 79
fruit-filled meringue, 178–179
fruit-flavored ice cream, 142
fruit-glazed cheesecakes, miniature, 54
fruit pies:
    Cranberry Pear Pie, 101
    Double-Crust Apple Pie with Custard,
        92–93
    Pineapple Banana Pie, 96
fruit tarts:
    Apple Streusel Tart, 94–95
    Berries and Cream Tart, 97
    Brandy and Ginger Peach Tart, 99
    Caramel Custard Fruit Tart, 106–107
    Cherry Quiche, 100
    Pear and Cheddar Tart, 102
    Purple Plum Tart, 98
fudge cake, Bourbon Street, 39
fudge coffee ice cream torte, 115
fudge frosting, for Devil's Food Cake,
        14–15
fudge mocha torte, 26–27
Fudgy Brownie Soufflé, 174

garnishes, 225
    Candied Lemon or Orange Peel, 229
    Chocolate Curls, 21
    Chocolate Dough, 226–227
    Chocolate Leaves, 228
    Chocolate Shavings, 228
    glazed nuts for Chocolate Nut Torte,
        24–25
    Notched Lemon or Orange Slices, 229
gelatin:
    cheesecake set with, 53
    mousses set with, 141
    unflavored, to gel, 3
ginger cake, apricot upside-down, 36
ginger peach and brandy tart, 99
Glazed Almond Date Cake, 38
glazed fruits as garnish, 225
glazed nuts, for Chocolate Nut Torte,
        24–25
glazes:
    apricot, for New York Cheesecake, 49
    apricot–Grand Marnier, for bread
        pudding, 72
    blueberry, for New York Cheesecake,
        49
    chocolate, for Chocolate Nut Torte,
        24–25
    chocolate, for truffle-filled pears,
        208–209
    orange, for Orange-Apricot Bundt
        Cake, 42

glazes *(cont'd)*
    orange, for oranges, 100
    orange, for Persimmon Spice Cake, 40
    for pastry, 84
    pineapple, for piña colada cheesecake, 55
    rum-brandy, for Holiday Egg Nog Cake, 41
    strawberry, for cream sponge tart, 38
    strawberry, for New York Cheesecake, 49
gluten in flour, 3
goat cheese cherry strudel, 131
Golden Delicious apples, 7
    Viennese Apple Strudel, 130
Gorgonzola Pear Dumplings, 135
graham cracker and nut crust, 97
graham cracker crust, for cheesecake, 53
Grand Marnier, crème de, 223
Grand Marnier–apricot glaze, for Olde English Bread Pudding, 72
Grand Marnier Nut Cake, 43
Granny Smith apples, 7
grapefruit, baked, with streusel topping, 206
graters, 6
greasing of pans, for cakes, 11
Greening apples, 7
grinding of nuts, 8

hardened brown sugar, to soften, 9
Hawaiian Fruit in Honey-Nut Yogurt, 195
    Baby Papaya Birds for, 200
hazelnut cream, coffee meringues with, 186
Hazelnut Meringue Torte with Apricot Cream, 184–185
Hazelnut Praline Cheesecake, 60
Heavenly Fruit-Filled Meringue, 178–179
Hershey's cocoa, 8
Hershey's unsweetened chocolate, 7
Holiday Egg Nog Cake, 41
Honeydew Melon Sherbet, 213
honey-nut yogurt, Hawaiian fruit in, 195
Honey Walnut Tartlets, 118
Hot Apple Cake with Caramel Pecan Sauce, 34–35
Hot Bittersweet Fudge Sauce, 220
Hot Chocolate Fudge Sauce, 220
    crunchy meringue ice cream sandwich with, 181
    peanut butter ice cream pie with, 114–115
Hot Chocolate Sauce, 215
hot soufflés, 169
    Amaretto Soufflé, 175

hot soufflés *(cont'd)*
    Candlelight Chocolate Soufflés for Two, 177
    Fudgy Brownie Soufflé, 174
    Hot Raspberry Soufflé, 176–177

Ice Cream Cone Pie, 116
ice cream pies:
    Coffee Fudge Ice Cream Torte, 115
    Peanut Butter Ice Cream Pie with Hot Fudge Sauce, 114–115
    Praline Ice Cream Pie, 112–114
ice creams, 142
    Cantaloupe Alaska, 194
    chocolate cups for, 154
    chocolate meringue shells for, 187
    chocolate shells for, 152–153
    Crunchy Meringue Ice Cream Sandwich with Hot Fudge Sauce, 181
    Fresh Peach Ice Cream, 166
    Incredible White Coffee Ice Cream, 166–167
    Irish Whiskey Ice Cream, 164
    Marvelous Mango Ice Cream, 165
    meringue swan containers for, 188–189
    Oreo Espresso Ice Cream, 164–165
    Peach Melba, 205
    Pineapple and Bananas Flambée, 206
    White Chocolate Ice Cream, 167
    see also frozen desserts; sherbet
ice cube trays, egg whites frozen in, 2
Iced Lemon Soufflé, 171
ices:
    Fresh Strawberry Ice, 212
    fruit, 191
    Tangerine Slush, 210
    see also ice creams; frozen desserts
Incredible White Coffee Ice Cream, 166–167
ingredients, 7–9
    combining of for baking, 11
    cream cheese, for cheesecake, 45
Irish Cream Liqueur, 223
Irish Cream Mousse, 146–147
Irish Whiskey Ice Cream, 164

jelly-roll pan, cake baked in, 20
    see also cake rolls
Jonathan apples, 7

Kahlúa-chocolate cream torte, 20–21
Kaye, Danny, 108
Kirsch-orange marinade for fresh fruit, 197
Kiwi Mousse with Kiwi Sauce, 144

Lacy Almond Cookie Cups and Saucers, 139
    Incredible White Coffee Ice Cream in, 166–167

lacy doily, powdered sugar decoration, 225
Land O'Lakes butter, 7
large eggs, 8
lattice biscuit, rhubarb peach cobbler with, 78
layers of cakes, aligning of, 11
leaves, chocolate, 228
leftover egg whites and yolks, to freeze, 2
Lemonade Chiffon Cheesecake, 53
Lemon Almond Tart, 109
lemon apple tart, 91
Lemon Chardonnay Snow, 211
Lemon-Cream Peaches with Blueberry Sauce, 204
lemon custard pie, 108
lemon juice, 5
Lemon Meringue Spiral, 27–28
Lemon Mousse with Crème Fraîche Sauce, 145
lemon peel:
    candied, 229
    grated, 6
Lemon Sauce, 220
    steamed blueberry pudding with, 66
lemon slices, notched, 229
lemon soufflé, iced, 171
lemon-vanilla syrup, fresh figs in, 201
Light and Dark Steamed Pudding with Brandy Cream Sauce, 64–65
light brown sugar, 9
lime sour cream tartlets, 116
Lindt Blancor white chocolate, 8
liqueurs:
    Crème de Grand Marnier, 223
    Irish Cream Liqueur, 223
lumpy cornstarch sauces, 4
lumpy flour, 4
lumpy melted chocolate, 4–5

macadamia coffee torte, 12–13
macadamia nut crust, for Pineapple Banana Pie, 96
Macaroon-Filled Apricots, 195
mandarin orange soufflé, chilled, 172
Manell, Rosemary, 14
mango ice cream, 165
maple praline mousse, 148–149
margarine, as butter substitute, 4
marinades:
    brandy and ginger, for peaches, 99
    orange-Kirsch, for fresh fruit, 197
Marvelous Mango Ice Cream, 165
measuring of flour, 4
melon baller, fruit cut with, 191
melon melange, minted, 194
melon sherbet, 213
melting of chocolate, 4–5

meringues, 169, 170
  Cantaloupe Alaska, 194
  Chocolate Meringue Butterflies,
    182–183
  Chocolate Meringue Shells, 187
  Coffee Meringues with Hazelnut
    Cream, 186
  Fresh Raspberry Alaska, 198
  Hazelnut Meringue Torte with Apricot
    Cream, 184–185
  Heavenly Fruit-Filled Meringue,
    178–179
  ice cream sandwich with hot fudge
    sauce, 181
  Lemon Meringue Spiral, 27–28
  Raspberry Floating Islands, 180
  Toffee-Crunch Meringue Torte, 179
meringue shells, superfine sugar for, 9
Meringue Swans, 188–189
Mexican Bread and Cheese Pudding, 73
Miniature Fruit-Glazed Cheesecakes, 54
Minted Melon Melange, 194
Mixed Fruit Cobbler, 74–75
mixed fruit ices, 191
mocha chocolate mousse, 147
  balls of, 147
  chocolate cream puffs with, 136–137
Mocha Fudge Torte, 26–27
mousses, 141
  chocolate, chocolate cream puffs with,
    136–137
  chocolate cups for, 154
  chocolate meringue shells for, 187
  Chocolate Mocha Mousse, 147
  Chocolate Peppermint Angel Dessert,
    154–155
  Chocolate Raspberry Dessert, 149
  chocolate shells for, 152–153
  Citrus Mousse, 143
  gelatin in, 3
  Irish Cream Mousse, 146–147
  Kiwi Mousse with Kiwi Sauce, 144
  Lemon Mousse with Creme Fraîche
    Sauce, 145
  lightness of, 2
  Southern Praline Maple Mousse, 148–149
  white chocolate pie, 104–105
My Favorite Cheesecake, 58–59

napoleon, strawberry phyllo, 133–134
Nectarine Cobbler, 76
nectarines, with lemon-cream and
  blueberry sauce, 204
New York Cheesecake with Choice of
  Toppings, 48–49
Notched Lemon or Orange Slices, 229
nougat-chocolate fondue with fresh fruit,
  196

nut cake, Grand Marnier–soaked, 43
nuts, 8–9
  ground, torte of, 12–13
nut tarts:
  Lemon Almond Tart, 109
  Regal Pecan Tart, 110–111

Olde English Bread Pudding, 72
Open-Face Apple Tart, 124–125
Orange-Apricot Bundt Cake, 42
Orange Custard Filling, for sponge cake,
  17
orange dip, fluffy, 197
orange glaze, for Persimmon Spice Cake,
  40
Orange-Glazed Oranges, 199
orange-Kirsch marinade for fresh fruit,
  197
orange peel:
  candied, 229
  grated, 6
orange slices, notched, 229
orange soufflé, chilled, 172
Orange Sponge Cake, 16–18
Orange Sponge Pudding, 68
Oreo Cheesecake, 50–51
Oreo Espresso Ice Cream, 164–165
Oriental food, desserts for:
  Chilled Mandarin Orange Soufflé, 172
  Pineapple Banana Pie, 96
oven, position of cake in, 11
oven thermometers, 7
overbeaten egg whites, 2
overwhipped cream, 9

pans, preparation for cake baking, 11
Papaya Birds, 200
Papaya-Yogurt Freeze, 211
parchment paper, for cake pan lining, 11
pastry, 83–84, 121
  Chocolate Pastry, 89
  chocolate shortcake, 80–81
  Cookie Pastry, 88
  Cream Cheese Pastry for Tartlets, 90
  freezing of, 84
  for Fresh Blackberry Cobbler, 77
  for Fresh Peach Cobbler, 76
  gorgonzola, 135
  for pies, 83
  rich, all-purpose, 85–86
  rolling difficulties, 5
  Shortening Pastry, 86–87
  see also Crusts
pastry bags, 225
pastry cream, for phyllo napoleon,
  133–134
pastry flour, 3
pâte à choux, 121

Pavlova, 178
peach, ginger and brandy, tart, 99
Peach Cobbler, 76–77
peaches, lemon-cream, with blueberry
  sauce, 203
peach ice cream, 166
Peach Melba, 205
peach rhubarb cobbler with lattice biscuit,
  78
Peanut Butter Chocolate Chip Cheesecake,
  56
Peanut Butter Ice Cream Pie with Hot
  Fudge Sauce, 114–115
pears, 9
  coring of, 191
  Pear and Cheddar Tart, 102
  pear cranberry pie, 101
  pear dumplings, gorgonzola, 135
  Pears in Praline Cream, 202–203
  truffle-filled, chocolate-glazed, 208–209
pecan caramel sauce, hot apple cake with,
  34–35
pecan meringue torte, 185
pecan praline candy, 148
pecan tart, 110–111
peels, citrus, grated, 6
Pépin, Jacques, 122
peppermint chocolate angel dessert,
  154–155
The Perfect Chocolate Dessert, 149
Persimmon Spice Cake, 40
phyllo, 121
  Almond Paste Chocolate Chip Strudel,
    128–129
  Black Forest Soufflé in Phyllo, 134
  Cherry Goat Cheese Strudel, 131
  Pineapple Cheese Baklava, 132
  Strawberry Phyllo Napoleon, 133–134
  Viennese Apple Strudel, 130
pies, 83
  Cranberry Pear Pie, 101
  Double-Crust Apple Pie with Custard,
    92–93
  Ice Cream Cone Pie, 116
  Peanut Butter Ice Cream Pie with Hot
    Fudge Sauce, 114–115
  Pineapple Banana Pie, 96
  Praline Ice Cream Pie, 112–114
  Pumpkin Praline Chiffon Pie, 103
  White Chocolate Mousse Pie, 104–105
Piña Colada Cheesecake with Pineapple
  Glaze, 55
Piña Colada Sherbet, 212
Pineapple and Bananas Flambée, 206
Pineapple Banana Pie, 96
Pineapple Cheese Baklava, 132
pineapple glaze, for piña colada
  cheesecake, 55

pineapple rickshaw, tropical fruit in, 192–193
pippin apples, 7
plum tart, 98
poaching of fruits, 191
port, prunes in, 203
pots de crème:
    chocolate, 163
    coffee, 162–163
    vanilla, 162
powdered sugar, 9
    decoration with, 225
praline cream, pears in, 202–203
praline hazelnut cheesecake, 60
Praline Ice Cream Pie, 112–114
praline maple mousse, 148–149
praline pumpkin chiffon pie, 103
pre-sifted flour, 4
prunes in Port, 203
puddings, 63
    Caramel Pumpkin Pudding, 69
    Christmas Cranberry Pudding, 70–71
    Orange Sponge Pudding, 68
    steamed, see steamed puddings
    see also bread puddings; custards
puff, warm blueberry, 79
puff pastry, 121
    Apricot Strudel, 127
    Easy Puff Pastry, 122–123
    Fresh Blueberry Turnovers, 126
    Open-Face Apple Tart, 124–125
Pumpkin Praline Chiffon Pie, 103
pumpkin caramel pudding, 69
Purple Plum Tart, 98

quiche, cherry, 100

Raspberries in Crème de Grand Marnier, 196
Raspberry Alaska, 198
raspberry chocolate dessert, 149
Raspberry Floating Islands, 180
raspberry-rimmed zabaglione, 156
raspberry sauce, 218
    Chocolate Raspberry Dessert, 149
    Peach Melba, 205
raspberry soufflé, hot, 176–177
Regal Pecan Tart, 110–111
Rhubarb Peach Cobbler with Lattice
    Biscuit, 78
Rich All-Purpose Pastry, 85–86
rimmed baking sheets, 6
rolled cakes, see Cake rolls
rolling of pastry, 5, 83–84
Rome Beauty apples, 7
Ruby-Red Raspberry Sauce, 218
Rum Sauce, 222

Sabayon Sauce, 221
    see also Zabaglione

salt:
    in butter, 3
    in dessert recipes, 3
San Francisco, Stanford Court Hotel, 113
Satin Strawberry Sauce, 218
    with Meringue Swans, 188–189
sauces, 215
    Berries and Cherries Jubilee, 219
    Blueberry Sauce, 218
        lemon-cream peaches with, 203
    Brandy Cream Sauce, 222
        for Light and Dark Steamed
            Pudding, 65
    Caramel Pecan Sauce, hot apple cake
        with, 34–35
    Creamy Vanilla Sauce, 217
        Bittersweet Fudge Torte, 23
        Fudgy Brownie Soufflé, 174
        steamed chocolate pudding with, 67
    Crème de Grand Marnier, 223
    Crème Fraîche Sauce, 219
        lemon mousse with, 145
    defrosted egg yolks in, 2
    Hot Bittersweet Fudge Sauce, 220
    Hot Chocolate Fudge Sauce, 220
    Irish cream, 147
    kiwi, kiwi mousse with, 144
    Lemon Sauce, 220
        steamed blueberry pudding with, 66
    Ruby-Red Raspberry Sauce, 218
        Chocolate Raspberry Dessert, 149
        Peach Melba, 204
    Rum Sauce, 222
    Sabayon Sauce, 221
    Satin Strawberry Sauce, 218
    Vanilla Custard Sauce, 216
savory cheesecake, 47
semisweet chocolate, 8
separating egg whites from yolks, 1
shells, chocolate, 152–153
sherbet, Fresh Raspberry Alaska, 198
sherbet, honeydew melon, 213
Sherbet Alaska Roll, 31–32
shortcake, strawberry chocolate, 80–81
shortcake roll, strawberry, 29–31
Short Crust Pastry, 83
shortening, pastry made with, 83
Shortening Pastry, 87
sifting of flour, 4
sizes:
    of baking pans, 11
    of springform pans, 7
soufflés, 169
    Black Forest Soufflé in Phyllo, 134
    cold, see Cold soufflés
    Espresso Chocolate Soufflé Roll, 32–33
    hot, see Hot soufflés
Sour Cream Lime Tartlets, 116

Southern Praline Maple Mousse, 148–149
Southern Praline Pecan Candy, 148
spice cake, persimmon, 40
Spiced Fruit Compote, 207
sponge cake, orange, 16–18
sponge pudding, orange, 68
sponge tart, strawberry cream, 37–38
springform pans, 6–7
    to remove sides, 45
Stanford Court Hotel, San Francisco, 113
steamed puddings, 63–64
    Steamed Blueberry Pudding with
        Lemon Sauce, 66
    Steamed Chocolate Pudding with
        Creamy Vanilla Sauce, 67
    Light and Dark Steamed Pudding with
        Brandy Cream Sauce, 64–65
stiffly beaten egg whites, 2, 141, 169
storage:
    of brown sugar, 9
    of flour, 8
    of unsalted butter, 7
strawberries, almond cream puff ring with,
    137–138
Strawberries in Crème de Grand Marnier,
    196
strawberry chocolate shortcake, 80–81
strawberry cloud, frozen, crunchy, 151
Strawberry Cream Sponge Tart, 37–38
strawberry filling, for orange sponge cake,
    18
strawberry glaze, for New York
    Cheesecake, 49
strawberry ice, fresh, 212
Strawberry Phyllo Napoleon, 133–134
strawberry sauce, satin, 218
Strawberry Shortcake Roll, 29–31
streusel:
    for apple tart, 95
    cheddar cheese, 102
    grapefruit baked with, 206
    for Purple Plum Tart, 98
strudels:
    Almond Paste Chocolate Chip Strudel,
        128–129
    Apricot Strudel, 127
    Cherry Goat Cheese Strudel, 131
    Viennese Apple Strudel, 130
sugar, 9
    in beaten egg whites, 170
Sugar-and-Spice Baked Apples, 210
superfine sugar, 9
sweet butter, 7
syrups:
    Grand Marnier, for nut cake, 43
    orange, for Orange-Apricot Bundt
        Cake, 42
    vanilla-lemon syrup, fresh figs in, 201

Tangerine Slush, 210
tart green apples, 7
tartlets, 83
    Amaretti Fruit Tartlets, 117
    Chocolate Truffle Tartlets, 118
    cream cheese pastry for, 90
    Honey Walnut Tartlets, 118
    Sour Cream Lime Tartlets, 116
    Toasted Coconut Cream Tartlets, 119
tart pans, 7
tarts, 83
    Apple Lemon Tart, 91
    Apple Streusel Tart, 94–95
    Berries and Cream Tart, 97
    Brandy and Ginger Peach Tart, 99
    Cherry Quiche, 100
    Open-Face Apple Tart, 124–125
    Pear and Cheddar Tart, 102
    Purple Plum Tart, 98
    Regal Pecan Tart, 110–111
    Strawberry Cream Sponge Tart, 37–38
Teflon-coated baking sheets, 6
temperature:
    for baking cheesecakes, 45
    for bundt pans, 6
    for cake ingredients, 11
    of ingredients for pastry, 84
    of oven, 7
    for poaching fruits, 191
    for puff pastry, 121
    for whipping egg whites, 1
10X sugar, 9
thermometers, 8
thickening of sauces, 4
tips:
    for baking cakes, 11
    for custards, 142
    for fruits, 191
    for ice creams, 142
    for meringues, 170
    for mousses, 141

tips (cont'd)
    for pastry, 84, 121
    for soufflés, 169–170
Toasted Coconut Cream Tartlets, 119
Tobler Narcisse white chocolate, 8, 46
Toblerone Blanc white chocolate, 8
Toblerone chocolate, for fondue, 196
Toffee-Crunch Meringue Torte, 179
toppings, 215
    chocolate, for peanut butter cheesecake, 56
    for New York Cheesecake, 49
    whipped cream, for fruit trifle, 157
    white chocolate, for cheesecake, 46–47
tortes, 11
    Bittersweet Fudge Torte, 23
    Chocolate-Kahlúa Cream Torte, 20–21
    Chocolate Nut Torte, 24–25
    Coffee Fudge Ice Cream Torte, 115
    Coffee Macadamia Torte, 12–13
    Coffee Meringues with Hazelnut Cream, 186
    Hazelnut Meringue Torte with Apricot Cream, 184–185
    Mocha Fudge Torte, 26–27
    Toffee-Crunch Meringue Torte, 179
trifle, Duke of Nottingham's, 157
Triple Cheese Flan, 47
Tropical Fruit in Pineapple Rickshaw, 192–193
Truffle-Filled Chocolate-Glazed Pears, 208–209
turnovers, fresh blueberry, 126

ultra-pasteurized cream, 2, 9
unbaked pastry, freezing of, 84
unflavored gelatin, to gel, 3
unsalted butter, 3, 7
unsweetened chocolate, 7
upside-down ginger cake, apricot, 36

Vanilla Custard Sauce, 215, 216
    Chocolate Velvet Crown, 150
    Raspberry Floating Islands, 180
vanilla-lemon syrup, fresh figs in, 201
Vanilla Pots de Crème, 162
Viennese Apple Strudel, 130

walnut honey tartlets, 118
Warm Blueberry Puff, 79
Warm Champagne Zabaglione, 155
whipped cream, 2
    for mousses, 141
whipped cream frosting, for orange sponge cake, 18
whipped cream topping, for fruit trifle, 157
whipped egg whites, 1, 8
    for mousses, 141
whipping cream, 9
white chocolate, 8
White Chocolate Cake, 21–22
White Chocolate Cheesecake, 46–47
White Chocolate Ice Cream, 167
White Chocolate Mousse Pie, 104–105
white coffee ice cream, 166–167
whites of eggs, 141
    folding in, 2
    frozen, uses of, 2
    to whip, 1, 8
    whipped, 169
winter fruit, cinnamon-scented, 201

yogurt, honey-nut, Hawaiian fruit in, 195
yogurt-papaya freeze, 211
yolks of eggs, 141
    frozen, uses of, 2

Zabaglione, champagne, warm, 155
Zabaglione, chilled, raspberry-rimmed, 156
zesters, 6
Zesty Lemon Custard Pie, 108